SECOND EDITION

ONE
SMALL
SACRIFICE

A MEMOIR

**Lost Children of the Indian Adoption
Projects**

Trace A. DeMeyer

Blue Hand Books
Greenfield, Massachusetts

Memoir/Native American Studies

ISBN-13: 978-0615582153 (Blue Hand Books)

ISBN-10: 061558215X

DeMeyer, Trace A. [1956-]

Cover design: Barb Burke. Cover Beadwork: Ellowyn Locke, Oglala Lakota, Cover: Family Photo

Publisher: BLUE HAND BOOKS, PO Box 1061, Greenfield, MA 01302, www.bluehandbooks.com, bluehandbooks@hotmail.com

2nd Edition: 2012

Published in the United States

Dedicated to

Cameron, Wild Cat and in memory of Kim Peterson
(1956-1978)
(Shown here in her high school graduation photo)

"My problem is secrecy. I believe that perpetually secret adoptions assure un-accountability and lack of transparency. And secret adoptions are only the tip of the iceberg. The secrecy permeates the process: secret identities, secret parents, secret records, secret foster care providers, secret social workers, secret judges and lawyers (all their identities are sealed, typically), secret physicians, secret statistics and, in the case of some adoption-oriented organizations, secret budgets and secret boards of directors. In any social practice, when people in positions of power hide behind masks, one can be pretty sure that they have something to hide."

-Albert S. Wei, Special Advisor to the Bastard Nation Executive Committee

"Storytelling is an important aspect of Ojibwe culture. My ability to tell a good tale can be used as a tool for teaching and connecting. Even though I grew up outside of my Native community and culture, my stories helped me to become a part of the community that I had lost. Adoption is part of the contemporary tales that Native people need to tell…"

- Tamara Buffalo, published author-poet-visual artist

"Everyone has a right to knowledge about their lineage, genealogy and identity. And if they don't, then it will lead to cases of incest…"

-Lord David Alton quoted after married adoptee twins were granted annulment in Great Britain (January 2008)

"We, as adoptees and birth mother's, have become so conditioned to keep quiet and take the living in shame as just a part of our life that we don't unite. As if we are not allowed to unite. The fear and stigma is so incredibly strong, it is all controlling. I truly don't think adoptees realize this."

- 73Adoptee Blog: Chynna Girl, November 14, 2008 [www.blogger.com/comment]

ADOPTION RECORDS

Here is a list of states where **adoption records** for all or some years are open. In some states, birth parents can sign a no-contact veto:

Alabama – Adoption records are open.

Alaska – Adoption records are open.

Colorado – Adoptions records are open for adoptees whose adoptions were finalized between 07/01/1951 to 06/30/1976 and 09/01/1999 to present.

Delaware – Adoption records are open. Birth parents can sign a no contact veto.

Illinois – Adoption records are open. Birth parents can sign a no contact veto.

Indiana – Adoption records prior to 1940 may be open.

Iowa – Adoption records are open prior to 07/01/1941

Kansas – Adoption records are open.

Maine – Adoption records will be open beginning in 2009.

Maryland – Most adoption records prior to 06/01/1947 are open.

Massachusetts – Adoption records are open for birth years prior to 4/14/1974.

Michigan – Adoption records are open if the birth parent's rights were terminated prior to 05/28/1955 or on or after 09/12/1980.

Montana – Adoption records are open for adoptions finalized prior to 2/2/1964.

New Hampshire – Adoption records are open.

New Jersey – Adoption records prior to 1940 may be open.

Ohio – Adoption records are open for adoptions finalized prior to 1/1/1964.

Oregon – Adoption records are open.

Tennessee – Adoption records are open. No-contact vetos are available to birth parents if the adoption was finalized after 1951.

In other states, adopted persons are provided with a fraudulent birth certificate under their adopted name and showing the adoptive parents as the natural parents of the child.

Contents

PREFACE (2nd Edition*)

*The first edition will be retired and replaced with this new book.
(Hold on to your first edition.)

Welcome to the **Second Edition** of "One Small Sacrifice." Second editions are usually a cause for celebration, because there is either big news or big change...

Sadly, the situation for Native adoptees has not changed much at all since my first book came out in 2010 and since adoption records are still sealed in all but eight states. In fact, if records were opened in America in 2011, every single adoptee I know would be celebrating.

Big change will happen when there is public awareness and mainstream education will teach about this ongoing and very troubling chapter of American and Indian history. Knowing about the genocidal effects of the Indian Adoption Projects, and the humiliation affected children (now adults) suffered in silence and isolation, deserves international recognition and big news. It won't be easy. Evidence of these projects is still sealed, along with our adoption files and birth certificates. We also need more and more survivors to come forward and speak out. Contact me please.

The community called America needs to help every Native American child who was placed in a closed adoption. This type of adoption erased our identity and denies us our ancestral treaty rights. Healing survivors will happen when successful reunions happen.

The time for big change is now. Adoptees need original birth certificates to return successfully to our tribes.

Why a second edition? There was more to share. For example, I now have a copy of my formerly-sealed adoption file to share with readers. I also made some changes to the organization of this book, which I hope my readers will appreciate. With this new edition and my blog **www.splitfeathers.blogspot.com,** I hope to keep our story in the news...

PREFACE (1st Edition)

I'm a fly on the wall, one who listens, the observer of the absurd, and a young girl wearing braids. That's me standing in front of an Ojibwe wigwam with my adoptive mother Edie and my adopted brother Joey. I'm the only Indian in this family. It was 1969. I'm 12 and the family is attending the famous Lumberjack Festival in Hayward, Wisconsin. Then I heard the drum. The Lac Courte Oreilles Ojibwe powwow was happening on the same grounds. The sound of the drum, the men singing filled me, like my heart opened up and the sky fell in. I could not tell anyone what I was feeling that day but it made me feel good, proud, and different. I knew I was an Indian girl just like the other girls I saw there but no one could tell me anything since I was adopted.

Back then life was about mystery. I knew little to nothing about being adopted or Indian, just that I was.

North American Indians call adoptees Lost Birds, Lost Ones or Split Feathers. Adoption messes with the brain's natural order so we Split Feathers get two experiences. I explain how later. One could argue which experience is best.

Adoption practices affecting one race of people had a specific purpose—the break-up of Indian families, to disrupt tribal culture across North America. I guess the idea was to assimilate us, tame us red devils and dirty savages. No kidding. So what is known about the Indian Adoption Projects and the aftermath, it's pretty much been secret. Few books acknowledge it happened, but it did...

It hurts to think secret adoption files (thick binders of papers with real names and the identities of real people) are still guarded (sealed by law) in

2011. This pretty much guarantees adoptees won't be rejoining their tribal nation or family any time soon.

Wisconsin was my home. I was transracially adopted and I'm American Indian and Irish. I am one of the lucky few who opened my adoption in a sealed record state. I explain that later.

Someone blogged in 2008: "Anyone who questions the Adoption Game gets thrown in jail or called crazy." Call me crazy then. Ground Zero for me was 2004, when I decided to write about it. Adoption "secrecy" made that nearly impossible. As a journalist I soon discovered nothing about adoption is simple or open; not after 1,000 drafts of this book; not after reading my file at age 22 back in 1979.

I expected little help or new discoveries. I didn't know there were six to ten million adoptees in the USA (alone). Some are blazing hot new trails on the internet global highway. I make friends, both Indian and non-Indian. Nor did I expect to find so many of us. We're all clinging to the same boat. Some even blog about it.

One in three Americans has an immediate family member who has been adopted...

Every Indian reservation in North America has a story about missing lost children and future generations who carry the stigma of lost language and culture. Some say Indian reservations were baby factories for social workers to fill their orders, or the place where churches and government abducted children for residential boarding schools.

Very few Americans witnessed this upheaval firsthand. Very few saw the Indian boarding schools and assimilation by whip or by washing the child's mouth with lye soap. Few knew that the Indian Adoption Projects and Programs were an orchestrated act of genocide, the same as ethnic cleansing. Many friends remember when they were abducted as children, not babies, virtually erased from tribal rolls, not told their tribe or their family's name.

These children, now adults, are expected to accept this? Funny thing is lost birds/adoptees don't look like adoptive mom or dad. So we are not supposed to notice this or dare to ask?

I strongly believe adopted children are in training to become warriors. I know many strong courageous adoptees.

Who said wild animals bred in captivity can never return to the wild? Can an Indian child return to the wilds of Indian Country? Sure, but not without baggage...maybe a language barrier, maybe a fear of the unknown.

Indian Country is still our home and adoptees like me will not be satisfied until they get some answers and meet some family.

This book could have many names: *Innocent Kid Running into a Minefield; Outside the Circle; Adoption Didn't kill our Spirit; Orphan Trauma; Babies to Distribute: Cultural Genocide; Not Exactly Grateful; Our Ancestors Prayed for Us to be Born; The Only Good Indian is a Dead Indian; and Adoption Reality is No Place for the Weak.* All would fit.

My Irish blood advised, tell your whole story. The Indian in my heart cautioned me to stay balanced, humble. Shame tried to interfere and told me to keep quiet. I took my old humiliations and used them like keys. I open up my life like a can of worms.

Take a journey with me. Keep reading.

Trace A. DeMeyer/ Laura Thrall-Bland/ Winyan Ohmanisa Waste La Ke

ACTS AGAINST INDIAN PEOPLE

By Terry Cross (Seneca tribe)

As European migration increased, to what is now the United States and Canada, traditional tribal practices in child rearing became more susceptible to the influences of the dominant society. Efforts to "civilize" the Native Indian population were almost always focused on Indian children.

The "Civilization Fund Act" was one of the first federal laws targeting Indian children. Passed by Congress in 1819, it authorized grants to private agencies, primarily churches, to establish programs to "civilize the Indian."

Later the federal government and private agencies established large militaristic boarding schools or institutions where Indian children were placed involuntarily and forced to abandon their traditional beliefs, customs, and traditions. Severe punishment in the forms of beatings, being chained and shackled, bound hand and foot, and locked in closets was not uncommon.

By 1900, after decades of forced removal of Indian children from their families and communities and the stripping of their culture from them, the natural child protection system that once flourished in every tribal community began to break down.

During the next half-century, tribal traditional practices continued to be discouraged and banned by federal and private agents, while oppression, alcoholism, disease, and poverty were allowed to take hold in most tribal communities. As these destructive elements took hold in Indian Country, child abuse and neglect became more prevalent too.

Government policies shifted in the 1950's towards a more humanitarian view, but not without serious consequences. Humanitarians still viewed assimilation as the best answer to the "Indian problem" and viewed tribes as incapable of caring for their children. New projects began, such as the Indian Adoption Project, which used public and private agencies to remove and place hundreds of Indian children in non-Indian homes far from their families and communities. Few efforts were made or resources committed to help tribal governments develop services on tribal lands that would strengthen Indian families.

As efforts to outplace Indian children continued into the 1960's and 1970's, the Association on Indian Affairs conducted a study in the 1970's that found between 25 percent and 35 percent of all Indian children had been separated from their families. This study also found that in **16 states** in 1969, **85 percent** of the Indian children were placed in non-Indian homes. The long-term effects of these massive out placements of Indian children were only just beginning to be understood in the 1970's, which included effects not only on individuals, but also the well-being of entire tribal communities.

Not until 1978, after the passage of the Indian Child Welfare Act (P.L. 95-608), did the federal government acknowledge the critical role that tribal governments play in protecting their children and maintaining their families.

The long-term effects from these removals and efforts to strip Indian children of their culture produced generations of Indian adults who have weak ties to their families and tribal communities, unresolved grief and trauma, and few supports or resources to help them. Other factors that are attributed to the rise of child abuse and neglect in Indian Country include the inappropriate interpretations of Indian parenting practices; exposure to known risk factors for abuse and neglect, such as alcoholism, poverty, and unemployment; federal policies that have supported family and community disintegration, such as termination and relocation; and learned responses that result from oppression and exploitation.

Written by Terry Cross (Seneca Tribal Nation) in a STATEMENT OF THE NATIONAL INDIAN CHILD WELFARE ASSOCIATION PRESENTED BEFORE THE SENATE COMMITTTEE ON INDIAN AFFAIRS Regarding the REAUTHORIZATION OF THE INDIAN CHILD PROTECTION AND FAMILY VIOLENCE PREVENTION ACT S. 1601, SEPTEMBER 24, 2003

WARNING to READERS

This memoir contains explicit graphic material that includes emotional and sexual abuse, and the cruel exploitation of Indian Children. This is not written as a chronology but rather as a memoir as I'm able to recall certain events and experiences. Trauma has a way of making our minds work in a non-linear fashion. Other Native adoptees helped me see this commonality in a non-judgmental way. We are called Split Feathers for this shared experience. Many adoptees I interviewed for this book are still unable to remember certain events of their childhood.

One Small Sacrifice

Who are you?

Stop and think about this... Who are you?

Think about your parents, your grandparents and great-grandparents, who you knew when you were growing up. Remember the stories of when, where, even how you were born.

Now... imagine you disappear, you're erased, no longer a part of your family history and genealogy. How would you feel? Grateful? I don't think so.

Now ... imagine an adoptee who doesn't know who they are ... nothing, anything, zilch... Can you imagine looking in the mirror, not knowing anything? How might that feel?

A fairytale? You think?

"Adopted people" are the only people in the world without free or unlimited access to their personal history.... we simply vanish into thin air.

This decision was made for us. Someone decided this long ago. Someone decided adoptees were better off not knowing anything. Someone decided this for me – I'd be fine, never knowing my identity.

Wait ... I was dead without my identity, without my name. I can't live like this.

My adoptive family had their stories, their names, their parents and grandparent's names, where they were from, how they lived, died, everything.

Like my adoptive mom and dad, many families are very proud of their stories. There could be bank robbers or horse thieves or rich barons or fancy politicians. Mine could be, too.

To tell my story, I needed more than their story. I needed my own.

Chasing Ghosts

"You must know where you came from yesterday, know where you are today, to know where you're going tomorrow." – Cree saying

I'm over 50 now. Helen, my birthmother I never met. I know she was 22 when she had me and gave me up. I know this since I read my sealed adoption file. I share the contents later in this book.

She was not what I expected. Ok, I'm not what I expected.

Getting this life and this experience is no coincidence. This makes me an adoptee uniquely situated. I experienced two worlds growing up, American and Indian, being raised in rural northern Wisconsin. Today I'm a journalist and write exclusively about Indian Country. I'm good at chasing ghosts.

But how do I write about Native American genocide? I ask Indian friends. They say, "Well, it's not exactly the Jewish Holocaust. It's bigger."

I did not see film footage when a ship pulled up on Turtle Island, but the story lives on. There are no photos of when early invaders arrived here and began their land grabs, collecting bounties on Indians, conducting military massacres. Indians fought long and hard. Tribes did Winter Counts, a kind of Indian Census and narrative. Photos and papers exist of Indians signing white man treaties to enact removals to lands called reservations. I've been to the graveyard of the last Indian uprising, the Wounded Knee Massacre in 1890.

As for the Indian Adoption projects, I needed a calculator. If the Native American population was 2 million and if just one quarter of *all* children were removed before the Indian Child Welfare Act of 1978, then on-paper, 80,000+ children were removed from their families during the early to mid-1900s. If the population of American Indians was 3 million, then over 100,000 babies were removed. I hated this math...85 percent of children were removed by adoption in 16 states. That's genocide.

Genocide, by my definition, means a community of people were culturally killed, wiped out or literally made dead for political and/or economic reasons. Strong words but true. Some of us are your next door neighbors. Some of us are not correctly listed on the census. Some of us are Indian only when we look in the mirror.

Pretend
You must stay drunk on writing so reality cannot destroy you... - Ray Bradbury

There were no cell phones to warn other Indians in 1491 or earlier. There were no text messages. There were no cameras rolling when the missionaries, militias and later social workers came for children. CBS, ABC, NBC did not film news documentaries. It's a miracle Indian people survived America's bad history.

So, yes, I did pretend to be someone – and live a lie – because I'm adopted, because I was supposed to be kept a secret. Ask any adoptee who has tribal ancestry. If you are not told, you're just another dead Indian, at least on record and on tribal rolls. America is like that. Adoptees of all skin colors in the United States are now estimated to number between six and ten million. That's a lot of bogus ancestry.

The 2000 census says there are 2.5 million Indians. I'd say many more if you count me and the thousands of Lost Birds from all across North America.

America would prefer every one of us to live as an American citizen as if none other were as good or as important. America forgets it's very new by all standards; it just acts like its old.

Indian Country is ancient. Our cells are identical to those of our ancestors of 30,000 years ago. Indian kids who are adopted and raised outside Indian country eventually get it—more or less.

We get that less Indians around is best. We get that America didn't respect us or our culture. We get that America tamed us, took our land, and then revised our history. We get that more Americans prefer us tucked away somewhere. They'll teach us their version of our story. We get that it's wrong but it's America. It's been this way a long time, over 500 years.

No one is exactly sure how many Indian children were taken, but thousands are gone and probably living on the fringe as urban Indians. That is how I see myself. I get that.

Chickens and Ducks

Alright, here's an analogy that woke me one night—can a duck raise chickens and the chickens forget they're chickens? That's a definite no.

I considered this at age 48 when I started writing this memoir. Steve Elm, a member of the Oneida Nation, and an editor in New York City, asked me to write a story about Stolen Generations, about American Indian children adopted by non-Indians, for his publication *Talking Stick* in 2004. The idea generated lots of comments from friends so I tried a few drafts of a story. I found no one had tackled this particular subject, what really happened to all these missing kids.

I never knew how or if I fit into this picture. I'd been working as an editor and journalist since 1996, first in Wisconsin, then Connecticut. I never imagined there was something specifically called the Indian Adoption Project or Indian Program, not when I was a kid, not when I started writing about it. But there was proof and I found it eventually.

Indian people disappeared—many did—all across America. Not all were adopted. After a few centuries, Indian Country better known as Turtle Island, apparently dissolved into America. After numerous relocation programs were created, Indians were told to move off their reservation so many did.

So, can an adoptee return to a reservation community as an adult when America raised us and changed us? Not that easy. I thought our bond is everything, our blood is everything. I get that someone came along and changed that, too.

Never before had I experienced such difficulty with one story. I repeat: never. I took to writing like a duck takes to water. Most days, writing and doing research is like breathing. This time was different. I struggled. I knew I'd hit something so I had to slow down, to process, to dig. This history, my history, similar stories, had to be somewhere.

Global

How many countries do not allow adoption? Several. Iraq is one. No children from Western Europe, Australia, or Canada are eligible for adoption by Americans right now.

Nonetheless, America's adoption reach has been global, widely publicized, some insist saintly, God-like of those who adopt orphans, even if money is exchanged for babies.

International adoption really began after the Korean War, when American GI's left numerous orphans with their poverty-stricken mothers; then Korean and American-Asian orphans were brought here to be adopted in the United States. After that, Americans adopted thousands of children from Africa, Asia, Eastern Europe, and Latin America. There is no bigger adopter. In 2002 alone, U.S. families adopted over 20,000 children from various Third World nations. [Americans use fertility doctors, too; they can't seem to make enough of their own babies.]

The overall topic of adoption begged one question for me. "Wait, how do adoptees feel?" No one had asked me when I was young or old. I wanted this answered so I dug in.

An adoptee movement makes headlines these days. Adoptive parents are usually shocked to hear their adopted child say they need to know who they are and what happened.

My Alaskan Native-Celtic friend Anecia says, "The power of identity is stronger than fear." That's a powerful statement about adoption, yes. Anecia went full circle as an adoptee and met her birth mom and dad. Her adoptive dad helped her.

The reality is adoptees do have a strong biological curiosity. It's awful scary not to know who you are. My first goal was discovery —how I lived a mystery and solved it, and I survived spiritually intact and remarkably well. Other Split Feathers need to know how this is possible, even after our pain.

This memoir is not about my recovery from depression or addiction or self-mutilation or suicide attempts, not at all. Apparently adoptees do suffer from these more than the rest of humanity.

Facing my own situation head-on, what choice did I have? I was an abandoned baby—it was my initiation into being human.

So I will share how my book started, my experience (as a child, a survivor and a journalist) and my friendships with other American Indians who were also adopted. I learned much more about the business and history of adoption so I include some of this, too. This might be controversial since it concerns mysterious (some say hard-headed, some say unethical) adoption practices, with unknowing Americans raising indigenous children who come from a distinct culture; and in a very real sense feel persecuted for being Indian. This story might contradict some popular beliefs, myths that persist about adoption.

Years ago I was embarrassed to say I was adopted. I used to think, "What made me such a loser?" I did not feel lucky. I did not have a clue that my adoption hurt me so badly, its tentacles reached into every aspect of my life, even as an adult. I ached to know my own mother, the woman who created me.

One expert wrote, "Loss of the most sacred bond in life, that of a mother and child, is one of the most severe traumas and this loss will require long-term, if not lifelong, therapy."

Really? No one helped me with my loss.

For years I just wanted to find the truth. I did not disrupt anyone's life, showing up on their doorstep unannounced.

For adoptees I write about each step to reunion with my birth family and relatives. For those who attempt to open their own adoption, or simply want to understand, I explain many stages. And I mention other adoptee stories, people I know.

Even now there is persistent rampant poverty in Indian Country. Even now it isn't easy being Indian, let alone poor. But it is better to know, and not be a mystery.

Adoptees with Indian blood find out soon enough their reservations are closed to strangers. Without proof, you're suspect. We don't always get our proof since state laws prevent it. Just one Minnesota tribe, White Earth, decided to call out to its lost children; this made news in 2007. Just a few showed up. Why? Adoption files are still sealed in Minnesota.

For any adoptee going back, this requires a special kind of courage. Adoptees know this.

Rhonda, a Bay Mills Tribal member, an adoptee friend of mine, was told early on—be happy, be white. Ask yourself, how would you react? When did Indian Country become such a bad place to be from? When did this happen? How did this happen?

Writing the Adventure

Keeping journals all my life, I'd never actually told anyone of my own harrowing adventure, my illegal pursuit of strangers who share my blood. It always bothered me I looked like no one I knew. I was pretty sure I had a tribe but was not sure which one.

When I started writing for Steve Elm in 2004, I didn't really want to look at my own perceptions or lack of them. Was I afraid? Yes. I didn't want to appear less than grateful to the DeMeyer family who adopted me. But I wasn't exactly grateful.

What had my "non-Indian adoptee status" done to me? I wasn't exactly sure.

I'd blocked out a lot. I prefer to think of my younger self as brain-dead or crazy. The past was a dark place to visit. Most of my earliest child memories were vague, even blank in places. I had shut down mostly what hurt. Some things, ok, many things, I didn't want to face again.

Early drafts of this book were fragmented. That's what one nice editor said. I kept patching memories together like a quilt. I remembered slowly, not seeing the whole picture of what had actually happened to me. Again I did not want to appear less than grateful to my adoptive family. It was good they adopted an orphan.

What this did, writing about it, is not what the adoption flyers said. Adoptees are expected to be happy, grateful—not devastated, not in shock, not horrified. To find any kind of sequence to this, I had to remember how I felt. Then it hit me—I didn't want to remember. I'd left the past behind for a reason. Too much hurt.

Writer's block was not what I needed. Months passed. Steve was waiting. Maybe I didn't want to ruffle any feathers, least of all my own.

Finally, one year and counting, after numerous mind-bending wake-ups at 4 a.m., I was writing again. First, I remembered the steps, opening my adoption, how I handled it, the good, bad, who I met, etc. In fact during 2004, I was still meeting new relatives.

What I encountered—besides shock—was me, barely alive, living dead.

Let me explain. I started to see that I was usually caught up in other people's lives just to avoid living my own. Under layers of denial, I conveniently forgot what I didn't like to remember. I had stopped caring about the past but it had me, all of me.

To piece together this life, I needed to step back, to connect the dots. I wasn't exactly ready to meet her—my newly-resurrected Shawnee-Cherokee. I had buried her. I didn't know how to be her. By the way, we're only dead to our tribe.

That is, until we return as ghosts.

Revelations

"...well I reckon I got to light out for the territory ahead of the rest because Aunt Sally she's going to adopt me and civilize me and I can't stand it. I been there before. – Huckleberry Finn (Mark Twain)

Only two categories of American citizens cannot obtain a copy of their original birth certificates: people in the FBI witness protection program and adoptees.

As a kid, I'm unaware of this. As an adoptee, I'm full of illusions. Now an adult, I see how illusions spared me from pain I could not yet comprehend or process.

I was emotionally stalled at 20, then 30, then 40. In other words—a wreck and I didn't like it. I'd found lots of books on what to do if you adopt a baby. There weren't any on how to live like this. Revelations were happening at all stages of my life. The internet helped, revealing a big picture of how I fit into this.

I'm no kid now. Thank God I've had Indian friends all my life. I hated being a stranger to my own tribe. I knew more about other tribal nations than my own. I looked like a success story, successfully assimilated.

By America's standards, I'd lost more than my parents. I lost my language, my ability to pray as a Shawnee-Cherokee. I lost my passport back to Indian Country. I had no right to be Indian anymore. In this way, adoptee culture is unique. In many ways it's like torture.

Two ducks raised me, two (chickens) walked away. I think all four parents were totally unaware how my "being adopted" affected me. No, this was not about fault or blame. They knew and I knew adoption was the way it was done; in the 1950s, a bigger system decreed let someone else raise your baby. Single women should not keep their babies. No one questioned adoption since it was done in the best interest of the child.

For Indigenous people around the globe, far too many moms and dads had no choice, truly no choice. Even uneducated Indian people are not stupid. Giving Indian babies to white families was part of a larger plan: colonization. It worked. It ultimately did change our future.

This was quite a revelation for me, being one of the colonized.

Further Reading: Of 'Sluts' and 'Bastards': A Feminist Decodes the Child Welfare Debate by Louise Armstrong (1995). The author reveals the critical link between the issue of welfare and that of child welfare: between the will to punish sluts and intervention to remove their "bastards." Armstrong guides the reader through the nightmarish foster care system. With razor sharp wit, she exposes the prejudices—and professional pride —that infests the social services bureaucracy and destroys so many children's lives.

Sacrifice

I maintain that most of us could have kept and raised our children with just a little support from our families. That being denied, perhaps if we had been treated like other mothers—allowed to see and hold our babies, have some memento of their existence—we might not have been so

traumatized. —Denise, Arizona Birthmother,
www.blogger.com/profile/05105971355542234723

Some unmarried mothers were told, in so many words, "Sacrifice your baby and save your reputation." Adoption officials assured them their privacy, "No one will find the baby once they're adopted. Records are permanently sealed so no one will ever know."

Some of these women were treated like savages, knowing their only option was to abandon their baby and forget it happened; easier said than done, right?

My birthmother's sacrifice, abandoning me, was a decision she made for herself. I was small compared to the rest of her life. She had no clue how I'd feel. After I disappeared, she had no idea if I would look for her, or my dad and my siblings, if I had any. I was supposed to live happily ever after.

It's sad to say my birth mom didn't seem real when I was young. She was a slut, painted for me by the Catholics who raised me. When did these ideas get planted?

If she was so horrible, what did that make me? Then why was my birth dad left out of my early thoughts? I don't know.

I hoped meeting some of my relatives I might feel human again.

After I read my adoption file in 1979, it was very hard to accept why my own birthmother abandoned me. "Let go... Abandoned...Orphaned." Those words echoed inside me like an infection, like I was defective.

At times I did act like an emotionally battered and beaten dog. I do remember. I felt terrible as a kid. It wasn't safe to be me, so sad. I remember living with my adoptive parents. I held back more anxiety than they or I could handle. I buried that too, filed it away, and pretended it wasn't there.

As a young girl, I lacked the tools necessary to handle or repair my damage. Sure, if I were a Vulcan on Star Trek, not feeling would be normal. I was supposed to feel grateful, not cold. What I could not see or hear was controlling me. I didn't know anything about birth psychology or soul sickness or other medical terms for my injury which felt like an open wound.

Sev and Edie, my new adoptive mom and dad, pretended too, hiding their own pain, her infertility after her two miscarriages. She could never have her own babies.

Every heart was broken in our family.

For Joey and me, we grew up their adopted kids, their only kids, replacements for dead babies. We lived their secret fear we might not turn out OK so Joey and I tried to be perfect.

Now this makes me sick. I didn't know others kids who had to try so hard.

Sure I could function. I was a musician, a model and a writer, someone my family could brag about. My face was in *Good Housekeeping* magazine. There's no question my adoptive family gave me many things—and the confidence that they loved me. Yet growing up, no one said how deeply disturbed I was.

Right above my office chair is an African mobile called the Circle of Joy. A circle of straw dancers sway above me. A poet friend Erin gave them to me. Her dancers gave me great pause.

I finally figured it out. I'll dance my way home.

Connecting the dots

Usually parents, adoptive or natural, are never held responsible or accountable to anyone but God. It's an enormous, thankless job raising kids. It's learn-as-you-go.

All my adoptive parents knew was: I grew up. I seemed OK. I wasn't their duck anymore.

This wouldn't be the first time someone in my family forgot to ask me how I felt. There were probably afraid to ask. Back then I doubt I could have explained it anyway. I couldn't say, "No one has to take this ridiculous journey but me, challenging religion and law just to know my own name, just to gain any semblance of human dignity. Where is my mother? Why is searching for her illegal? I need to find her."

Growing up DeMeyer, relatives talked for hours about their ancestry. Every word hung in the air, and stung like a bee. Obviously, they were oblivious to my pain as I became distinctly numb. They had no clue.

As they talked ancestry, I deciphered their words: "You belong to someone else." I felt so tiny, unimportant, like a stranger, though this was my home.

Writing this book meant writing about stuff I'd buried. Writing this required re-living that past, with no proof of what I believed to be true. Until I was 40, I knew nothing about my tribal relatives on paper. Perplexed, sure I was, but I never gave up.

A chronology wasn't what my editor Steve wanted. (Three drafts he returned, gently suggesting, "try again.")

By 2005, it hit me. I needed to connect with other Split Feathers/Lost Birds. I needed to know if they were experiencing what I was experiencing. It took me awhile to get all my ducks (and dots) in a row. The row became more like a circle.

By the end of 2005, I was writing at all hours, usually in the middle of the night. I submitted *"Generation after Generation, We are Coming Home"*; Steve Elm finally published it. It wrote itself. At 3 a.m., the story flowed out of me like a geyser. (You'll read it later.)

I inadvertently started a fire. My re-connection to self didn't stop or end. Two, then three more years flew by, still sitting at this computer, dots connecting me all over the place, to more people and more fires.

Coast to coast, people could read my *Talking Stick* story online. Friends emailed my story to their friends who were also adopted.

Paul DeMain, the publisher of *News from Indian Country,* is also an adoptee, so he published my story. Then more adoptees popped up, slowly like baby turtles. Then more found my blog. Then more found me on Facebook.

By 2009, the circle spread like a web. I'd not only found me in this story, or a new sense of it, I found other adoptees just like me... hopefully with this book, I'll find even more.

Mosaic

Writing, I think, is not apart from living. Writing is a kind of double living. The writer experiences everything twice. Once in reality and once in that mirror... – Catherine Drinker Bowen

There's no way someone can work on processing emotions, day in and day out, without some kind of mental health break. I tore out my bathroom. Even though this book was waiting to be written, I slowly and carefully installed mosaic tile around my old bathtub. I ripped away the 70s wallpaper, slapping adobe plaster on the walls.

I'm sure the plumber and electrician thought, "Trace is a little crazy."

Hard physical labor—keeping my hands busy—helped me think. I worked six long months on that mosaic. That you can't rush. Like the Seal song, "We're never gonna survive... unless... we are a little crazy..." Well, maybe I was a little crazy.

I call the mosaic a labor of sanity.

Since 2005, I wrote and rewrote. Each day was becoming a mosaic of adoptees; some might call me, or we email or we visit in person. Some share their pain and the complexity of being lost or they tell me about their happiness (or the tragedy) after reunions with their birth family and relatives.

A shy lost bird in British Columbia emailed me right after the *News from Indian Country* story was published. She shared her mystery and said no one had ever talked to her about being a Lost Bird. No one had ever helped her deal with her sense of loss. That's how insane this is—being isolated, perilously alone, powerless.

An adoptee survival mechanism (and patience) seems to kick in when we need it. Lost Birds/adoptees, even in remote places, do figure out the internet. More than one emailed me: "I never told my adoptive parents. I waited a long time. I used the internet to search. I used a registry. I had a friend who used a lawyer..." they wrote.

If they need it, I offer my help.

They ask me, "How would an American handle being taken to India or Iraq... to a completely new culture? How would they handle this situation if it happened to them?"

My answer: They'd adapt, yes. Ask a lot of questions? Sure. Miss home? Definitely.

Each Lost Bird/adoptee has a unique story. Some tell a horror story of searching for answers and their tribal identity without instructions, receiving rare encouragement. There is no passport back to Indian Country. Very few found help. I met a few who successfully opened their sealed records and some did get enrolled in their tribe. Some found out they were already enrolled.

It amazes me how clever and creative adoptees are. We are never really lost, they say, just missing a huge chunk of our life and the people who have answers. Our identity becomes both Indian and non-Indian. Some adoptees feel moving back to our reservation will replace some of our pain. Some are hopeful, and cling to the idea they'll find living (or dead) relatives. Some adoptees figured out Indian people are more likely to be in cities, and not on the reservations. A few adoptees said they were children, not babies, when they were adopted, and remember being taken. More than one told me "fight-or-flight" was how they felt as a child. Some ran away as teenagers.

For any adoptee still searching, the information you need is the name of your mother or father, and which tribe.

It hurts me so much I can't help every adoptee. It pains me more birthparents aren't trying to find us. It kills me the Bureau of Indian Affairs, an American agency created for Indian people, isn't set up to offer resources to help Lost Birds. Adoption laws prevent us from ever knowing our true identity.

Lucky birds who do find their family name often do make contact. Several make regular trips home to their reservation to see family. Slow migrations are underway. At this very moment, someone brave is reconnecting past to present.

Many more pray for a sign. *The Morning Show* on NBC ran a series on *Lost Identity* in November 2008. One Oregon adoptee hired a private detective and in three days found his mother who is a member of the Klamath Tribe. Oregon passed legislation for adoptees to gain access to their sealed adoption records. Many more will succeed with these new laws.

We'll guess why the Indian Adoption Project files remain sealed and closed.

I'm not giving up. I want the government *and* tribes to open records for every adoptee. I will never give up until this happens. I want Senate hearings on this issue!

A Lost Bird I know in Connecticut travels around Eastern reservations looking for people who look like her, since a priest had handled her adoption 56 years ago and no paperwork exists. I pray for Mary Ann to reconnect with her tribe every day. She has asked Maine and New Hampshire to find some record of her birth.

Hearts heal when you find your tribe, when relatives welcome you home, when you find someone who looks like you, when you learn words of your ancestor's language.

Grass Prisons

By treaty, America created oppressive dirt-poor grass prisons they called Indian reservations, isolated far away from the American pilgrim-pioneer.

Poverty is poverty and looks pretty much the same in Indian country. From that perspective, most Indians have lived poor since treaties, moving from a hunter-gatherer society to organized concentration camps.

The Indian Program was one of the Indian Adoption Projects I researched. It was different for Native mothers, many judged for poor living conditions on their reservation or in their urban ghettos. The pioneer judge and jury did nothing to stop missionaries (then social workers) from coming to take (others say steal) children, with the promise of a good Christian upbringing, or a Christian home, or a Christian boarding school.

There was nothing wrong with the way Native people prayed to their Gods. Indian people do raise children differently because grandparents, aunties, uncles, your mother and father's kin act as parents to every child. No child was ever lost or without relatives since the entire tribe was your family. There was kinship adoption.

Americans and Canadians didn't understand Indian people. Indian culture was judged inferior— so they scooped up Indian kids for boarding school and adoption, to assimilate us, make us white and to take more and more land.

Tribes are still on the lookout for others who come for their children, a few hundred years later. In many ways, poverty was a powerful weapon. It still is on many reservations.

Excerpt: "Our Indian Program" 1960, New York

A pioneer in offering adoption to mixed-race children and children of color, Louise Wise Services placed a large number of children through the Indian Adoption Project. The following excerpt describes the agency's early role in that effort and suggests that matching played a somewhat different role in adoptions of Native children during this period than for other children marked by visible differences.

"Miss Jenkins discussed our Indian Program as a whole, giving the background of the project which was created a little over a year ago (1959) by the Bureau of Indian Affairs and the Child Welfare League of America. There are very few services offered to Indian unmarried mothers who may want to give up their babies for adoption. The mother has very little communication with the Indian Bureau workers who are not geared to the unmarried mothers' needs and the mother has had to be dependent on state resources which have provided a limited number of homes for Indian children, and who would more likely place the child in a foster home than in an adoptive home. The possibility of finding good Indian adoption homes has not been fully explored and not enough has been done in placing Indian children with non-Indian families. We are not sure how much prejudice has had a part in this and more interpretation is needed. It is hoped that some of these things may be resolved in this project.

The (1960) project is for a period of three years and it is hoped that adoptive homes can be secured for 50 children and that the project will stimulate additional placements by the local agencies.

To date our agency has placed six Indian children and at present we have one child in care. The first two children referred to us were half Indian and they were placed with Jewish families, who had one child from us. The third, a little full (blood) Indian boy was placed with an Indian family and it turned out to be very suitable as both the child and the adoptive father were from the same reservation in Arizona. The next two children, twins 2-1/2 years old, were placed with a Protestant family. The fourth child placed (with a Jewish family) was Peter, two years old.

Peter, a full (blood) Indian child, was born September 1957, came here October 1959, and was placed for adoption in December 1959. The ratio of Indian blood is determined because as a member of the tribe Peter shares in the money the tribe accumulates, and Peter had money of his own. Peter's parents were on the verge of divorce and he was always the center of controversy between his parents. They had married very young and have three children; they were not able to take on the responsibility of a family with the result that the children were shifted from relative to relative. Peter had been in a foster home when his mother took him back and shortly thereafter his parents surrendered him.

Peter was placed in a boarding home on an Indian reservation in Montana. The plan was for Miss Jenkins to visit him and to help him get to know her, and in short, to make him comfortable enough with her so that she could take him back to New York. The Bureau of Indian Affairs worker was very helpful to Miss Jenkins, and worked with the Indian boarding mother in order to get her assistance in helping Peter to relate to Miss Jenkins. The help the boarding mother gave was outstanding and much careful thought was given in planning for the big change in Peter's life.

Peter managed beautifully on the 9 hour plane trip to New York, even though he was very frightened when the plane took off. He adjusted well in our boarding home where Miss Jenkins visited him every other day so that she could continue her relationship with him thus serving as the connecting link between his past and his future.

The family selected for Peter had originally attended one of the group meetings for applicants interested in older children; they were over-age for our regular group of young children. The leader of the group had been favorably impressed by them and felt they might also be interested in an Indian child. When this was explored they were most enthusiastic and wanted Peter immediately. The adoptive father grew up in Canada and knows quite a bit about Indians. Peter was placed with them and they are already speaking of adopting another Indian child. The placement is working out very well and Peter is beginning to acquire a sense of permanency. The Committee found the presentation fascinating and enjoyed it very much."

[Source:

www.uoregon.edu/~adoption/archive/LWSOIP.htm]

Note: Louise Wise adoption agencies closed their doors more than a few years ago. Those adoptee records are now held by Spence-Chapin adoption agencies in the US.

Open and Honest

After I did my search, I found I was more open and more honest than I'd ever been. I felt whole.

My closest friend is another adoptee named Rhonda. Do we have a lot in common? Our story goes: our birthmothers never told our birthfathers about us. Both our dads were Indian men. I did a DNA test in 1994 with my birthfather Earl who was Shawnee-Cherokee-Delaware and Irish. Rhonda did DNA with her Bay Mills Indian uncle since her birthfather Teep had already passed on. Neither of us met our non-Indian birthmothers.

My dad didn't live on a reservation and Rhonda's dad did, on and off.

Raised white kids, we were not "recognized" as Indians. Each of us has a brother who was also adopted, probably not American Indian, but who knows since neither opened their adoptions.

I met Earl who was very sick, who died shortly after we met. Rhonda never met her dad Teep.

Very often Rhonda and I would talk about who cared for us prior to our adoption. We both had foster families. Who cared for us as newborns, before our adoption? Those months must have hurt if we bonded with them then were taken away again.

Together Rhonda and I vent our frustration over sealed records, paying for files, even the expense of DNA tests.

Rhonda called the Bureau of Indian Affairs in Michigan for information when she had her birthfather's name. The woman on the other end of the phone said if Rhonda's father was already dead, she'd never get tribal enrollment. Rhonda was smart not to listen. Rhonda's Uncle had her father's DNA. Rhonda was enrolled on Bay Mills tribal rolls in Michigan.

We talk about the ghosts of our dead relatives, our fate (some call salvation) being handed to strangers. In so many ways, adoption feels like abduction.

If we don't acknowledge the full extent of our wounds, we won't heal. Acknowledging the truth of my abandonment, I did begin to heal, but after I opened my file.

Adoptee Clarissa Pinkola-Estés, a psychologist who wrote *Warming the Stone Child*, said that those who have been "abandoned" and face it and work through it can become the strongest people on the face of the earth.

Finding my answers happened slowly, like detective work, facing what seemed impossible. I shed old skin. I had the splitting sickness, though many don't call it that, not yet.

My adoptee friends Rhonda, Adrian and Anecia said some of the same things I'd already put in this memoir. No, it wasn't just me; I'm not alone. It helps to know you're not alone.

Once I finished the writing for *Talking Stick*, I went further, scouring Internet records, adoption stories, newspaper articles and laws and decided a book might help other adoptees as much as my search, research and reunion helped me.

I had to buy a filing cabinet. There was so much adoption history; I read more than I could ever write.

Post-Adoption Depression

Splitting sickness is defined by Indian people as soul sickness. Anyone can split, even adoptive moms. When you can't handle some part of your life, a part of you shuts down.

The *Globe and Mail* newspaper in Canada published a story in June 2009 about adoptive mothers who suffer from post-adoption depression, what I call the splitting sickness.

Apparently, more than a few adoptive moms didn't feel any love for their new adopted child, even after years of waiting, often at huge expense. Afraid their new adopted child might be taken away, or how they might be judged, adoptive moms would not seek help for their symptoms. The story said an estimated 11 to 18 percent of adoptions break down during the first six months. American researchers found two percent of adoptive families cannot cope after an adoption is finalized. In some cases, the child is returned to authorities and readopted.

So adoption isn't perfect? No, it's forced. Adoption creates a "fantasy family."

Women who suffer with this new disorder "post-adoption depression" have numerous symptoms: feeling sad, tearful, irritable; self-imposed isolation from family, friends, spouse; anger at the adopted child, spouse or other children for no apparent reason; desire to leave home or have the adopted child removed; loss of interest or pleasure in most activities; significant changes in appetite and sex drive; insomnia or a marked increase in sleep; fatigue, lack of energy; feelings of worthlessness or guilt; and thoughts of suicide.

But wait. These symptoms exactly describe what many adoptees experience, but it lasts their entire lives.

What looks like a fantasy can really be a nightmare.

Warning Labels

"Take the first step in faith. You don't have to see the whole staircase. Just take the first step." – Rev. Dr. Martin Luther King, Jr.

The adoption industry will not advertise that most patients in psychiatric care are adoptees. They don't warn adoptive parents their new child will suffer from "Severe Narcissistic Injury" or "Reactive Attachment Disorder." This news would not be welcome.

In fact, the adoption industry does not tell adoptive parents that adoption hurts adoptees so deeply they may consider suicide, self-medicate or commit criminal offenses.

Being an adoptee is a mind-altering experience, because the moment you are separated from your sacred space, the womb that brought you here—into this reality—into this world—being handed to strangers, given away, feels more like a nightmare.

I was terrified when *she* disappeared. No one could make *this* make sense.

I wrote in my journal, "Her rejection of you is the moment you become an orphan. The moment you become an orphan, your life literally rips apart."

Denial hurts, too, because the pain is more excruciating when an adoptee never finds answers. Pretending everything is OK does not make our adoptee symptoms go away.

Adoptive parents are assured adoptees won't need anyone but them, with little compassion for our complexities, or see our "soul sickness" as a ticking time bomb.

As a child I did not understand my emotional damage was a disorder nor did I receive treatment for depression. I've met many adoptees and none of us had treatment for severe narcissistic injury. We were never told.

It took me years to figure out how this happened. No one told me emotions, even extreme ones, could be expected at some point in my life. I was never allowed to express my fear, anxiety or confusion, or even admit these feelings existed. Like other adoptees, I might delay it until adulthood, or not express them at all.

Adoptees don't come with warning labels.

Maybe we should...

Baby Scoop Era

The "Baby Scoop Era" (named for the period, 1940s to mid-70s, during which adoption was virtually the only option for unwed pregnant women) ended after Roe v. Wade, as abortion was legalized and single motherhood gained acceptance. The resultant fall in adoption rates was drastic, from 19.2 percent of white, unmarried pregnant women in 1972 to 1.7 percent in 1995 (and lower among women of color). Adoption is big business— lots of money changing hands.

—DENISE, www.write-o-holic.blogspot.com

One White Newborn = $60,000-$80,000+ US

America's adoption industry earnings are approximately $1.4 billion each year. Every birth is a true miracle. We all know what a gift it is to have a baby. If famous people adopt, then it must be working, right?

After giving birth to one daughter then twins, actors Angelina Jolie and Brad Pitt are still madly in love with their three adopted children. I don't doubt that. But how do their adopted children feel? The press will never ask; I doubt we'll ever know. Of course, their children would say: "We are grateful, loved and happy." It's like a script. They won't say, "Get me outta here."

Being raised with nannies in a celebrity circus will be normal for some of them. Joan Crawford, Burt Reynolds, Rosie O'Donnell, Jamie Lee Curtis, Sharon Stone, Michele Pfeiffer, Calista Flockhart, Sheryl Crow, Barbara Walters, Tom Cruise and Nicole Kidman and many others in Hollywood made headlines when they adopted, shielding their precious darlings from the prying eyes of paparazzi. Madonna, Ricky Martin, and Meg Ryan made headlines when they adopted a Third World orphan.

Wealth and prestige might mask or delay symptoms in certain orphan adoptees.

Regardless, adoptees will have emotional difficulties, regardless of who adopts them, including Hollywood.

Bad Seed

I'm glad I don't recall the time I spent in a Minnesota orphanage. I won't deny adoption is necessary. Every child on Earth deserves a good home.

Since my adoptive parents never met my birthparents, they didn't know what kind of people they were. How heroic for them to adopt me when I might be flawed, or bad seed. Yes, it was dangerous to adopt a stranger's child. In the white America of my parent's era, "beware" and "be careful" was whispered about adoption since these babies might turn out to be genetic lemons.

Social workers might concoct a story, to sell us as white, even though Rhonda and I had our Indian blood, too. Our adoption files do not mention that fact.

Since America was founded, it wasn't safe to be anything but white. The Eugenics Movement enforced involuntary sterilizations of minorities, particularly indigenous people (Indians) and Africans Americans.

Growing up, I never heard, "Tracy was illegitimate or Joey is someone's dirty little secret!" but I knew it's what people were thinking. People at church watched us with either scrutiny or pity. If Joey and I did not turn out OK, using the genetic lemon theory, it wouldn't be our parents fault.

Today an adoptive parent can return flawed orphans who don't bond well or act out. There are special lawyers who sue adoption agencies when an adoptee is imperfect in some way.

To protect ourselves, adoptees will train themselves to look happy. I know I did.

Funny, I always seemed to know who was adopted. Our parents usually introduced us or we introduced ourselves as adopted children. I had two friends named Kim and another named Lisa and we all knew we were adopted.

This became our bond, our shared identity.

Indians Never Forget They Are Indians

For any adoptee, opening an adoption is like opening Pandora's Box. You just never know who—or what—will fly out at you. Since this story means a lot to Split Feathers, I couldn't stop until I knew everything I could.

America's Indian Adoption Project was not publicized or well known, just like a few more secrets I found buried along the way. Congress heard Indian leaders complain in 1974, "In Minnesota, 90 percent of the adopted Indian children are placed in non-Indian homes." I was born in Minnesota.

The adoption industry won't say exactly how many Indian children were adopted. They'll say adoptees were raised by people who wanted us. They'll say our birthparents were poor. They'll say adoptions were done legally.

Wayne Carp, an adoption advocate and author who went "undercover" to compile his book on adoption history kept running into secrecy problems. Unlike Carp, I am the story. I didn't go undercover. I dove in headfirst.

"Be kinder than necessary, for everyone you meet is fighting some kind of battle." I don't know who said this but it says so much. Regardless if you're Indian or non-Indian, adoptees from closed adoptions do battle with the same things.

Even if the people who adopted us were kind, generous, thoughtful people, can they imagine what it feels like being adopted? Hardly. Wearing this "secret adoption" mentality is like wearing a strait-jacket. It wears you down. I tried to avoid it but couldn't.

When uncertainty becomes insecurity—that is not good for anyone, especially for those families who live with or love an adoptee.

In 2009, Amazon.com had over 5,000 books on adoption. The majority written by adoptive parents, professionals and the system designed to promote more adoptions. Far fewer books are written by adoptees. I'm not surprised.

I am not designating myself an expert here, since I know many adoptions happen for different reasons with different results. Too many people, even Indians, take their identity for granted which makes it all the more frustrating. America has amnesia about lots of things, especially American Indians. Americans will need to wrap their minds around some very troubling history.

By the way, Indians never forget they are Indians, even when they are raised by non-Indians—or ducks.

Adopt, Adapt

...Leo Her Many Horses, an Arapaho who lives in Wyoming, says the men's chicken dance starts with the story of a boy who was feeling badly because he didn't belong to any tribe. He sat outside the powwow and watched the prairie chickens for a bit before coming back into the powwow, emulating their movement. At first, other dancers were appalled at this dance, but the elders said no, let him be, he represents the bird nation.

["American Indian dancers keeping it real," by Shauna Stephenson, News from Indian Country, Aug. 20, 2007, page 26]

My husband Herb calls me a bird. I know he's right.

Every bird has a song. Birds learn to sing listening to their parents who learned it from their parents. Each generation, birds make nests, roost and sing in the season of spring. Baby birds hatch in sync with migrations. Each chirp is a signal, warning of danger or predators. Birds must sing or they'll surely die.

Orphaned birds can't sing. They can't without parents to teach them. If baby birds are abandoned, they'll die. If raised by foster bird-parents, they'll sing just like them. Baby birds mimic and adapt.

Like an abandoned bird, I was fostered (then adopted) by strangers. I learned to sing like them. Adoptees mimic and adapt.

In Indian Country, grieving grandparents call us Lost Ones, Split Feathers or Lost Birds; they say we come from two worlds and there are so many of us, they call to us in dreams, as ghosts.

Birds do hold a special place in many cultures. In Hindu myth, birds are the messengers of the gods. Bird clans are alive today in many tribal nations and indigenous cultures. Singing is not just sacred, it's ceremony.

I am a Lost Bird and know the history of America is a history of possession, not just land, but perception. I know Native people get upset when our cultural beliefs are misinterpreted, even misused. I get that those who control the land control the history. If we don't know this, we are doomed.

Many Lost Birds I've met are my age, in their 30s, 40s or older. We have our own story now, and our own honor song. We live two cultures. We understand what adoption did to more than a few American Indian families.

Knowing you're not alone works like medicine.

NANCY VERRIER M.A., PSYCHOTHERAPIST

"The chosen child and the grateful child myths are two beliefs that die hard. Although made to feel as if it were the case, most adoptees do not feel chosen so much as they feel **unchosen** by their birth mothers. To be chosen by anyone else after that is anticlimactic. So far as being grateful, it is the adoptive parents who should be grateful. They are the ones pursuing the adoption. They are the ones who got what they wanted. No child would choose to be separated from his biological mother. That she/he may have to be separated from her is a different thing altogether. That is an intellectual, adult decision, not an emotional/sensual baby experience. Although grateful for many things his/her parents may have done for them, no child should be obligated to feel grateful for having a loving set of parents. That should be his right."

Four Traumas

More and more of this adoption reality is coming out on the internet, which means more and more adoptive parents and birthparents are in for a few more surprises. One study claims adoptees are more traumatized than a prisoner of war. We suffer from post-traumatic stress disorder. A prisoner of war may escape or be released, but an adoptee will suffer its effects our entire life. There is no known cure.

Now I believe there are four distinct traumas in being an adoptee.

They are: 1) in utero, when you hear what is happening to you or sense what is coming; 2) when you are delivered, abandoned, and handed to strangers; 3) later when you are told you are adopted and realize fully what being "adopted" means; and 4) when you realize you are different, from a different culture or country, and you can't contact your family, or know them, or have the information you need to find them.

It took me years to get this. There were more traumas, too—like when I'd fill out forms at the doctor's office. I had no medical history. I had no idea if I was sitting next to someone who could be my biological brother, mother or father. To think I could marry my own relative and not even know it, that idea was horrifying.

I could carry a gene that I pass down to my own children—but I wouldn't know until it's too late. My child could suffer since I didn't know. If my birthparents were alcoholics, then I really shouldn't drink. I could be pre-disposed to diabetes or heart disease or cancer or depression and not know this. My list went on and on.

Adopted daughter gets what's rightfully hers

[THE CONNECTICUT LAW TRIBUNE, Scott Brede, August 20, 2007]

Loranda Kay Costello is $180,000 richer and met her birth father for the first time, all thanks to her attorney's successful efforts to open Costello's adoption records.

Born a member of the Yakama Indian Nation in Washington State, Costello was whisked away to Connecticut at the age of 6. Her birthfather was imprisoned and her birthmother had a drinking problem. Here she was adopted by a Stratford couple, and her name changed from Laronda Peter to Loranda Neupert. (Later when she married, she took her husband's last name.)

Growing up, she and her brother, Joseph, had vague knowledge that they were Native American, but didn't know the name of the tribe to which they belonged and had no contact with their birth parents, according to Costello's attorney, Allison M. Near, of Hurwitz, Sagarin, Slossberg & Knuff in Milford.

In college, Costello grew more interested in her heritage and learned that members of certain tribes may be eligible for scholarships, Near said. As it turns out, members of the Yakama Indian Nation receive financial payments from the tribe generated partly from the tribe's timber lease. "That's something that would have been paid out [to Costello] in various installments throughout her life, had [the tribe] known her whereabouts," Near said.

Over the years, the installments added up. Online, Costello eventually learned the U.S. Office of the Special Trustee for American Indians was holding benefits under her birth name that had amassed to roughly $180,000, according to Near. The problem was she needed proof that she was, indeed, that little girl who was separated from her biological parents some four decades earlier.

The agency that handled Costello's adoption attested, in a letter, that her parents were, indeed, Yakama tribal members, and gave her some other non-identifying information about them. To satisfy the requirement for proving her name change, however, she needed to obtain a copy of her adoption decree. In April, the Stratford Probate Court directed the adoption agency to release a copy of the decree with non-identifying information about her birth parents pursuant to C.G.S. § 45a-748. That still wasn't good enough to satisfy the Yakama tribe. It required a copy of the decree certified by the probate court itself.

Costello's husband is a longtime Hurwitz Sagarin client. Represented by Near, she petitioned Probate Judge F. Paul Kurmay to allow her access to her court adoption record under the Indian Child Welfare Act (ICWA).

"Under Connecticut law, you really can't get anything without parental consent," said Near. But in the interests of promoting the stability and culture of Indian tribes and families, the ICWA provides Native Americans who were adopted access to information about their biological parents 'as may be necessary to protect any rights flowing from the individual's tribal relationship.'

Kurmay found Costello had a 'powerful due process and equal protection of the law argument' and held that the federal law took precedence in the matter before him.

Last month (July 2007), with a certified copy of her adoption decree in hand, Costello traveled to Washington and collected what is owed to her.

Though her birth mother has since passed away, she and her brother reunited with their biological father who had long been in search of their location. "She's got siblings she didn't even know about," said Near. "It's really been an incredible experience for her."

> American Indian and Alaska Native children had the highest rates of victimization (abuse) by white Americans nearly 2 to 1 over their Euro-American counterparts.
> - A study from the National Clearinghouse on Child Abuse and Neglect

Treaty Rights

Never in my wildest dreams did I expect — or imagine—how writing this would impact my life, or change me—again. I have not met one Native adoptee who is interested in claiming money. Like me, most want to meet relatives, relearn language, know their history, and know how to pray. Most of us want to be enrolled in the tribe (on paper) and attend ceremonies.

The tragedy? So many Lost Birds are still lost. The vast majority of tribes are struggling and do not have the means or money or the interest to find us. The Lost Birds I've met could not afford to hire detectives or a lawyer. Adoptees will remain invisible without the government-issued tribal enrollment card.

Enrolled tribal members do have guaranteed treaty rights. What Indians gave up in land and territory was exchanged for the rights to hunt, fish and gather. It may sound primitive but it still exists. By treaty, the American government guarantees every Indian has health, education and welfare guaranteed in those treaty rights.

Most Native people I know paint, bead or write for a living. The Native American Arts and Crafts Act passed in 1990, and made it illegal to label or market "art" or "crafts" as Indian-made except by federally-recognized and enrolled tribal members.

Crazy Horse Didn't Have a Tribal ID

Indigenous people of North America don't all look a certain way, and quite honestly they never did! Crazy Horse had long reddish-brown wavy hair. That pretty much describes mine.

Indians come in all colors, shapes and sizes. Anti-Indian attitudes flourish across America and Canada, and Indians are now the only people in the *world* to have to constantly prove their identity or show some kind of identification (ID) card.

Indians clearly understand why the federal and state governments want less of us on the tribal rolls —it's less work. Accounting for land leases and repaying millions (possibly billions) in unpaid Indian trust funds, perhaps the American government hoped Indians would be too weak to remember, or too cautious to fight back, reminded of past treatment.

In any case, adoptees will remain lost with sealed adoption records. None of us will be entitled to promises made in the treaties. Indian identification cards are now a re-quirement in this century. Looks don't cut it anymore.

It's just one more obstacle for Native adoptees to overcome—no identification card. Obviously Africans Americans don't have to show an ID card to prove their identity or tribal ancestry.

I doubt that Crazy Horse ever had to show identification to anyone. Crazy Horse didn't have a tribal ID card anyway.

My Maliseet friend Russ called his tribal ID his "Holocaust Card."

Religious Freedom
"I think the spiritual values come first and everything else follows..."
— Leonard George, Chief Councilor

One Indian Adoption Project relocated almost 400 Indian children to families in New York.

Two close friends, both adopted and Native, were raised in New York in the late 1950s, early 1960s; one with a Jewish family; the other with Christian parents. Neither was told anything about being American Indian, but both men could *see* that they were.

My Apache friend eventually met his biological family and traveled to his reservation; while my other friend, the Lakota, opened his adoption records with the help of the T.R.Y. agency (located in Massachusetts) but he learned that his Lakota birthmother didn't want any contact with him. His uncle agreed to speak with him. My friend has no idea who his biological father might be, or if he is Lakota plus something else.

Many Lost Birds feel ceremonial practices are an integral part of their spirituality and growth. These men missed those experiences growing up, and felt robbed of their identity as Native men. My Apache friend did attend ceremonies, after a period of adjustment, getting to know his ancestral Apache family.

There was a time when all tribes' were banned from having ceremonies, when the Sundance, Ghost Dance, Midewin, Sweat lodge, Vision quest, Powwow and others, were illegal in America. This discrimination was finally reversed in 1978.

> *Henceforth it shall be the policy of the United States to protect and preserve for American Indians their inherent right of freedom to believe, express, and exercise the traditional religions of the American Indian, Eskimo, Aleut, and Native Hawaiians, including but not limited to access to sites, use and possession of sacred objects, and the freedom to worship through ceremonials and traditional rites.*
> *—American Indian Religious Freedom Act of 1978, Public Law 95-341*

Fellow journalist Suzan Shown Harjo, Hodulgee Muscogee/Cheyenne, founder of the Morning Star Institute in Washington, D.C., gave this testimony to Congress on the history of the American Indian Religious Freedom Act:

"This Act was necessary in 1978 because Native Peoples were still suffering the ill-effects of sorry policies of the past, intended to ban traditional religions, to neutralize or eliminate traditional religious leaders and to force traditional religious practitioners to convert to Christianity, to take up English and to give up their way of life. Even though the federal Civilization Regulations that first criminalized traditional religious expressions in the 1880s were withdrawn in the mid-1930s, laws and practices impeding Native Americans' free exercise of traditional religions persisted. Native sacred objects continued to be confiscated and graves looted. Those objects stolen in earlier times filled federal, state and private collections, as well as museums and educational institutions in Europe. Native sacred places continued to be desecrated and damaged. Those annexed during the formal "Civilization" period remained in non-Native governmental and private hands, and Native people risked stiff fines and imprisonment for fulfilling religious mandates at those sites. Native traditional people organized a national coalition in 1967 to gain protections for sacred places and ceremonies, to recover Native human remains and sacred objects and to promote respect for Native people and rights in general society."

About The Indian Adoption Projects and Programs:

Working Together to Strengthen Supports for Indian Children and Families: A National Perspective, Keynote Speech by Shay Bilchik at the NICWA Conference, Anchorage, Alaska on April 24, 2001

For a long time in the early history of child welfare, many educated middle-class Americans sincerely believed that the world would run smoothly and sweetly if everybody would just make the effort to think and behave like they did. In the name of improvement, Irish and Italian children were scooped up from city tenements that looked crowded and dirty, away from "unfit" single parents and the smells of unfamiliar cooking, taken to the countryside in orphan trains, and parceled out to rural families. Most of them never saw their parents or siblings again.

These were terrible acts, no matter how noble or "professional" the intentions of their perpetrators. Next to the death penalty, the most absolute thing a government can do to an individual is to take a child away. But these were acts against individual immigrant families, and no European national group was singled out for these removals to the point of being imperiled.

One ethnic group, however—American Indians and Alaskan Natives—a people of many cultures and governments, and the original citizens of this land—was singled out for treatment that ranged over the decades from outright massacre to arrogant and paternalistic "improvement." CWLA played a role in that attempt. We must face this truth.

No matter how well intentioned and how squarely in the mainstream this was at the time, it was wrong; it was hurtful; and it reflected a kind of bias that surfaces feelings of shame, as we look back with the 20/20 vision of hindsight.

I am not here today to deny or minimize that role, but to put it on the table and to acknowledge it as truth. And then, in time, and to the extent that each of us is able, to move forward in a new relationship in which your governments are honored and respected, our actions are based upon your needs and values, and we show proper deference to you in everything that concerns Native children and families.

These are the facts. Between 1958 and 1967, CWLA cooperated with the Bureau of Indian Affairs, under a federal contract, to facilitate an experiment in which 395 Indian children were removed from their tribes and cultures for adoption by non-Indian families. This experiment began primarily in the New England states. CWLA channeled federal funds to its oldest and most established private agencies first, to arrange the adoptions, though public child welfare agencies were also involved toward the end of this period. Exactly 395 adoptions of Indian children were done and studied during this 10-year period, with the numbers peaking in 1967. ARENA, the Adoption Resource Exchange of North America, began in early 1968 as the successor to the BIA/CWLA Indian Adoption Project. Counting the period before 1958 and some years after it, CWLA was partly responsible for approximately 650 children being taken from their tribes and placed in non-Indian homes. For some of you, this story is a part of your personal history. Through this project, BIA and CWLA actively encouraged states to continue and to expand the practice of "rescuing" Native children from their own culture, from their very families. Because of this legitimizing effect, the indirect results of this initiative cannot be measured by the numbers I have cited. Paternalism under the guise of child welfare is still alive in many locations today, as you well know.

EARLY YEARS

"I'll Take That One"

So how does this work? Was I like a lost-and-found item in a department store then put out on display? Did strangers come in, spot me and point, "I'll take that one." How did they know it was me they wanted? Why me in particular? It's not like an interview if I can't talk yet.

Actually, my parents didn't choose me. I was available and the Catholic Charities people brought me to them and sold them on me. After this transaction, I became invisible, unidentifiable and perfectly suited to blend in with all the other children. I was in a real sense legal property, given a new name and identity and supposedly matched to look like my adoptive parents.

How strange, really. Then I'm supposed to thank them and love them for buying me and giving me a home. Of course I did. I did love them with all my heart. There must be a rule book on this somewhere, right?

My birthmother Helen was Catholic. Marriage was an institution, central to many religions. Had this religion instructed everyone to judge a woman with an illegitimate child? Make this baby a sacrificial lamb? Did they say to her, "You get a do-over if you abandon your baby... No one will ever know they existed... You'll never find a husband with a bastard kid."

It was different in Indian Country. Native women would choose a father for her children and if he didn't work, she'd choose another one. For many Native mothers, the rule book changed when organized religions took over. Native mothers had many things working against them, like the plague of poverty and persistent oppression, and the wrong ideas about customs and savage Indians.

I finally saw the myths created for me. Gratitude is easy when you're young. Impossible when you're an adult. My gratitude silenced me, almost permanently.

When I reached adulthood, the words "this was done in your best interest" felt like pure nonsense. Clearly that wasn't enough information to build a life on.

I was not their legal property but a human being.

State Secret

After my 1958 adoption hearing in a Wisconsin courtroom, I was legally re-named Tracy Ann and handed to Sev and Edie DeMeyer. An orphan boy they named Joey arrived in 1958.

Trained as foster parents, Edie and Sev, my mom and dad, had tried to have their own babies but couldn't. Adopting me meant they'd have their family, first me, then hopefully a boy.

Amid the oohs and ahhs of this joyous occasion, had my new family considered my heredity, or the egg and sperm that created my body, and my DNA? Had anyone considered what I'd experience being thrust into a sea of new faces?

No, they celebrated. They had no idea I was devastated by the loss of my own mother.

Edie and Sev knew they had a big job ahead, raising me and Joey (who they named Joseph

William). They assumed we'd be ok. No one said otherwise.

They didn't know (or seem to care) who I really was. My Indian blood was secret. We did not talk about it.

Obviously I'd adapt. Their identity would become my identity.

As a teenager, I decided to open my adoption. I knew it would require patience and probably miracles.

Remember a chicken raised by ducks? This is where it gets interesting. It's hard to tell the difference when you're tiny, hungry, helpless. Edie and Sev nursed me back to health after the orphanage and two foster homes. I guess I worried them because I didn't cry. I didn't for a long time, mom said.

Other Split Feathers say we don't cry because we're "in shock."

Today I cry rivers.

Mom

It took me awhile but today I see my mom as her own person and less as the woman who adopted me. No one will ever replace her in my life, while I'm sure both of us would like to go  back and do many things differently. When I write about Edie, a jar of her homemade applesauce is on my desk or on the kitchen counter. It reminds me of the nice things she did. I do remember her breaded pork chops, chicken and rice, homemade bread, and lemon meringue pies. Dad said mom couldn't boil water when they got married.

Our house was beautiful, and at the appropriate time, full of holiday decorations; we threw big parties; and we always had a packed refrigerator so we never went hungry. Mom cleaned like a fanatic and cooked like Martha Stewart.

I don't believe Mom thinks she chose badly in a husband. Maybe Sev was really something when they were in their 20s, when he was courting her.

Edie (short for Edythe Mae) was a beauty with brains. She excelled in math, English and music. She had top security clearance at Hanford, the country's first nuclear power facilities. She knew shorthand and took dictation — the nuclear physicists only had to correct her spelling of the words she never understood. She wrote 10+ letter words phonetically. She signed an agreement she would never discuss what she did at Hanford, where they developed the first nuclear weapons.

Edie told us stories about her father Edward, an auctioneer after the Great Depression and how he managed pro-wrestlers. Mom claims she was her dad's favorite. Grandpa held her for three days when she had scarlet fever as a baby, when she was not expected to live.

Oswego Mafia

I loved mom's stories. One summer in Oswego, Illinois, Mom was running through wet grass and fell on a milk bottle, severely cutting her right arm near her elbow. She was 11 or 12 and described seeing her bone through bloody shreds of skin.

Dr. L. J. Weishew, a mob doctor, clamped mom's bloody mess together. If the regular town doctor hadn't been away or drunk, mom believes she would have been permanently disabled, unable to use that arm. She said Doc Weishew used clamps and poured disinfectant in her wound.

Weishew was the second generation in a family of doctors in Oswego, outside of Chicago. I did some digging and emailed Roger Matile, director of the Little White School Museum in Oswego. He wrote, "While Dr. Weishew was rumored to have treated various members of the Dillinger and other gangs; no real proof was ever produced, although the circumstantial evidence was pretty strong. For instance, John "Three Fingered Jack" Hamilton, one of Dillinger's gang, was killed while the group escaped from the Little Bohemia resort in northern Wisconsin. Hamilton's body was buried in a shallow grave along Illinois Route 25 less than a mile north of Dr. Weishew's home."

When the cops found Hamilton's body, burned beyond recognition with lye, mom and her siblings hung out by the funeral home, hoping to catch a glimpse of the Oswego Mafia. Edie believed Doc Weishew was arrested (though I couldn't confirm this with Matile) and mom wondered what happened to his beautiful wife and two young daughters.

Don, Doc Weishew's son, was very sick with tuberculosis, so mom and her sister Marj visited him and sang to him in the hospital. A cure for TB didn't exist and Don died as a child.

How ironic mom and dad built a lake home in northern Wisconsin where the Dillinger gang was suspected of hiding out in the 1930s.

Joey and I listened as mom told her stories.

She had one boyfriend, Eddie, who flew his own plane. They met when she and her parents lived in Richland, when the first Nuclear Reactors were being built in the desert. Mom said Eddie really wanted to marry her and flew her to lunch on the Oregon coast.

We wondered if she regretted her decision not to marry Eddie. She said no, but there was this strange wistful look in her eyes.

Bob and Delores Adopt Four

When mom was 22, she and her sister Marj moved to Los Angeles. They applied for a job giving music lessons at Bob Hope's house in Toluca Lake.

Mom saw stacks of Bob's new book sitting on a table near the door (possibly this was his third book, *So This is Peace* in 1946). Bob, whose real name was Leslie Townes, wasn't home. Bob and Delores had adopted four children, Linda, Anthony, Nora, and Kelly; all from the same orphanage in Evanston, Illinois. Mom saw their photos in the living room. Delores, Mrs. Hope, told them she needed just one music tutor for her kids so Mom and Marj gracefully declined. Delores drove them back to Redondo Beach when mom told her they'd taken the bus.

Mom, Marj and girlfriend Cathy all shared a house on Redondo Beach. They could walk down the boardwalk to hear the Jimmy Dorsey Orchestra and see all kinds of movie stars. Mom had a civil defense job, working as a private secretary to a top boss. Lucille Ball and other entertainers visited where she worked.

Mom could have been a movie star, she was that photogenic. She bragged how tiny her waist was; she said one boss had a huge crush on her.

While riding bikes in the mountains, Mom, not realizing how sun-burned she was, accidentally cut her own thigh with her fingernail. Her leg took a long time to heal. Mom showed us how to tan using olive oil, plus it worked as a bug repellent. Flies hated it.

Joey and I would listen as we sunbathed in our backyard in Wisconsin, Mom sprawled on her redwood lounge, with Bubbles our dog napping underneath.

Mom said her mother Kathryn was from Keswick, Cumberland, England. Her maiden name was Usher-Pearson. Kathryn had two sisters, Edythe and Ann.

Auntie Ann sent us gifts from England. I still have a cedar pencil box with my name on it. Auntie Ann wrote about mom's aunts and uncles in her letters.

We learned how mom's mother Kathryn studied opera in Edinburgh, Scotland and went to college there. Grandma sang like an angel and mom would say, "When she sang 'Oh Danny Boy,' people would cry." We heard how grandma played opera on 78 records when she'd clean and bake on Saturdays. I vaguely remember her upswept hair and British accent. She died when I was young. I promised mom I'll find the graves of her grandparents in England, and leave them flowers.

Mom's father, Edward, had a twin sister. Joey and I laughed since he was over six feet tall and his twin sister was barely five feet. Edward's family had lived in Indiana and Illinois. Edward's father died from eating poisonous mushrooms. Edward met Kathryn during WWI when the three British sisters were sent to the US for their safety.

Mom always told great stories.

Infertility

Mom never told me about the two babies she lost. For her, infertility must have been heartbreaking, a pain I can't fully imagine.

I heard about mom's miscarriages from Joey's wife, Tracy Lea, my sister-in-law. When Joey married Tracy Lea in 1980, I became "Trace" and have used this name ever since.

Tracy Lea heard how doctors did a total hysterectomy when mom was just 28. Mom probably had endometriosis, which is operable, even curable. That had to be hard on mom, probably why she never mentioned her miscarriages to me.

The 1950s were primetime for the adoption experiment since there was baby formula and babies waiting. Edie was 31 and Sev was 35 when I was born in 1956. Mom converted to dad's Catholic religion before they married in 1948.

I don't think it was mom's idea to adopt. It's what infertile couples did in those days.

Before I arrived in 1957, they were foster parents to a little girl named Cathy. Mom remembered, "Your dad told the social workers if Cathy stayed any longer, we were going to keep her. Catholic Charities took her away the next day. She was not adoptable, or legally free, like you."

There are moments when I do remember Cathy. I named a doll after her. I just can't remember her face. If my parents loved her, where are Cathy's baby photos? I could never find any. There is no trace of her. There are no newborn baby pictures of me, either.

Why did it take so long for me to be adopted? I may never know.

Sickly

When I arrived in 1957, I'd scream when mom tried to lay me on my stomach. I didn't cry. The back of my head was bald. I suffered with chronic ear infections, stomach aches, constipation, skin rashes and itchy hives well into grade school but mom said they loved me through it.

Of course, our family doctor gave me antibiotics in those days, now considered ineffective, and possibly dangerous. Over-use of antibiotics was common then; I was already allergic to penicillin. Very early my immune system was not working well. Now I find out my skin was telling me I had allergies.

It was hard to tell when I was sick, Mom said, but she could tell by looking in my eyes. (What was I, a zombie?) I look sad in many photos, but apparently this was no cause for alarm. They figured I'd grow out of it.

My first Christmas, I had a high fever and wasn't excited at my new toys or the frilly dresses. Immediately Edie figured out I was sick. They called the family doctor. Sev demanded he drive out in a snowstorm on Christmas Eve, yelling "Get out here now."

Sev was always the doting dad. Mom claims he'd get up and give me a bottle, change my diapers, and rock me back to sleep. I could tell my dad loved me. I was sure.

First Memory

My first real childhood memory is in 1961. Joey accidentally knocked the wind out of me as we're tossing an inflatable ball around the backyard. I fell backwards, dizzy. Sev screamed. Immediately he grabs Joey, tiny at age three, cursing and yelling as he carries him into the house.

Mom, upright from sunbathing on her lounge, yells to him, "Tracy's fine."

I suddenly realize what Sev might do to Joey; and that scared me more than anything.

This is my first memory of us as a family. We're outside, we're playing, and then I'm terrified.

Joey is fifteen months younger than me. After that day, I never wanted Sev to hurt him, or scare him, ever again. It became my job to protect him.

Birth Defects

I wasn't exactly happy when Joey entered the picture in 1958. I was jealous over all the attention he was getting. Mom remembers I was curious at first; then Joey bit me so hard I bled after I tried to steal his bottle. I never tried again.

In no time, Joey was my very own baby.

At home, we'd usually have an early supper, with plenty of fresh game, fish and vegetables. Our home-cooked dinners were perfect but that half-hour wasn't the most relaxing. Many arguments would happen over supper, seated at our dinner table.

I could always tell when Joey was nervous; he'd eat too fast. Once he bit his own thumb so hard it bled. Joey stuffed himself, which experts claim is emotional; it just looked like he was starving. There was always enough food.

The minute Joey finished eating, he'd rush off to the bathroom, same time every night. You could set a clock by this boy's colon.

Years passed before Joey learned he had a birth defect. He had major surgery in his 40s to correct it.

After my frequent painful bladder infections, I had my own birth defect; my urethra was too small. I had surgery at 19 to correct it.

Medical history is essential to every human being. For adoptees with sealed adoptions, this basic human necessity wasn't ever taken into account.

Good Daughter

Over time, our little family of four grew inseparably linked. I flourished, yes. As quickly as I grew, uneasiness grew too. I knew I was different. Something wasn't right.

My friend Rhonda remembers at age four she wanted to run away. I had the feeling too that home wasn't really home. I wanted to be someplace else.

Perhaps Edie felt this, too. Mom would say to me, "You act like you don't like me."

There was a reason. She was not my birthmother. Children are quite honest when they are confused. I had questions. So much didn't make sense.

I hid any sign of desperation and confusion. There were no words for my uneasiness, nor could I fathom how to deal with it. While my friends were running around thinking about grades and boys, I just worried about everything.

Not quite sure what my brain was telling me, I acted normal. Well, at least I thought I did.

I never had a bad experience with my extended DeMeyer family, really. I was treated just like the rest of my cousins. All my aunts were kind. Some paid very close attention. I'm sure they watched with curiosity—since ours was the only family with adopted kids.

I got real good at hiding my thoughts which were locked up just like my adoption records, tucked away in a courthouse vault, buried in total darkness. Sometimes it scared me. Why was I adopted? What was wrong with me? It had to be horrible.

Part of me lived while the other part stayed hidden, pretending to be a good daughter, sister, classmate, friend.

Someone called me "bubbly." I was that good as a kid. Luckily I discovered I could become a new person at will. I could create a happy personality who could handle anything, do anything, and be anything. I looked fearless.

Blocking confusion from my mind was sick but a safety net. No one knew how lousy I felt. I had no clue I was grieving. Parts of my brain didn't function until much later, not until I started to wake up all these buried memories.

This is the splitting sickness; it can be dangerous, even fatal.

Maybe...Maybe...

That's me in 1961, with my makeshift microphone, crafted out of a stick and small plastic shovel. I'm singing on our picnic table. Edie and Sev's taste in music had rubbed off. Both my parents were talented musicians, great singers who threw all-night parties on the weekends.

By age 4, I could sing every song on their favorite album, *Top Hits of 1959*, including "*Primrose Lane*" sung by Bobby Darin. The nuns at school were impressed when I sang "Mack the Knife" instead of a nursery rhyme in first grade; one nun even called our house, laughing. Honestly, I didn't know any nursery rhymes. Singing was good for me. In the book *Mozart Effect*, music therapist Don Campbell claims the ear grows the brain. At 18 weeks and still in the womb, a baby's ear develops. If we can hear in the womb, obviously we can hear our parents talking. Maybe I heard music.

At home, Edie played organ and Sev played drums while our guests would drink and dance. Joey and I listened from our beds. We ate their cold hors d'oeuvres before they woke up.

Very young, I invented maybes. Maybe my mother wasn't able to keep me. Maybe something bad had happened. Maybe she was a teenager. Maybe I was sick. Maybe she regretted letting me go. Maybe they were looking for me. Maybe she died...

Thoughts went back and forth in my young head, not every day but often. Maybe was all I could come up with. I just didn't know. Trust me, maybes were torture.

But there were signs. When I told my little brother I could make it rain, making him sing and dance in a circle beside me, Joey believed me when the sun disappeared, and clouds filled the skies.

"Dance with me, Joey, dance …" and so we did.
Then the sky opened and sprinkled rain on our
heads like a baptism, a blessing.

I'll never forget the look on his little face.
Joey still remembers. Nobody taught me to dance. I
just knew.

Mrs. Sanders

I grew up in the Arrowhead region, the
home of the Chippewa Indian; they call themselves
Anishinabe, the First People. Clans of Algonquin-
speaking people live near and around Lake Superior
in the US and Canada.

Lucky for me, Mom and Dad weren't
adverse or racist toward Indians. I always knew
who the Indian people were. Indian people were
everywhere, especially in Douglas County.

Many of our neighbors had Indian blood.
They knew me well, especially Mrs. Sanders who
babysat. Lloyd and Dorothy Sanders, an Ojibwe
couple with three kids, lived next door. Dorothy
knew I was Indian and showed me so much love
and interest; I am humbled to remember her.

I remember Dorothy, always smiling at me,
encouraging me without words. I was blessed to
know her and have this acceptance as a young child.

Eventually, I developed Indian radar. I
sensed when others are around. It took years
before I realized how many Indian people I knew
and how many did watch over me when I was
young. I always felt more comfortable, more
myself with Indian people.

Much later when I was fostered by my
Lakota friends, this helped me understand the

beauty of those early relationships with women like Dorothy.

My mind simply blocked out what I was unable to handle, so I split for my own protection. That's normal, experts claim. Parts of me grew, while other parts shut down.

Shocked

Very early it was explained to me and Joey that we were adopted. Mom and dad told us because they didn't want the kids at school (or anyone else) to blurt it out and embarrass us. The social workers told them to tell us early so we wouldn't be shocked. I was very young and it was confusing but I got the picture. For a while their news felt special but that wore off in a hurry.

Joey and I could have passed as their biological children. Back then babies were apparently "matched" to look like their adoptive parents. That way they wouldn't have to tell us, "Oh yeah, we adopted you."

I heard often, "you look just like your dad." I knew better. Our physical bodies weren't that different. Mentally, we were worlds apart. I did have dark hair like Sev and Edie in her pre-blonde days. Joey still looks like Edie in many ways.

In fact in 2009, Joey's identity is still a mystery. He didn't open his adoption like I did. Some experts claim adopted boys don't want to hurt their adoptive mothers. Mom and dad could have lied and not told us, which is unimaginable, knowing what I know now. Not knowing you're adopted can still make you crazy. No one ever said I was Indian. I just knew.

Braids

By the 1st grade I told mom I wanted to wear two braids. She braided my hair until I could do it myself.

There was no kindergarten class so I started first grade at St. Anthony's Catholic Grade School, my dad Sev's alma mater. Our parish had a church, rectory, convent and grade school in Allouez, a Belgian enclave in a suburb of Superior, Wisconsin.

Dad's parents, Henry DeMeyer and Romanie "Rose" Baert, had both migrated from Belgium. Henry was killed in a tragic accident in 1923 when dad was just three. Henry's horse and buggy was smashed between two trolley cars in south Superior. Rose, my grieving grandma then lost the baby she was carrying. To feed her six hungry kids, a friend loaned Rose money to open a chicken restaurant and she secretly bootlegged beer in a back room during Prohibition. Dad and my uncles gathered coal off railroad tracks, even burning the basement stairs one winter to keep their house warm.

Dad's habit of burning things continued; our basement incinerator was always blazing and burned little Joey's arm (accidentally) more than once. Our house was never cold.

Though he never talked about it, Dad studied eight grades at St. Anthony's then quit school. I saw a photo of him bartending at Rose's tavern. Then he worked on the Great Northern railroad, probably when he started drinking so heavy.

I knew his history.

Jealous Bastard

Many adoptees would be satisfied just to know the truth. Contact is a different matter and no reasonable person on either point of the adoption triangle expects a relationship to automatically develop with strangers, even strangers who are biologically related. Adoptees, generally, are not seeking a family, but themselves. —Bastard Nation.org

As I got older, I became jealous of kids who lived with their biological parents. I hated being a mystery.

My adoptee friends remind me of what we heard. "You can't help but envy those kids who look exactly like their mother and father, because you don't look like anyone… kids on the school bus and at school who call you a bastard or an orphan, you grown deaf to it. You grow deaf to their questions — 'don't you wonder who you are?'"

Adoptees heard the same things I did, wherever they grew up.

They remembered, "Our parents told us what to do, what to think, how to feel. 'Be happy you're here with us. We choose you. We love you.' Any doubts we have, we're not able to express them. When you are not allowed to know who you are—parts of you go numb."

No orphan can escape this—a heart broken too often turns to stone.

I didn't know what to say to my friends when they asked me about being adopted, other than it was embarrassing and something bad must have happened.

The kids on the school bus did call me a cat-tail —which meant Catholic.

My closest friends in grade school didn't question me. I knew before 1st grade I was adopted. One classmate Kim from St. Anthony's told me in 2009 that her parents explained Joey and I were adopted and to never bring it up.

Joey and I did talk about it. It just didn't make any sense. What was wrong with us? Why were we given up? This nagging fear never left us alone.

Eventually it hit us we were not really brother and sister, by blood. That hurt both of us. Yet we never hesitated in being best friends, or fighting like cats and dogs.

We approached Mom (cautiously) on adoption. We waited until she brought it up since it made her so uncomfortable.

"Is anything wrong... with us?" She'd answer, "No. There's nothing wrong with you." I eventually figured out there was definitely something wrong with our biological parents or else we wouldn't be in this situation.

"Nothing is wrong" was so wrong. Lies don't help. Dreaming up questions for her was tough. Sometimes mom would say, "It's because your parents couldn't keep you, they weren't married, or maybe, maybe, maybe...."

The truth would have been better, much better.

Reasons

Mom gave us lots of valid reasons for them to adopt. Edie and Sev tried to have babies but couldn't. They were Catholic and wanted kids. That was their reason. So we believed it. They wanted us. Our other parents didn't.

So by trial and error, Joey and I learned not to bring it up the subject and act grateful. We understood our predicament had conditions; if we became a problem we'd be on our own, possibly abandoned again, or put out on the street or sent back to the orphanage or foster care. No way. We could not risk that.

We could not protest the absurdity or secrecy we lived under. It was never clear how mom and dad might respond to questions. Mom was usually bothered by something or sick. Dad could get real angry. We knew showing too much interest in our adoption was definitely risky. If we asked too many questions, they'd think us ungrateful; then if it's our bad attitude, then we're their problem.

I wonder how many kids out there acted like I did. I was confused, very sad. Some kids possibly overreact, or won't pretend, and do act bad.

I got cold. I told myself — "remember they gave you a home. Only ask questions at the right time, whenever the subject comes up. Don't act overly interested, just curious, ha-ha-ha...." It seemed necessary to disguise my need for an identity early. My parents had absolutely no idea how I really felt or what this charade was doing to Joey or me.

I remember thinking, "My family is out there. I was taken from them. I never said it's ok with me. They might miss me."

The threat of being abandoned again hurt so much I silenced my curiosity and I grieved in stages. Edie often said I was moody.

Alcoholic

Oh, yeah, Sev was an alcoholic. This must have been carefully disguised before the social workers did their rounds of home inspections before Joey and I were adopted.

Dad controlled our environment, whether Joey and I felt safe or scared to death. When he was sober, he was very strict, especially with me. He was not nice to Joey. Maybe dad thought abusing him verbally would toughen him up.

To this day, I have a very low tolerance for alcoholics. I do understand how we learn from the mistakes of others. The spirit in alcohol is very destructive so I avoid it.

Sev never talked about hunger or the poverty his family endured in Wisconsin. I do not know what caused Sev to drink or take such a self-destructive path. Was it because of mom's infertility? Was it because they argued a lot? Why does anyone self-medicate? They are in pain. Watching him taught me important lessons early.

Sev did quit drinking "cold turkey" when I was in junior high. He went to one Alcoholics Anonymous meeting, insisting vehemently —one meeting was enough. Then he said he wasn't an alcoholic.

Denial worked for him. His drinking was a disease and we all knew it masked something. I could never quite figure out what it was... what pain drove him to drink.

Sev slaved over 30 years on the railroad, and it was a dangerous job. Alcoholism was a serious problem for many railroad men. There were more bars and taverns in Superior than any other business. Our little port town had ore boats and the Great Northern railroad, the only jobs with good pay and pensions.

Joey and I would spend an entire Saturday or Sunday afternoon waiting outside a tavern, waiting patiently to go home, sometimes begging a quarter to play pool or pinball. Mom and dad's tavern-hopping-weekends went on for years. One night we were pulled over by a cop and I remember his flashlight shining in my face. He told dad to drive home safe. Even though Sev was smashed, he was not taken to jail or even given a ticket.

Abstain

I never really knew why Sev obsessed about my insides. He told Joey never to hurt me or punch me in the gut—ever. I never heard an explanation of why this was so important —unless it had to do with Edie's insides, maybe her failed pregnancies.

At St. Anthony, every girl in my class was warned to abstain from sex. Many of us, 12 and 13, had just started to menstruate (or have our monthly moon) so the nuns organized a reproduction class, girls only, my last year at St. Anthony's.

Children raised Catholic are instructed very young to wait until they are adults to get married then have sex—not the other way around. Despite frequent warnings, one of my classmates was 14 when she got pregnant. The nuns running Cathedral Junior High were not happy having her around so our pregnant friend suddenly left. Many schools have rules about this, yet a double standard persists because her boyfriend was not expelled or forced out of his school. There was no stigma for him.

My pregnant classmate's mom decided to raise her granddaughter, after she was born. Eventually our classmate did return and planned to get married after high school. She and her husband would raise their daughter together, which they eventually did.

Back at home, Sev lectured me, "a man will not want you unless you are a virgin."

By then he'd already molested me. I remember the first time like it was yesterday. I was maybe 13. It was a Saturday and Edie was at work. Sev took of my shirt and sucked on my breast. I froze. As he talked dirty, I blocked him out. I didn't hear him. My mind went to other places, somewhere far away. I knew this was not going to be a one-time thing. The sheer horror of that was another reason I went numb and split into pieces.

Virgins

I guess Sev didn't rape me so I'd remain a virgin. We were such good practicing Catholics. Parents and priests said all kinds of things. Do not kill, do not steal, do not lie, respect your parents. We memorized all Ten Commandments at St. Anthony's.

Despite frequent warnings, I fell in love. Artie was my first real boyfriend, my first kiss, my first escape. I sinned when I had sex with Artie. We were 14. There was no condom. There was no planning. There was curiosity. There was no experience in what we did. I was babysitting my cousin's kids. Artie came over and we did it.

I didn't think about pregnancy. It seemed worse to lose my virginity. I imagined Sev would kill me if he found out I lost my virginity. I'd embarrass my entire family. I'd never find a husband. There was no doubt if I were pregnant (which I wasn't) that my baby would be taken away from me and adopted. I never ever wanted to get pregnant.

Remaining a virgin was deeply engrained in my head. Only married people had sex but it didn't stop Artie or me. It happened three times.

Long story short: I found out Artie was two-timing me with Luanne so I dumped him. This killed me.

I may have lost my virginity with Artie but my innocence was already long gone. Sev had killed it.

"I'm your father... you need to know about this, sex this and sex that..." He said so many things, I lost track. Dad always tried to get me alone.

I thought, "He isn't my real dad. In his sick twisted head, molesting me isn't wrong, it's not incest. I'm not his real daughter."

I grew up so fast. I tried desperately to avoid him. I had headaches. I never wanted to be alone with him. I couldn't tell anyone why.

Since I couldn't avoid him completely, I blocked him out.

I found someone to replace him in my life. Artie was the only one who could rescue me, I thought. Artie was my prince in shining armor, as was my next boyfriend and the next.

Shirley Temple

How many children pray to be kidnapped? I used to. When life got to be too much, I'd pray someone would kidnap me or show up to claim me. I thought my adoption had to be a mistake. I got this idea from the Shirley Temple movie, *The Little Princess*, when she became an orphan. I identified with this little princess, poor and destitute, sent to live in the attic. Eventually her father, a wounded soldier, came to her rescue. I had this fantasy life playing in my head. I had to be brave like her. I never dreamed I was the child of Marilyn Monroe or anything foolish like that, but I hoped my being born wasn't a mistake. Even as a girl, I longed to meet an adoptee who opened their adoption successfully. I prayed my real parents regretted what happened to me and they would look for me. I was completely ignorant of what to do.

Afraid

It's strange and wonderful how a child can cope through their difficulty. I managed to invent my own sense of safety at home. This happens, no matter if you're their kid or their adopted kid.

I was afraid to leave the closet doors open when I went to bed. It became a nightly ritual, closing my closet door. No one ever questioned me. I just did it, no matter where I stayed or what type of closet.

The medical term for this is obsessive compulsive disorder or obsessive compulsive personality disorder.

For years, Sev walked by half-naked in a t-shirt, exposing his genitals on his way to the bathroom in the middle of the night. Even at 4, I didn't feel safe. I was afraid to sleep with my bedroom door open. This lasted well into my 30s. I'm not sure how I quit but it was after Sev died.

For a lot of reasons, I never slept well. If Sev woke me for school, he'd grab my legs and upper thighs. I was so scared of that. I wore heavy layers of clothes to bed, even as a young girl. By 14, I never let anyone see me naked, not even mom. Modest, yes, but I was protecting myself.

For many years I was afraid to go into stores, gas stations, restaurants and nightclubs alone. I finally broke this fear in my 20s.

Edie thought it strange when I refused to go into a store alone to buy milk or bread. Not only was I shy, I was afraid of men or being alone with one of them.

Near Death

My first near death experience happened right after they adopted me. Sev dove fully-dressed into a cold Wisconsin river to save me. I rolled off a blanket while the three of us were having my first picnic at Amnicon Falls. I don't remember how I nearly drowned. I do remember mom saying later, "Sev ruined a brand new pair of shoes."

In third grade, I broke my left wrist. Joey and I were ice skating one Friday night with neighbor kids on a pond across the road. Joining hands, I was at the end of the whip, and got thrown into a snow bank. Sev, already drunk, said my wrist was fine.

For two days I blocked the pain but my wrist swelled and turned black and blue. On Sunday at the Patterman's house for dinner, I tried to carry a tray of drinks to the dining room and dropped it. I never cried. Finally they noticed the swelling. The next day I was x-rayed then hospitalized. No one asked why it took so long for me to see a doctor for a broken bone.

Another time I got pushed over a fence and a stump punctured my leg. Dad, drunk again, said, "Put a Band-Aid on it."

I nearly drowned three times, in a river, a lake and another time at a swimming pool in Aurora, Illinois. I was hospitalized for convulsions when I was 14. They never said what caused them.

Years later a Seattle psychic told me I'm on "extended life," so I chose to live and not die. I had a purpose, a reason to be here. He said I wanted to experience every minute of this.

"NO"

Joey was definitely more shy than me. Joey and I knew Edie and Sev were just like bottle rockets, highly explosive, even when they were sober. When they did fight, they either yelled or stopped talking to each other. We heard from our beds. Dad never hit mom but their fights were brutal, loud, often about stupid things.

Joey and I knew when to tiptoe around them or when to hide. We had to be careful. Dad's biggest punishment was a strike with a belt. The easier was, "Go to your room without supper." I got belted once. I don't remember why.

It became a running joke that dad would immediately say "NO" to whatever we asked, so Joey and I would ask mom. On big stuff she went to dad. She was much better at getting him to say yes.

Since dad was home on weekends, Joey and I took off on our bikes. Binge drinking was heaviest on weekends. Sev was a very mean drunk. He would bear his teeth at us, like a rabid dog. We couldn't figure out what made him so mean. I thought sometimes it was us, like we were an intrusion.

Family vacations revolved around dad's drinking or his hunting and fishing in northern Wisconsin. Thanksgiving week was deer hunt season and a big drunk with his buddies wearing red hunting clothes. Spring and summer dad fished the Brule River for rainbow trout after work. He'd hit a few bars on the way home.

This was no Disneyland. We never camped in Glacier or Yellowstone like other kids. Our trips consisted of driving out west or we took the Amtrak train to visit Edie's parents in Washington. Dad's job allowed us to travel free on the rails. After mom's parents died, we drove south to see Edie's sister and brother in Aurora, Illinois.

Dad's mom and his sisters lived close-by in Superior.

On road trips, mom invented the radio game. Joey and I could win a nickel if we guessed the correct singer and song. Tony Bennett, Robert Goulet, Ray Charles, Pat Boone, Bing Cosby, Mario Lanza, I knew them all by the distinct timbre in their voice. I studied them and won lots of nickels.

Anti-freeze

Sev drank anti-freeze once, by mistake of course, then was rushed to the hospital, paralyzed on one side of his body. It looked like a stroke but it wasn't. Already drunk out of his mind, dad thought he'd found booze in our garage. Joey found the opened Prestone bottle.

At the same time, Edie was hospitalized, having yet another back surgery. Mom might be gone a month, sometimes longer, after each major surgery. Dad took Joey and me to visit her but usually she was too out of it, in too much pain. She had numerous operations when we were kids.

By the time Sev drank the anti-freeze, I could keep house, make meals, and do laundry. This time, Joey and I were not sure either would recover. We were old by then; I was in 8th grade, Joey was in 6th. Joey was a much better cook than Sev anyway. It was a relief to have the house to ourselves, even for a few days.

With both Edie and Sev hospitalized, daylight was spent in school. The school bus drove us. When word got out to our new parish priest, he made surprise after-school visits. Sev's oldest sister Mary stayed overnight when she could.

Aunt Mary and Uncle Chet drove Joey and I to Memorial Hospital in Superior to see dad paralyzed. I didn't cry. I could barely manage my disgust. I didn't feel sympathy for him.

Mom, doped up on painkillers in a Duluth hospital, wasn't told, not right away.

After the antifreeze incident, I thought, "Maybe this was it. If dad recovered, it might bring our family closer. If he's paralyzed, it could end his drinking."

It was just hope. Sev didn't stop, not right away. He fully recovered from the anti-freeze.

Edie had already tried a separation the year before. Right away, dad made us feel guilty, then tried pitting Joey and I against mom, making her the bad guy for kicking him out. Dad was gone just a few months. Our old parish priest told mom she had to take him back. Edie couldn't divorce him—she was Catholic. After seven years of knowing our family, this priest was gone, transferred to a new parish.

With their long list of sins, I never read one about alcoholism or incest. I never told anyone Sev was molesting me, especially mom. I couldn't say when he French-kissed me, I gagged and almost threw up. Dad told me once to be careful when I changed his sheets since he'd had a wet dream. He made me sick. I knew mom couldn't handle it, not after so many surgeries and mini-nervous breakdowns. There was no doubt mom needed more help than me. She was married to him.

Mom played it up as a hypochondriac, too sick to notice us or too distracted to see what was happening to us. Children were meant to be seen—not heard—at our house. Better to be invisible, I decided.

One night a voice drew a shield, a guard tower around me. It said wait, this won't last forever. I trusted this voice. It never lied to me, ever.

Big Game Hunter

Dad always wanted to be a big game hunter and go on a safari, but he never got the chance. But he knew the name of every animal on the planet. We tested him.

Every Sunday, Sev sat us down to watch Mutual of Omaha's *Wild Kingdom*, and later Marlin Perkins' *Wild World of Animals*. Both shows traveled to Africa, South America, the Arctic, Alaska, Canada, and the Soviet Union. Animals were losing territories and forest habitats that were burned, slashed for homes, logged or mined.

We watched every *National Geographic* special, and learned about anthropology, biology, history and culture, first on CBS (1965-73) then on ABC (1973-74). Capturing wild animals, Marlin's men trapped them for zoos, claiming they'd be safe from extinction, so their breeding would continue. They didn't understand that some animals could never reproduce under those conditions, behind bars and glass. I learned zoos made big money if they had enough of these wild animals. Trapped and caged, many struggled, some quickly died. I never wanted to go to a zoo.

It was too horrible, too sad.

Kings

Dad spent most of his free time outdoors and was particularly good at training hunting dogs—I watched. Dad raised two black labs, each named King, and later a yellow lab named Buck. Dad spent hours training each one to retrieve buoys and balls so he could use them duck hunting.

Our first Black Labrador was outside in the snow when Joey disappeared in the woods behind our house. An hour passed and Sev couldn't find Joey, who was maybe four years old. Like a trusty companion, King brought Joey back by the sleeve of his little red snowsuit on that dark winter afternoon. Mom cried and cried, repeating over and over, "King saved Joey's life." All our labs were gentle and protective. We'd climb all over them as toddlers and rode them like horses. After each dog died, we mourned.

Finally when Joey was 12, he convinced mom we needed a new dog, a mixed breed puppy from the neighbors a few doors down from grandma's cabin. We loved this puppy and named him Bubbles because his long fur had black and white spots.

Bubbles liked our neighbors, Church and Pearl, so he spent most of the day with them while we were in school.

I'd spend hours picking wood ticks off this dog. Bubbles, Joey and I were outside all day, whatever season it was in Wisconsin.

Baby Crows

One spring Dad brought us home a surprise. He'd found two baby crows near the railroad tracks on his job as a switchman.

Joey called his crow Blackie; I called mine Artie. (I had to name mine Artie since that was when we were first falling in love.)

Every day Joey and I softened dog food in ice cream pails so the crows could eat. Dad said we'd know if our crows were boy or girl when they had babies.

The crows grew fast. They took turns pestering Bubbles when he'd try to nap, hiding under Mom's lounge. They'd peck at him gently but never hurt him. They wouldn't leave the poor dog alone. Apparently crows do this to wolves in the wild—they are animal allies.

When Sev painted the garage that summer, Artie and Blackie got white paint all over them, then took turns plucking the white feathers off each other. They looked awful but all their feathers grew back. Dad thought it was better to have white paint on them so they wouldn't get shot. It didn't work; Artie and Blackie knew they were meant to be black; thankfully, they never were shot.

Our crows waited on the telephone poles until we climbed off our school bus. Apparently Artie and Blackie flew house to house when we were in school, neighbors said.

Crows are especially clever. When Alex, a carpenter, came to put a deck on the back of our house, our crows stole a pack of his cigarettes and his shiny metal lighter. The evidence was strewn all over the grass. Mom said the crows stole dishcloths off our clothesline and hung them in trees. Crows will take shiny things, easy to carry. They had no sense of what was our stuff or theirs.

Late summer, we drove south to see mom's family over Labor Day weekend. We didn't know until later that Bubbles was hit by a car and killed on our busy rural road.

When our neighbors found out, Frank went to get Bubbles off the road. But the crows wouldn't let him. Artie and Blackie guarded Bubbles as he laid there. Our crows didn't touch him, though instinctively crows eat road-kill.

Finally, wearing a thick jacket with a hood, Frank and his wife Dottie hatched a plan. He'd grab Bubbles then run up his long driveway into his garage.

As he ran, the crows dove at Frank the entire way. It must have been a scene out of the Hitchcock film, *The Birds*.

When we got back, Joey and I called and called but couldn't find Bubbles or the crows. Frank heard us outside and phoned dad with the whole story.

The crows were waiting, perched on the roof of Frank's garage.

Dad and I went to get Bubbles, stiff and wrapped in a blanket. As we walked home, the crows followed. Joey and I cried as Dad buried Bubbles in our backyard. It took a long time to grieve; even Artie and Blackie were sad.

When autumn turned the leaves red and gold, Artie and Blackie left, migrating with other crows. Joey and I came home from school one day and they were gone. We hoped they might return, maybe the following spring. Maybe they did. The crows were never really ours and we knew that.

Every crow interests me now. I still call them, imitating their "caw-caw." I feed crows wherever I live.

I read a funny article about crows long after Artie and Blackie. Apparently crows have incredible memories. They remember people who are nice to them. Crows live together in a large family flock. They study us. If they don't like us, crows might do nasty things to our yards or cars.

I do appreciate them. Crows taught me to be gentle, kind and respectful. I'd stroke their heads and look in their dark mysterious eyes. I never felt fear of their strong claws or sharp beaks. They were real friends.

Happenings

When diocese budget cuts forced St. Anthony's to close when I was in 7th grade, I transferred downtown to Cathedral Junior High for 8th and 9th grade.

I managed to fit in with jocks, freaks, rich kids, poor kids, preppy kids, even class presidents. Sev was so likeable he talked to nearly everyone. I learned that from him.

My first year at Cathedral, I asked our principal Sister Diane if our school could have what I called "Happenings," held during the last period on Friday. Students could use the gym, dim the lights and dance to 45rpm records we brought from home. I was surprised when Sister Diane said yes. One friend ran the stereo and we danced non-stop an entire hour, like a powwow.

My second year I ran for Student Council Vice President and won. Miss French held a competition for best short story in her 9th grade English class so I wrote about a young voyeur living in his apartment building. She read my story. Winning her contest stuck with me for years. It grew my confidence; I knew I'd write more. When my guidance counselor said I was reading and writing at high school levels, I decided I'd go to college.

In my first theatre class, I landed the leading role in *Sorry, Wrong Number*. I'd watched Barbara Stanwyck in the movie version. My scream at the end of the play drew an entire shop class out of their classroom during a rehearsal. Edie and Aunt Mary attended opening night. I liked applause and all the attention. I knew I'd act again.

Not everything was acting. I did turn green the day our chemistry class dissected frogs. I was excused to sit in the hall. By 9th grade, I knew I'd never be a biologist.

I liked to make people laugh. I also knew being class clown was a disruptive influence on the other students. It was not funny when Sister Gladys tipped me out of my desk onto the floor during a math test. I'd asked Chuck for an eraser and she ran up to my desk and flipped me. Sprawled on the floor, my underwear exposed, this was not funny but a real disaster. This nun hated me. I ran to the office, humiliated, embarrassed, dreading the phone call home. Dad drove to Cathedral and got the whole story. Sev and the principal agreed that Chuck and I would have our own private math class and tutor in 9th grade.

I'm sure Sev made quite an argument. Dad made a definite impression on Chuck who later became a lawyer.

That same year, Sister Gladys retired.

Demons

One recurring dream I had as a teenager was Mom, Joey and I careened off the "Singing Bridge" into the Nemadji River.

I dreamt we were trapped inside our Buick, seeing blinking orange yellow lights and bubbling green water outside the window.

The singing bridge was a steel-covered bridge in Allouez. Car tires made the bridge sing. When we drove over it, the first one to touch the roof of the car made a wish. The singing bridge was torn down eventually. Even now, I can close my eyes and see the bridge and then feel us sinking in the car.

Sev was not in my dreams, not until after he died in 1985.

No one explained how Sev's disease would affect us or our future. No one had therapy back then. No one, not even the priests, apologized for Sev's behavior or tried to get us help. This was the only family I had. We were all very sick.

I didn't know my low self-esteem would attract demons. It was like I had a target painted on my back: "Perverts, Predators, Pedophiles, come get me." That truth was well obstructed. I was attracting the one thing I didn't want, becoming a victim, a target, a doormat for men to control.

Never told I was sacred, or that my body was my own to protect, I had no power to control that as a girl. We heard sex was dirty. So my dad was a dirty old man.

When I was 13, Joey and I faced a new demon. That summer a new friend phoned and said her father was visiting and wanted to take us swimming.

Never having met him, Edie said, "Fine, go."

This man drove us to a lake, no one around— not even a house. Joey and I wore swimsuits under our clothes so we quickly undressed and jumped in the lake with my girlfriend. In minutes, her dad was in the water next to me. I struggled to pull away but he was strong and held me. Then he tried to put his hands inside my swimsuit.

From a distance, Joey saw the look on my face and immediately swam over. My little brother saved me from this sick bastard. We got out of the lake, grabbed the towels mom packed for us and we dried off. The man knew he was caught but acted like nothing happened. He was watching us, yelling, "Hey, come back in, we just got here."

Still shaking, I couldn't talk. Joey stood next to me by the car, maybe 10 minutes. Joey finally got up his courage and walked to the beach and told him, "Drive us home."

No one spoke in the car.

In the front seat, my friend looked so small and helpless. I knew what the demon had done to her.

Joey and I never told our parents anything.

DEFINITION: Reactive Attachment Disorder
RAD is characterized by the breakdown of social
ability of a child. It is associated with the failure of
the child to bond with a caretaker in infancy or early
childhood. This can be caused by many factors,
ranging from child neglect to the child being
hospitalized for severe medical problems. The
children may display either indiscriminate social
extroversion as they grow older (treating all people
as if they were their best friend) or showing mistrust
of nearly everyone. In Plain English: RAD is the
Splitting Disease, Soul Sickness, Post Traumatic
Stress Disorder, and the Split Feather Syndrome...

Confession

Mom said Joey and I would go up to perfect
strangers as toddlers, which seemed odd to her.
We didn't cling to her knees like her sisters kids
did. Obviously, we hadn't "bonded" with anyone,
she told me later.

I was named Tracy after our parish priest,
Father Tracy, though I don't remember him. He
was the editor of the Superior diocese *Catholic
Herald* newspaper. Father Tracy died young, just
37 years old. Mom remembered he came to the
house and told her he was dying and asked her to
pray for him. She cried whenever she talked about
him.

Many priests came to our house, and quite
often they drank late into the night with my
parents. It didn't appear they saw through our
barriers, hiding our dysfunctions as a family unit. If
they did see through us, they never intervened.

Our house was a few miles from the church
yet out in the country, somewhat isolated. Sev and
Edie's parties lasted all night sometimes. After

music, they'd play smear (a Belgian card game) and drink. The priests did nothing to hurt us or help us; maybe they were too inebriated to notice.

Unfortunately I do remember the kiss between Edie and one parish priest from Chicago, on the stoop behind our house at dusk, one early summer night.

I became an adult in seconds. The image of them kissing stuck in my head. Not one word was said. All I knew was—I'd carry on as if I didn't see it. I knew that it would spell disaster if Sev or anyone else found out. I knew the part about priests not having sex or having wives.

By 14, I already knew how to say things people wanted to hear. I became adept at lies, half-truths. I survived that way, so I did not arouse suspicion.

A mix of fear and gratitude silenced my desire to tell other relatives what was going on at our house, so I never mentioned mom's kissing the priest or dad's alcoholism or being molesting.

I had no choice but to lie. All though school, many years, the nuns had no clue how we were living. Our clothes were clean and pressed. Our homework was done. I was not beaten or bruised; emotionally-distraught, sure, yes, but that was much easier to hide. The nuns didn't scold me for chewed raw fingernails or chewed pencils or incessantly twirling my hair. Maybe they did notice but never said anything.

In 6th grade I did get busted shooting spit balls into the piano. The nun caught me and two boys. She said we had to write the same sentence (something about spitting) 500 times, have it signed by *both* parents and bring it to school the next morning.

Nope, Sev didn't belt me. Edie shook her head in disgust.

I handled the trouble I was in, or whatever trouble my parents were in, pretty well.

I decided, "come on, it was just a kiss." I seriously considered what might happen if people found out, and how this man might not be our priest anymore.

Sometimes Mom did secretarial work at his rectory. My classmates saw her car but didn't ask me anything. When this priest was transferred, Edie confided in me he never stopped loving her, not for a minute, even years after the kiss.

When we visited him at his new parish, he took mom aside and said he considered leaving the priesthood for her.

She told me everything.

Priests still transfer to a new parish every seven years, even with a priest shortage in several states.

Back then I wished the priest would have married her and became my dad. How different our lives could have been. When this priest left, I despised him, this man of God, for his lies, his double life, his forked tongue, for abandoning us and sending us back to the monster. He was the one who told Edie she couldn't divorce Sev.

Life was like that. Adults lied when it was convenient.

In those days, I went to Mass six days a week. I remember stepping into the dark confessional every week, thinking, "I don't have anything to confess to this man."

My Favorite People

Writing back then was like having my own psychologist. I filled several spiral notebooks with entries about the crows, Bubbles dying, when Artie and I broke up, even when I was losing my grip. Yes, I wrote silly awkward teenage poems, but writing them did help.

I often wrote about my favorite people. There was Grandma Sevvy (dad's mom) and my Uncle Chet (Sev's brother-in-law) who was Anishinabe and Scottish. Mom told me Chet's mother was an Indian. She'd actually lived on the shores of Lake Superior. Her Fond du Lac tribe was eventually relocated from Wisconsin to Minnesota. Mom said Chet's mother was different; "wild hair" she remembered. I did ask mom why Chet's mom acted so shy. I met her a few times.

I was deeply connected to my Uncle Chet. He let me hold my first garden snake. Mom was horrified when she saw the little snake wrapped around my neck. Chet took us berry picking and taught Joey and I about bears.

He was my real protector, though he didn't really know it at the time. Or maybe he did, which was why we spent so many summers at Grandma Sevvy's cabin in Solon Springs.

Every Friday night, Grandma, Uncle Chet and Aunt Mary (Sev's oldest sister) came for hamburgers, homemade fries and beer. And they were with us just about every holiday.

Once, Uncle Chet saved my life. When I was 9 or 10, I was viciously stung by hornets; one got me on my left eyebrow. I'd hit their nest with a stick because Sev said he didn't want that hive under the garage eaves. Sev heard my screams and called Chet who applied red clay to my numerous bites. Sev was too upset to yell at me. My long hair kept the majority away from my face.

Chet made Joey and me giggle. He was Santa Clause. Chet would do just about anything for a laugh that included wearing a wig, stuffing a giant bra, throwing on a hula skirt, wearing a lampshade for a hat. Laughter is big medicine in Indian Country. Chet made us cry with laughter.

Really, I wanted to be like him. When Uncle Chet died in a car accident, I had just started high school. I couldn't breathe when I heard. I imagined Chet was in heaven so I knew he was OK.

Bubble Butt

Few people knew I could survive a whole day on a bag of potato chips. I became "weight obsessed" in 9th grade, between junior high and high school. That summer I dropped 25 pounds of "baby fat" as Edie called it. I drank coffee in the morning and nothing else until dinner. Then I might eat four bites of something. Mom and I drank diet rite cola instead of water. I hated to eat because I thought being fat would ruin my future. Obsessed, I didn't want my thighs to rub together. I wanted to be Twiggy, or other stick-thin models i studied in magazines.

Sev said no man would want someone who wasn't a virgin. Being thin was something I could control.

Edie was "built like a brick shithouse," Sev would say. When their friend Jim was visiting from California, he called me "Bubble Butt." He told me I was going to be trouble (not in trouble) but greatly desired by the opposite sex. Was he hitting on me, too? I was 14.

His words weren't a comfort. I didn't want that kind of attention. I was self-conscious enough. I had only one thing on my mind, survival. I didn't dwell on what I looked like, or think I could use beauty to get what I wanted, to control someone else.

I chose to carry a lot of responsibility. I didn't sink into addiction like Sev, but became rather a control freak. I concocted a thick blanket of illusion to hide under. I could have become many things - bitter, depressed, addicted, suicidal, or possibly homicidal. Many times I wished Sev was dead.

I believe my ancestors took a hold of me and kept me sane. Sane is a relative term when I really consider it now.

Crazy is more the way I'd describe it.

The Velvet Dress

For the Christmas dance at Cathedral Junior High in 1970, I needed a very special dress—and found one, an expensive $50 crimson velvet mini-dress with elaborate gold stitching. Wearing it made me feel like a princess but that was a lot of money. Sev said I should have it so he bought it.

Mom never let me forget how much it cost. After this major purchase, I wore my 9th grade velvet dress for every holiday, every special occasion, even my high school graduation portrait (in the photo). Forty years later, I still have it. I might still be wearing this dress if it fit me.

Mom had amassed her own dazzling wardrobe and a spectacular collection of hats that she wore to mass every Sunday. Edie, serious about clothes and sales, inherited her taste from her British mother.

I perfected my grandma's heavy accent watching a Yardley lipstick commercial on TV. Then I decided to study French in junior high and two more years in high school.

After Peter Pan blouses and navy jumpers or some variation of a Catholic School uniform, I was ready to wear my own clothes in high school. I wore blue jeans and dresses. I coveted racks of vintage rayon at the Salvation Army, Goodwill and St. Vincent de Paul. In high school, I borrowed from every closet at home. I devoured 1970s magazines like *Glamour* and *Mademoiselle*, reading about celebrities, actors, models and musicians. One boyfriend said I became whatever I read about in those days.

Nerves were eating at me by high school. I developed a strange rash on my skin anytime I got wet. Red welts would appear after I'd swim in fresh water, in the chlorinated pool, even after a shower at home. Even my own sweat made me break out. The rash wouldn't last long but it looked bad. I

called the red blotches on my face "nerve zits."
The rash would cover my face, arms and chest.
They'd go away after about 20 minutes, after my
skin dried.

High School Musical

By high school, mom and dad had lost all
interest in us and our activities. They rarely
attended a recital, play or school event. By then,
Joey and I simply stayed out of their way.

I auditioned for my first high school musical
Camelot in 10th grade. I was cast in a chorus part
but Sev said NO. There wasn't a school bus for our
after-school activities.

Lucky for us Sev's rules changed when I got
my driver's license. At 16, I could borrow Edie's
Buick, since she'd stopped working nights on the
ore docks in Allouez. Joey and I had a new method
of escape.

My junior year I successfully auditioned to
be an alto in the Concert Choir and one of eight
Spartan Singers, and we all wore matching
costumes. After I won three medals in state vocal
competitions, I seriously considered becoming a
musician. I had a solo, *One Tin Soldier*, on the
Concert Choir album. I decided music was my
ticket out of Wisconsin.

In my senior year, I landed the lead role in
the musical *Annie Get Your Gun*. I sang "Anything
You Can Do, I Can Do Better," and "There's No
Business like Show Business." For five
performances, I lived and breathed Annie Oakley.

Sev banned all makeup in junior high. By
high school, I wore eye shadow, mascara and a

sequin on the corner of my eyes, affixed by fingernail polish. I braided my wet hair to get a crimped look. I carried a big white furry purse I named Rufus. (It looked exactly like a sheepdog.) I watched Dick Clark's *American Bandstand* every Saturday and knew the best clothes and best dance moves. I seldom wore the winter white "go-go" boots Edie bought me. (Oh God, she loved those boots.)

When mom's parents died, she took a train out west as a brunette and came back a blonde. By high school, she dyed my long dark hair to a streaky dark blonde.

Since I had enough credits to graduate my senior year, I started classes at the University of Wisconsin in 1974. Both campuses were within walking distance so my friends Kat, Lila and I walked or we drove together.

Edie and Sev both worked but we never had a lot of money. For at least five years, I babysat. I watched kids during mass then got night-time babysitting jobs. I even sold Bingo cards in the church basement once a week. During high school I worked part-time, first stocking shelves at a grocery store, then as a salesgirl at a shoe store.

Passive Aggressive

Adoptees agree with me we create a personality we use with our friends, a personality that is more honest than we can be at home. I know I did this. I didn't want to hurt my parents but I wanted to be real or genuine, or at least try. I needed a personality that could deal with both parents.

Mom was in every way a Hollywood starlet, always cool, always tan, and living in some other universe. I loved her so much. But I figured out early how not to upset her. It was better to lie or tell her what she wanted to hear.

If anyone—friend or relative—upset her, oh my God. She'd *never* forgive them. I watched it happen over and over. She would not tell them why she was so upset—she'd tell me. I heard stories about this sister-in-law or that friend, who did this or said that... mom would avoid them—permanently. She'd never tell them off to their face. She made them guess.

I was asked far too often, "What did I do to her?" I might know but could only shrug.

I was mom's constant companion. I caught the brunt of her various emotional outbursts instead of her directing anger at the people who upset her. If a man made a pass, I knew about it. If a woman was jealous of her, I knew that. Dad's sisters sure knew how to push mom's buttons. One of dad's best friends flirted too much. I knew mom needed attention. I knew she needed me more than I needed her.

I always wanted mom to say what was on her mind. I wanted her to stand up for herself. Back then, she'd avoid every uncomfortable conversation, every sticky situation.

This is how I inherited her passive aggressive approach. I'd run at the first sign of trouble. When people would upset me, I'd use it, even when dealing with her. I hate this. This is not good and very hard to get rid of once you learn it. I try to be assertive now but it's not easy.

Mom's glamour girl image was nearly as big a problem as her temper. She was never really home in Wisconsin. She needed to be in a big city where she could shine. To her, being attractive was a priority.

Mom inhabited a different world than I did. She lived for love. If men weren't in love with her, something was wrong. When dad died in 1985, Mom read a romance novel every day. Then I heard about this guy or that guy who would drive to her house and pester her constantly. She'd just lock the door and wait for them to drive away.

It was never easy for me to tell her anything big. The good stuff, sure. That was all she wanted to hear anyway. I'd wait a long time before mentioning anything that resembled the truth with her. I found it was easier to write her a letter— then let her cool off.

Mom never really knew me or what Sev did to me. I decided the truth would have killed her. I hated that she treated me like a friend when I needed her to be a mom.

Sadly, I could never tell her anything she didn't want to hear.

Pedestals

Sev did put Edie on a pedestal, a place for saints and unusually attractive people.

Mom needed a friend like me. I knew when our family doctor was in love with her. Doc kissed her when she came out of surgery after they removed a (non-cancerous) lump out of her breast in the 1960s. Edie fluttered to attention, like a moth to a flame. I'm not saying she had affairs but the potential was always there.

I didn't know how to help her at times, which was all the more frustrating. It was hard to tell who the parent was. During one heated fight at home, Mom, Joey and I got in the car and we drove hours. Another time the Chicago priest took us waterskiing and dad was not invited. At her worst, Mom either threw stuff or screamed. When mom said she'd kill herself, and locked herself in the bathroom, Joey panicked but I knew she wouldn't.

We were as close as two women can get. I was there for her. Watching her gave me obvious lessons. Edie used beauty, as if it satisfied something in her. She instilled in me I had to be beautiful, too. Beauty would open doors for middle class kids like me.

Many women from the Tri-Cities developed breast cancer. Grandma Kathryn died from it — it was too late to save her because the cancer had spread to her lymph nodes. Mom developed numerous breast lumps over the years. One tiny breast lump in 1996 was cancer. She had surgery and there was no recurrence.

In 2006, doctors found papillary (cancer) cells in my thyroid. It's treatable but it makes me wonder if I was exposed to too much radiation when I lived in Richland-Kennewick-Pasco, right after college graduation. We visited our grandparents there many times.

Runaway

In 1973, Linda, my next door neighbor, called me to go out. Sev, as usual, said NO. Linda and I had breezed past the ID check at one Superior nightclub so we planned to do it again. I looked older than I was. Live music was great and Linda liked the keyboard player in this one band.

I'd "officially" begun dating at 17. I'd had a boyfriend Steve and could drive but I needed permission to do anything. I still had a curfew. Linda, 18 and legally an adult, had complete freedom. Sev wanted to know where I was, who I was seeing and what I was doing.

That summer I didn't know what he'd do to me or when. Sev had tried to convince me he should be my "first" as in intercourse. Dad had a dream that men in Sweden are the first to sleep with their daughters. Dad went psycho and couldn't wait to tell me he'd ordered me a vibrator. I grew more terrified each day.

When Linda called that night, I left though my bedroom window. As we drove to Superior, I told her I wasn't going home. She could tell I was serious about not wanting to live at home anymore. Linda's classmate, John, was bartending at his uncle's tavern so we went there. I asked John if I could stay in his apartment, above where he worked. He hesitated at first then said OK. Nothing sexual happened with John that Saturday night or ever, because he was my friend. John sensed my desperation, but I couldn't talk about it. The reality was I couldn't be on my own, not yet.

The next morning I wandered around downtown Superior, trying to figure out what to do. I knew Edie would be hysterical, screaming threats. Then Sev would corner me somewhere. I needed this nightmare to end.

Since I ran away, I could not go the police. I knew they wouldn't help me.

At a phone booth, I called Steve, my ex-boyfriend. I said I didn't want to go home. Steve said he'd already got a call from my parents. He promised them he'd drive me home once he found me. Edie said they were worried. As we drove, I grew more and more afraid. Steve knew it was going to be horrific so he left quickly.

Waiting for me at the back door, mom grabbed me by the arm then started yelling, "If you ever run away like that again, I'll have you arrested, you whore. I'll send you to reform school, you whore, you slut...," the usual.

Finally I decided mom needed to hear the truth. As she yelled, I yelled back he molested me. I yelled back, "He bought me a vibrator." Of course, she didn't believe me.

Joey ran out to the garage to search. The vibrator was hidden. Joey found it up under the seat in dad's Jeep. He showed it to Mom. This was it.

Slowly realizing what I said, what he'd done, what he'd planned, mom had no choice but to listen. She couldn't tune me out. Sev just stood there, busted.

After she called me a few more obscenities, and a liar, I sat silent. The fear felt like heat; my body hurt. I let her yell while the truth sank in.

Edie never paid much attention to me. I was a stupid teenager. The signs were everywhere.

She simply refused to see them. Now was the test. Would she protect me, and defend me? She did.

Edie turned her rage to Sev, telling him he'd see a psychiatrist the next day. I'm pretty sure Sev never went to a psychiatrist. I went to my room.

Nothing was the same after that day. The shockwave hit our family, felt many years to come. Running away worked. Sev finally left me alone.

This was my personal victory.

Steve

I'd met my second serious boyfriend after Artie in high school. Steve was a junior, I was a sophomore. Steve planned to be an artist. I planned to be a musician. Steve knew something was wrong when I didn't allow him to visit me at my house, even though Sev was sober by then.

He knew dad didn't allow me to formally date until I was 17. Steve and I did go to the Christmas dance in high school but it wasn't a real date since I was only 16. Steve and I found time to be together at lunch or after school. Sometimes he drove me home. I'd met his parents, his brother and sister, and we all got along fine. Steve and I never talked marriage. We talked future.

I was desperate to start a new life. My silence spoke volumes. I was like a car running on two cylinders instead of four. Everyone saw it but me. Steve finally figured out I was much too complicated; dating me was too much work.

Steve took an easy way out. His senior year he went out with someone else but didn't tell me. The next morning at my locker, Linda, his date, told me in person—just to see the look on my face. Of course, Steve and I broke up that day.

I knew our relationship was a mistake. We'd never have a future. I'd slept with him on more than one occasion. I knew it was a mistake.

Edie was furious when I bought Steve a Christmas present one year, with money I earned stocking shelves for the father-son grocers in Superior.

The grocer son hired me and asked me to sit on his lap in his office, just once. Oh my God, I thought. He was just like my dad, another sick pervert.

Back then I thought all men were like dad. I couldn't trust any of them. Not even Steve.

"You're only as sick as your secrets"

No one had ever called me an orphan to my face. That is until Archie, my uncle Chet's brother showed up for Joey's high school graduation, and told me how Joey and I turned out OK, considering how we were both orphans. I was stunned to hear someone say it. I was in college then. No one had ever called me an **orphan** to my face.

I can honestly say I never felt unwanted— never. They wanted "us," not just my adoptive parents but our other relatives wanted us. They truly did.

Carrie Fisher said, "You're only as sick as your secrets," discussing her new memoir "*Wishful Drinking*" on the *Today Show* with Matt Lauer in December 2008.

Yeah, I was sick, sicker than I realized, keeping so many things stuffed up and buried. I knew very little about the "real me." I had no idea as a teenager how my adoption scarred me. No one said being adopted was an issue. No one said I needed counseling.

Freddie Action

Joey and I were never told we'd go to college like other kids did. Dad wanted us to get out of Wisconsin, and said often, "There is nothing for you kids in Superior."

Grandma Sevvy told me I had to get an education. I'd ride my bike to her house on Saturdays and clean for her since she was almost completely blind. When I started taking classes at the university in Superior, she encouraged me to get a degree.

A few weeks after high school graduation, I joined my first professional rock band Freddie Action. Three guys (Mark, Hank, and Fred) with their 1970s long hair recruited me from Payless, the Duluth shoe store where I worked.

Desperate to find a girl keyboard player who could sing, they'd gone to see Mr. Pufall, my former high school choir teacher. Pufall gave them my name.

The guys easily convinced me I could do this. Mark (on guitar) wrote out the chords for me to play. I already knew how to play organ, learning on Edie's Hammond B3 with a Leslie. I would sing lead and back-up. We rehearsed four hours of songs every day at Mark's house for over a month.

By August 1974, I was ready for my first gig at the Yellow Submarine Nightclub in Superior. I did two solos, "*To Love Somebody*" by the Bee

Gees and "*Heatwave*" by Kathy MacDonald. Three nights a week, I was a real rock singer. Big names like Linda Ronstadt and Ann Wilson of Heart had not come on the scene yet. By the late 1970s, rock music hit its stride.

Since I was only 17, the band needed my parent's permission for me to play local bars. Sev told the guys I could not drink alcohol and only play in certain nightclubs. Not Darlene's. Sev's railroad buddies had told him Darlene's was bad. People had sex, boozing it up.

To fill in for another band last minute, we decided to play Darlene's anyway.

That Friday night, Sev showed up and removed me after one set, as the band and the audience, including my old boyfriend Steve, watched. Dad barely noticed how nice the three-tier stage really was, all lit up. Steve tried to talk sense into dad, pleading, "let her stay." Sev just grabbed my arm and walked me out the door. Joey waited in the Jeep. We drove home in silence. The band felt very guilty but couldn't stop Sev since I was still a minor. I had not heard about being emancipated like some teens that legally separate from their parents.

Mark came out to the house and apologized to Sev the next morning. Dad made everyone nervous but I did play Darlene's that night. Yes, it was probably the most embarrassing moment of my music career.

Not quite ready to be a frontman, I sang behind a tower of keyboards. At home, I practiced in front of the mirror. I'd found my cool band clothes, especially satin and rayon, at various thrift stores and in dress shops.

On my 18th birthday in September, the guys got me drunk on Black Russians.

Beauty Queen

I made about $75 a week playing in Freddie Action. My aunts, mom, dad, even some of their friends, came to hear me at the Yellow Submarine. That August I moved to Ostrander Hall, a co-ed dorm, about 20 minutes from home. It seemed so much further away.

Freshman year I majored in music, studying voice and opera, and minored in English. I loved everything about college, even my eccentric English professor Dr. Gott and I earned his A's.

Edie and Sev helped out with tuition, the meal plan, dorm costs and books in my freshman year. On the meal plan, I could enjoy three starchy meals a day. Lunch was my usual bag of potato chips. I still gained 10 pounds. When I wasn't singing, I could survive on $10, or whatever mom mailed me.

By 1975, no longer their dependent, I applied for 100% financial aid. The university Office of Financial Aid arranged school loans and work-study jobs. Besides work study, I worked nights for Pete, a Greek who owned King's Inn, at his restaurant bordering the campus. Pete fed me one meal daily.

My sophomore year I switched my major to theatre and acting. I had no plans to be an opera singer. I'd sing in rock bands and act. I landed starring roles in college productions *Godspell*,

Damn Vikings (adapted from *Damn Yankees*) and *Hot L Baltimore*. My favorite movie back then was *Annie Hall* so I adopted Diane Keaton's eccentric style; baggy clothes were cool then.

After Freddie disbanded, I was recruited for a new band right away and became a frontman. I moved in with my college boyfriend Barry at age 19 but didn't tell my parents. We rented a one bedroom apartment on John Avenue in Superior. For better pay and more nights, I sang lead in Chameleon. After that I was hired as lead singer in Magic, then Three's Company.

Singing four sets, six or seven nights, I started to lose my voice. This was not good since I was required to speak and sing in my theatre classes. My opera/voice professor got me an appointment to see his throat doctor. I had "hamburger throat," the doctor said. "Your vocal cords are raw and exhausted."

My voice professor taught me to speak a few notes higher than usual, to curb my chronic laryngitis. I cut down singing to two hours a night in Three's Company. I had to, if I wanted to graduate from college and not cause permanent damage to my vocal cords.

Joey started attending U.W.S. in 1976 and moved to the dorms, so mom and dad were empty nesters.

Dad bought a new fishing boat, mooring it in Cornucopia on Lake Superior. Mom took up pottery.

Like Everyone Else

I managed pretty well. I developed an outgoing personality—split into two people — happy on the outside, sad on the inside. Back in those days, no one was going to give up family secrets. There was no Dr. Phil or Oprah. I had no idea we weren't like everyone else. I wasn't sure our family unit was abnormal. I maybe had a glimpse of "normal" when I stayed the night with one of my classmates. But even then I didn't trust appearances. I knew people often hid their bad behaviors and deep dark secrets.

Since I was a teenager, Grandma Sevvy supported my choice to find out who I was. We talked openly about my being adopted. She encouraged me to find answers, "my people." I had no idea how.

Rose wanted to me to graduate from college, which I did. I was her first granddaughter to get a college degree, too. She didn't live long enough to see me get married.

Grandma and I had a very special bond, both of us born in September. Rose had a stroke, one of many, on my birthday in 1977. She died two weeks later.

I never told Rose her son molested me. I couldn't hurt her that way. I wanted people to think we were a good family, as normal as anyone. I wasn't about to break apart the only family I had.

In college I starred in Leo Zeck's student film *"The Girl,"* about a girl who walked forward while everyone else walked backward. Actually it was me he filmed walking backwards. Everyone else was normal.

I was walking backwards. I was stuck living in reverse, but afraid to look back.

Good Housekeeping Magazine

My junior year, I was voted the UW-Superior Homecoming Queen 1976. My picture ran in a special Homecoming Queen spread in the November 1977 Good Housekeeping magazine. My Aunt Laura unexpectedly found my face in her magazine on a flight to Wisconsin to see Grandma Sevvy in the hospital, when she had the stroke.

I waved from a convertible in the televised "Christmas City of the North Parade" in Duluth and another parade earlier in Superior as UWS Homecoming Queen. Besides my work study jobs, I did runway modeling for Jason's skiwear, then landed a few television commercials. My first big commercial was a "talkie" for the Duluth Transit Authority; that one was shot on a moving bus. The DTA bus driver performed magic. I was one of the lucky ones he helped to magically get a raise and job promotion while riding his magic bus. Edie and Sev loved it. My commercial aired on television after I'd moved out west so I never saw it. This was long before VCRs.

(next page, third row, far left is my photo, dyed blonde hair)

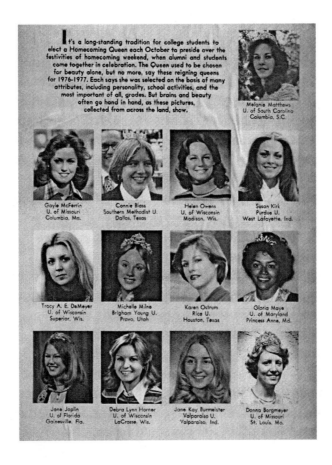

It's a long-standing tradition for college students to elect a Homecoming Queen each October to preside over the festivities of homecoming weekend, when alumni and students come together in celebration. The Queen used to be chosen for beauty alone, but no more, say these reigning queens for 1976-1977. Each says she was selected on the basis of many attributes, including personality, school activities, and the most important of all, grades. But brains and beauty often go hand in hand, as these pictures, collected from across the land, show.

Melanie Matthews
U. of South Carolina
Columbia, S.C.

Gayle McFerrin
U. of Missouri
Columbia, Mo.

Connie Blass
Southern Methodist U.
Dallas, Texas

Helen Owens
U. of Wisconsin
Madison, Wis.

Susan Kirk
Purdue U.
West Lafayette, Ind.

Tracy A. E. DeMeyer
U. of Wisconsin
Superior, Wis.

Michelle Milne
Brigham Young U.
Provo, Utah

Karen Ostrum
Rice U.
Houston, Texas

Gloria Maye
U. of Maryland
Princess Anne, Md.

Jane Joplin
U. of Florida
Gainesville, Fla.

Debra Lynn Horner
U. of Wisconsin
LaCrosse, Wis.

Jane Kay Burmeister
Valparaiso U.
Valparaiso, Ind.

Donna Borgmeyer
U. of Missouri
St. Louis, Mo.

"World Peace"

The Sigma Tau Gamma Fraternity made me a "Little Sister" to run as their University of Wisconsin-Superior Homecoming Queen candidate in 1976. I didn't know much about sororities or fraternities nor did I ever pledge for one.

Very busy on the Student Activities board, I booked coffeehouse acts, ran the film projector on free movie night and I served as a Fine Arts representative on Student Government. That didn't leave me much time.

Jim, my friend and frat brother, had the bright idea I should try out for the Miss Wisconsin-Miss USA beauty pageant right after homecoming. The frat-house would officially sponsor me. It costs money to compete for pageant scholarships, money I didn't have. They bought me an expensive advertisement in the Miss USA program and a brand new headshot at Jesperson's Photo Studios in Duluth.

Frigid Superior-Duluth wasn't exactly a bathing suit mecca. I looked everywhere for a pageant-worthy bathing suit and seamless invisible pantyhose. I was probably the first from Superior to wear nylons and a swimsuit at the same time. I already had my evening gown; my glitzy band clothes from Three's Company would work.

Even though I'd watched almost every beauty pageant on TV, I stammered slightly when the judge asked, "What would you do after you're Miss Wisconsin? ...If you could be anything?"

I didn't have a coach like other contestants, trained to answer "world peace" whenever asked a question. Instead I mumbled, "I'd be a doctor...nothing more important ...healing the sick....," covered in a sentence or two.

I surprised myself. I didn't know I wanted to be a doctor.

Well, that wasn't as hard as the fake smile. Contestants used "Vaseline" on their teeth to keep a permanent smile on pageant day. My face actually hurt.

Despite a pre-dawn beauty parlor appointment, the stylist shook her head at the mass of frizz I called my hair, the result of one of

Aunt Mary's home perms. My hair was dry and bottle-brown since I thought bleached blonde was too "rock star" for this crowd.

Jesperson, the photographer in Duluth, gave me his wife's post-pregnancy high protein diet so I managed to get to stick-thin 119-pounds.

I didn't win the title of Miss Wisconsin. I wasn't even a runner-up. Friends cheered me up saying, "the judging was rigged. The girl who won had a father who worked on Miss USA pageants in another state."

It wasn't a big deal. I wasn't devastated. I was planning to visit Joey. He had a job selling appliances out west and I had the big plan of moving out west, too.

I graduated in February 1978 but missed my college graduation ceremony in June. I was managing the women's clothing department at Wilson's in Duluth and my boss wouldn't give me the night off.

When Barry, my college boyfriend, got a job at Westinghouse, moving out west was in motion. We were both going and his new employers were paying for it.

Packing boxes for the movers, I got an unexpected phone call. Mom said my best friend Kim, an adoptee, had been murdered. Losing Kim was not lost on me.

Kim Peterson

In high school, my closest and best friend was Kim Peterson. Our lockers were close so we met the first day our freshman year. Just as fast, somehow we discovered we were both adoptees.

Eventually I met her parents and she met mine.

Truly, we were best friends but worlds apart in regards to our parents. She was an only child. Kim's parents were quiet, and very good to her, as far as I could tell.

Kim's mom made the best three-decker sandwiches and worked ridiculously long hours at a local restaurant. Kim's dad worked a night shift so I rarely saw him. She never had issues with her parents or complained; they gave her plenty of freedom—including her own car.

We didn't talk about my situation but Kim knew something wasn't right. She knew it was bad because I'd never give her any details. She was the same about her family. Secrecy was deeply ingrained in me, plus it was totally embarrassing how Sev had gone from being a drunk to a pervert. Somehow Kim sensed something was wrong when she'd call; immediately she'd drive out to see me. She was an angel to rescue me many times.

When I couldn't leave, we'd play badminton in my backyard. It'd get so dark we could barely see the birdie, but we kept on playing. I never wanted her to leave. Many times she saved me from going insane, just being there, getting me out of the house.

Ours wasn't typical teenage angst. Kim was like me in many ways—both of us had trust issues, and very low self-esteem. We were middle class kids, not rich, not poor. I thought Kim was smart, funny and sensitive. I didn't ask her why she never dated—I knew she saw herself as overweight. Kim was top heavy but never overweight. She always wore smock tops to hide her cleavage.

As Kim was shy and reserved over her appearance, I was nervous about Sev, jittery about even telling her. I was afraid the whole city would find out.

My father's obsession with me, and the threat of intercourse with him was getting more intense and frequent while I knew Kim, although I was never raped.

I couldn't bear to hear another word about sex. Edie would laugh at Sev's dirty railroad jokes. Mom never noticed the change in me. Kim did.

Then we graduated. I moved to the college dorms and became a full-time musician. Kim and I saw less and less of each other. We ran in different crowds. She didn't go to college. I'd occasionally see her at the Cove nightclub when my band Magic played there. She even asked to borrow some of my band clothes.

Kim looked great, wore contacts, had a new haircut and even lost a little weight, but most of all she seemed happy and more confident. One night she was especially glad to see me. Kim said she'd met someone, a biker named Alan. Right away they're getting married. I received an invitation to their wedding reception party at the Conaway Club. I got there late because Magic had a gig that night.

Less than six months later, I ran into Kim at the Piggly Wiggly; she was wearing huge dark sunglasses. I noticed she was hiding her face behind her long hair. Kim talked quickly, acted strange, and made some plan for us to get together. I knew something was wrong.

I didn't know what was actually happening to her. We lived just three blocks apart.

Finally, Kat told me. Alan broke Kim's arm and beat her and hit her in the face many times. Kat took her to the hospital more than once for x-rays.

Kim always made some excuse, saying it was her fault or she fell or ran into something. She never told her parents or me. Thank God, Kat was there for her.

The afternoon mom called, I was in the midst of packing. Mom told me to sit down. She had never said anything like this to me before. Boxes were everywhere. Finally I said, "OK, Mom, OK," and sat on my kitchen floor.

Mom told me Kim had been beaten to death by her husband. The newspaper said she suffered many broken bones and had tried to crawl for help. Neighbors heard a struggle but then silence, so they didn't investigate. Alan beat her up then left.

Kim was alone in the hallway, unable to scream or cry. She fell down a flight of stairs, crawling for help, finally bleeding to death from internal injuries.

I cried and cried to mom, "Where was I?" I got angry and wanted to kill her husband, the man who murdered her. At Kim's funeral, I vowed to her I would never live another minute in fear. I would live better than that. I would never take abuse.

Alan went to prison. I really would have killed him.

I kept the beige crocheted shawl Kim had made for me. Her graduation photo is up where I can see her. I keep her shawl on the back of my chair as I write, so I can touch it from time to time.

The shawl was my high school graduation gift. (shown left, I'm 22)

I got away from Sev. I escaped.

Kim was dead, and just 22 years old.

Secret Adoption File

One morning I woke up and decided I needed to do something about opening my adoption before I left Wisconsin. I walked to the Douglas County courthouse alone. I was thinking maybe a sympathetic judge would hear my request in private and let me read my file. It couldn't hurt that I was almost Miss Wisconsin and a UWS graduate.

Another word for miracle is synchron-icity. I had miraculously good timing.

Remember, adoptees are not trained genealogists, detectives or experts in searching for lost relatives. I'd kept a newspaper article about a woman named Florence Fisher, who successfully found and met her birthfather. That article gave me hope. Florence founded the Adoptee's Liberty Movement Association in New York (ALMA), to help other adoptees. I wrote ALMA who mailed me a brochure at my apartment and I'd put my name and birth date on their registry.

I wanted my medical history and I wanted my name. I wanted to know my ancestry and who my ancestors were...it was a long list. Somehow Florence Fisher in New York had found her father, and they were reunited. I wanted that, too. If she could do it, I could do it.

I was confused that a birth certificate would list someone as illegitimate when it takes two people to conceive a child. Even if they weren't married, why were they protecting my father's identity?

By age 22 I had tried the ALMA registry, wrote a few letters, made phone calls but nothing had worked. My birthmother wasn't trying to find me. That became apparent. I tried calling Catholic Charities who handled my adoption and they treated me like a leper. There wasn't an internet to consult. I thought I had exhausted all my options.

I didn't have papers from my adoption to know my real name. I had even tried calling hospitals in St. Paul where I was born; they said they couldn't help me since their records were sealed, too.

I had one last option—the Douglas County courthouse where they probably had my adoption hearing. They had to know something.

The Judge

I walked into the courthouse in Superior and found a judge in his office. I don't know how I chose him but I did recognize his name—his brother was the principal at my high school. I asked to speak with him in private then told him why I was there.

Being direct, not pushy, I said I needed my medical information since I was adopted.

The judge explained adoption files don't usually include medical history; he admitted to me that wasn't good. He seemed sincerely interested in what I had to say.

I also knew the judge was sizing me up. Was I mature enough to handle this request and what I was about to get? Standing there, I tried to disguise my racing mind: to hide the fear and anxiety that he would say, "No, go away."

I held my breath, composed myself and asked politely, "Please, sir, let me look at my file." It was up to him if he would open it. "I really need this information," I told him.

He nodded and called someone on the phone, and a woman entered. He told her to retrieve my file. God Bless this judge!

It took a while, of course. I'm sure there are stacks of adoption files in every courthouse across America, just waiting to be discovered, secrets exposed. This judge understood and showed his respect to me and my ancestors. This act was at his discretion since adoption files are still sealed in Wisconsin in 2009.

His clerk returned and the judge handed me my file, a few inches thick, at least two hundred pages!

The judge said I could only take notes but not have copies of anything. He gave me a pad and pencil and told me to take as much time as I needed.

I'll never ever forget his kindness.

I sat alone in his courtroom at a long wood desk. As I read the birth certificate and flipped through page after page, it just didn't seem real. Then it hit me. They were writing about me. I was reading my name for the first time.

Laura Jean Thrall.

It hit me so hard, I couldn't move. I just sat there. Then quietly, I started to cry. I needed to let it out. But I didn't want the judge to find me crying so I tried to compose myself. There were so many pages, dreary documents about placement and legal forms. I took a few notes on the pad the judge gave me. My hands were shaking. As I read, my heart was filling up. I was getting answers. Prayers were being answered.

I was shocked to read I was over 10 pounds when I was born. I must have been quite a baby and quite a burden, I thought. Diabetics have large babies, a friend told me later.

I was struck by the synchronicity that I was 22 and my mother was 22 when she gave me up.

Helen was from Minocqua, Wisconsin, a few hours away. I was illegitimate. My unnamed birth father, 28, was from central Illinois, from a farming family. They met in Chicago, got engaged, lived together at 2316 South Millard Avenue in Chicago, Cook County, Illinois, then she got pregnant. He took off and she went looking for him. She thought his family was hiding him.

This was her version, her statement to Catholic Charities. She went to St. Paul, Minnesota, had me, and gave me up.

My file said I was baptized Roman Catholic on Sept. 18, 1956 at St. Paul's Cathedral and I was kept at the Catholic Infant Home from 9-14 to 9-26. Then I was placed in two foster homes in Wisconsin from 9-26 to 3-15, 1957. I was born at 4:30 p.m., weighing 10 pounds 3 ounces, and was 21 ½ inches. One report describes me as a pleasant outgoing child, well-adjusted, large framed, with a high average ability – whatever that means. A social worker had written down physical descriptions of both my birthparents.

I went to his office off the courtroom, to return my file. Then he said he remembered me!

Twenty-two years ago, he'd met me cradled in Edie's arms, probably in the same courtroom. He had been my parent's attorney in the adoption proceedings. I thought, "This is another miracle."

My tears flowed for days, even after the shock of what had happened, what I had done, wore off. It was a miracle. God had answered my prayers.

I will always be grateful to the judge for letting me read my file.

It changed my world, and my life.

RELINQUISHMENT AGREEMENT BETWEEN CATHOLIC CHARITIES AND A BIRTHMOTHER

Know all men by these present:
That_____ the undersigned, being the parent of _____, a minor child born in the state of _____on the ___day of_____, 19-- being unable to adequately provide or care for said minor, hereby surrender the custody of said minor child to Catholic Social Service_____ a child welfare agency duly authorized under the laws of the state of _____ to care for, maintain or place children in family homes for care or adoption; and I also hereby relinquish to said agency all rights to every kind or nature which I may have to the custody services, earnings, or control whatsoever, over said minor child and hereby consent to the adoption of said child by any person or persons deemed by said child welfare agency to be fit and proper as adoptive parents. To the best of my knowledge said child _____ was/was not born out of wedlock. [Signatures, Witnesses, acknowledgement, date. This relinquishment has been duly recorded.]

Bottom of page: "The parent or surviving parent of a child, or the mother of a child born out of wedlock, may relinquish the child to a child welfare agency licensed to place children for adoption by a written statement signed before 2 witnesses and acknowledges before a representative of the child welfare agency. No such relinquishment shall be valid unless a copy be approved by and filed with the State Department of Social Security and Welfare.

[Source: www.adoptees.org/relinquishment1.htm]

Catholic Charities

I got to read my original birth certificate just once. I didn't get to keep a copy. I don't recall seeing any original adoption contract. It may have been in my file but I was too young to realize its importance.

Helen was my age when she filled out this contract. I wasn't sure if she'd be happy I was going to try to find her.

Catholic Charities Social Services handled the paperwork, though their typical contract doesn't exactly specify secrecy for the birthparent. "Know all men by these present..." it sounded like our Catholic religion (and men) invented this just for unwed moms and babies born out of wedlock.

Wait, it's not complicated. I just wanted to know my name, my identity. It had nothing to do with religion.

But it did matter since I was raised Catholic. In their box, what I was doing was evil and it was illegal, searching for people—and possibly violating someone else's privacy, exposing the secret that I am alive. By all accounts, I risked eternity in hell. In other words, searching for Helen could get me thrown in jail. Phone calls, letters, all attempts could get *me* locked up.

Back in my 20s it did look impossible.

My search meant I'd face my birthmother. This was most terrifying, even after hell. What lead her to abandon me; I had no clear understanding after reading my adoption file. Helen's relationship to my unnamed father seemed bitter but I wasn't sure.

I had no clue how to find her or if I should find her. Every state I visited, I looked up my name Thrall.

Child

Conspiracy of silence
Every story in you hides, surprise
Silent to the end,
No one knows what makes you cry
Trauma of a child

Running from the past. At last
Shadows hiding in the dark
The mind wounds fast, Child
Fears of what it will do to you
Scars underneath the skin
Secure in knowing you'll move on
Starting over, settling in
Abused neglected lonely soul
Bitter mystery, Child
Not forgotten... lonely child
Run, run, running on, running wild
Broken will, broken dreams
Sacrificed children, silent screams
Oh, child

Song lyrics I wrote about Kim and me, in my band "Sardaukar" in Kennewick, WA
©February 1980

Sardaukar

A few days after Kim's funeral, in the spring of 1979, I moved out west. At her funeral I vowed to live better, and be better.

In Richland, Washington, Sev's two older brothers had been professional musicians. My Uncle Joe had retired from playing saxophone. His wife Laura invited me for holidays and birthdays. We were especially close.

Sev's oldest brother, Puppy, was a professional drummer. His real name was Henry and he died while I was in college. His widow Betty still worked as a professional pianist in Richland. Dad's family visited us many summers in Wisconsin.

Once when I visited my cousins and Aunt Betty, she played the piano while two of her daughters and I sang. It was perfect harmony.

Edie's younger brother Charles, and her younger sister Pat, and their families, also lived in the Tri-Cities. Aunt Pat's husband grew rich growing grapes. I rarely saw them or my cousins.

Once I settled in Richland, I signed up for the Waterfollies Talent Contest, and won the trophy for Best Singer in the Adult Vocal division. Aunt Laura applauded from the audience.

With my new Bachelor of Fine Arts degree, I was hired half-time as office coordinator for the Arts Council of the Mid-Columbia region. The local newspaper ran a story about me when I started work at the Arts Council. The Columbia Center for Graduate Studies also hired me for part-time work a few months later.

Washington state was better for me and richer than Superior. To me, rich just meant experience. I'd met plenty of rich people. I wanted more life experience and knew someday I'd be a writer.

My first goal after college was to be a great musician. I went to hear live music in Kennewick and Richland and met other musicians so eventually I started my own band, Sardaukar. Our bass player Dave came up with our name and a logo. We hired a manager-agent. I wrote melodies and lyrics. Keith, the guitar player, wrote music.

Dave, Keith and I co-wrote twelve original songs, and recorded two demos in two recording studios. Soon a Richland-Pasco-Kennewick radio station played our demo. One night a friend Carol and I were driving to Pasco and we pulled over to hear me singing on the radio. The four guys and I shared a band-house in Kennewick and wrote music every day after work. I started jogging and dropped back down to 119 pounds.

At one of our concerts, an advertising executive recruited me for another TV commercial; this time I wore a bikini on the back of a moving motorcycle. My Suzuki commercial was shot along the Columbia River in Kennewick.

Success tasted better than food, so I wanted more.

I left Washington, my jobs, my college boyfriend Barry, my band Sardaukar, my aunts and uncles, and moved to the Big Apple.

Greyhound

In the spring of 1980, I went cross-country on a Greyhound bus to New York City. I planned to work as a singer-actor-model. I wrote to BJ, a theatre friend from college, whose mom was a musical agent. I asked to live with them in Bayside, Queens and offered to do whatever his mom Shirley needed me to do. BJ said he'd pick me up at the bus terminal in Manhattan.

Shirley suffered from migraines so I drove her to appointments in her Cadillac. My second day in New York, I drove us through Little Italy and Chinatown. Many times I drove to the Green Tree Country Club for her meetings and meals. I never once scratched or dented Shirley's car. I'd never seen anything like the streets of New York City. Parking was a nightmare.

Shirley was self-employed as a musician's agent and occasional wedding planner. We attended one gala wedding she'd planned in New Jersey. In exchange for room and board, I delivered contracts. Some days I rode into Manhattan on the Long Island Railroad – me, a kid from Wisconsin.

Shirley had raised two kids alone. Her son BJ had a production company and worked as a key grip on movie sets. Her daughter Robin worked in the garment district.

It was Robin who suggested I go see Elaine's Model Service who sent me on one modeling job where I wore expensive Italian shoes designed by Claudio Rocco and did reception, greeting buyers. The Rocco job paid me $100 a day for four days! I'd never made that kind of money before as a model.

"Whirlwind Shirl," as I called her, was a lovely blonde and former Playboy Bunny. She called me her WASP, her white Anglo-Saxon Protestant assistant. I'd say, "No, Shirley, I'm your WASC (Catholic) assistant." I tried her bagels with lox and cream cheese and ate my first pastrami on rye at one of Shirley's favorite kosher delis in Manhattan. We went everywhere together.

Shirley was exactly who I wanted to be. I had so much to learn. Very savvy and raised Russian Orthodox Jew, she trained me on all kinds of things, like "never pay full retail." Shirley bought all her designer clothes and perfume at cost. An entire line of designer rayon dresses arrived each season, brand new, through her daughter Robin's contacts.

Show Business

Moving from rock music to show business, I jumped at every chance Shirley gave me to sing. One evening I performed four numbers with an orchestra in a grand Manhattan ballroom. It was wonderful to sing with strings, even with my goose-bumps.

On the Circle K Cruise Line, I performed a set – unrehearsed –with a group of studio musicians. As our party-boat glided around Manhattan, I sang Debby Boone's *You Light up my Life*, and there she was, the Statue of Liberty, lighting the harbor. I thought of my Grandma Sevvy entering this same harbor as a little girl from Belgium. Mayor Koch and other Democrats were living it up onboard and dancing. I thought I must be dreaming. But I never dreamed this big.

Because of Shirley's connections, I was hired to hostess at the Sheraton Hotel's Kona Tiki nightclub on 7th Avenue. I seated the rich and famous wearing a one-shoulder Hawaiian dress, slit up the sides. Shirley and her friend Stanley Flato, a William Morris agent, were regulars and friends of Kona Tiki manager Cynthia, the daughter of famous Broadway producer Joe Kipness.

After work, the agents took me places I could sing. One night I did a Barbra Streisand number, "*The Way We Were*," in a fancy French restaurant. Another night, we went to the exclusive Friar's Club. (They had recently lifted their ban on women guests). My date was famous comedian Dick Capri who I'll never forget. Guiding me through secret rooms around the club, Dick reminisced about the club's famous "celebrity roasts."

Dick sent a car all the way to Bayside for our second date. The two of us went to see his friend Rodney Dangerfield at his nightclub. Dick Capri opened for people like Engelbert Humperdinck, Shirley Bassey and Tom Jones. Capri had me yell out a few "one-liners" so Dangerfield would shine the spotlight on us. Dick took a bow. I heard amazing stories about Rodney that night.

Not long after, Stanley had me audition for his Brazilian client, Jose Ferrar and the Highlights, getting ready to head out on another USO tour. Ferrar was famous in South America. Stanley said if I worked hard, I could be "an opener" just like Dick Capri at resorts in the Catskills or Poconos. I went to the Ferrar audition and they loved my rendition of *"The Rose,"* made famous by Bette Midler.

After a hair and make-up show on Long Island, Stan looked across his desk at me, my hair tightly braided in corn-rows and make-up just perfect, he said, "Kid, I see you on the big screen."

I was so blown away. I couldn't wait to tell Shirley what he said.

Helping out at one of Shirley's auditions, I met Georgette, who I nicknamed Gorgeous, or GG. Tall like an Amazon, GG sang in six languages, played guitar, had narrowly escaped her crazed Scientologist ex-husband, and had just returned from a solo trek through South America.

Shirley hired GG to play the Kona Tiki. I was there opening night and GG did great. Not long after, GG begged me to go with her on a job interview for a personal secretary position. The president of a coal company implied not-too-discreetly that GG had to live with him and do more than type. As I escorted her out of his apartment, it hit me that this city was the jungle. We both had to be more careful.

New York, New York

I celebrated my 24th birthday on a date with Dan, a model-actor I met while I was hostess at the Kona Tiki. I fell head over heels for Dan, quite a bit older (41), who had all kinds of advice for me. He'd been in movies, and collected residual checks from the *Godfather* sagas. He was a print model for Schick razors.

Dan and I went on all kinds of dates. He bought me my first sangria at a Mexican restaurant on the Upper East Side. One afternoon in Greenwich Village, we ran into Dan's acting teacher, John.

John said I reminded him of someone then looked closely at my fingers and palm. He told me, "Singing is a vibration, which is why you do it so well. It's good for you. Keep doing it."

Encouraged, I believed John's words. I could really sing. Stanley, Dan and Shirley also made me feel very confident. I was not living in fear.

Bad Choices

Often I didn't know who to trust. I was so fortunate to be surrounded by important people since New York was such a battleground. Actors and musicians would use anyone to get a break. I wasn't used to this.

Making bad choices was never a deterrent for me. I turned down Stanley's offer to become one of the Highlights (which I did regret). I'd met Rick, a country music composer who had a loft in Soho. We collaborated, sang a few duets and he took me to see music publishers. I never liked country music so that little deal with Rick went nowhere.

Answering an ad in Village Voice, I was hired to collect admission at Singles parties in upscale nightclubs, thrown by a promoter who lived in the same building as Rodney Dangerfield. BJ was keeping tabs on me, and sounded an alarm when he found out the promoter was a Hampton Heavy (like a Soprano). BJ found out I'd worked three weeks without a paycheck and felt I was in over my head. I assured him I was not afraid since the promoter never asked me to sleep with foreign diplomats or rich clients like he did his other female employees.

I was lucky again but these guys were scary, even dangerous.

When I first got to New York, BJ had asked me out and I refused. We had been friends a long time but never dated in college or had sex. Now we argued like my parents. I took on a very sarcastic tone with him and didn't back down. This made BJ fighting mad and furious. BJ was responsible for my being in New York. He said I had to leave, for everyone's safety, including my own. That promoter was the straw that broke the camel's back.

Dan said we couldn't live together because he shared his Upper East apartment with his mother. If I moved out of Shirley's house in Bayside, I had nowhere to go. Georgette was living with one of the singers from The Main Ingredient.

Unusually quiet, Shirley didn't argue for me to stay so I tucked in my tail, called UPS to pick up my boxes and left on a Greyhound.

New York was maybe too much of an experience.

Tropic Zone

Rock bands had a very short —a band would break up, get a few new players and a new name. Back in Wisconsin, I moved in with my musician friend Charlie and his girlfriend Molly, across the street from my old apartment in Superior. Charlie was booking bands. I joined Solitaire we renamed the band Automatic. We became so popular we had two agents—Debbie booked Ontario, Canada and Charlie booked Wisconsin and northern Minnesota. Our band Automatic had a house gig at the Eagles Night Club six nights a week in Superior when we weren't on the road.

For extra cash, I sang a jingle for Video Plus. I co-wrote with Denny, another musician friend, and two of our songs were recorded on vinyl by a local band named Hostage. For $18 an hour, I modeled nude for two art classes at my former university. New York had definitely changed me.

When Automatic split up in 1981, Charlie got me an audition for *Will Sumner and Tropic Zone*, the most famous rock-jazz-fusion band in the Twin Cities. Will had an album out so I drove to White Bear Lake in Minnesota to audition and was hired.

Within days, I moved to Minneapolis, got a new roommate, landed a part-time job decorating windows at a nearby drugstore and started rehearsals.

Tropic Zone, booked months in advance, played to huge crowds in Minneapolis and St. Paul. Some weeks we played six nights. Will wanted to get us on the college circuit which meant longer road trips and better paychecks.

Without warning, the day after Thanksgiving in 1982, I was fired. Not because I couldn't sing, Will said. He and the band decided to hire a guy who looked and sounded just like Al Jarreau, who was more their style. I didn't see it coming.

I sunk into a deep depression. I was not bouncing back. I wasn't sure I could do it anymore, not after Tropic Zone. I wasn't good enough.

For a paycheck, I worked retail at the Clothes Horse, near my apartment. Charlie, still my agent in Superior, assured me Tropic Zone wasn't a good fit anyway, not my style of music. He kept telling me it was their loss, not mine. I told him I wasn't ready to look for a new band or even start one.

Not long after, Will called out of the blue and hired me to do backup for his new Tropic Zone album. He promised if they did a national tour, I'd be hired back.

Wyoming Cowgirl

I wasn't recovering. My vocal cords needed a good rest, maybe a year. I wanted to try something new. After Tropic Zone, I moved back up north and stayed with Charlie who was renovating his new nightclub, the Norshor Theater in Duluth. I helped peel off the old paint and wallpaper, then I bartended beer and wine when his nightclub opened.

On a crazy whim, I answered an ad for the Heart Six Dude Ranch in Moran, just outside Jackson Hole, Wyoming. Then I got the call. One of the owners, Victoria, interviewed me on the phone. She called me at the Norshor to tell me I was hired and said, "Get out here, Pronto."

Ranch owners Carol and Victoria worked us six days a week. For five months, I was a cowgirl. I wrangled horses, cleaned cabins, did laundry and cooked breakfast over an open fire. I loved every minute. I had no idea the high altitude would help me drop 20 pounds!

Promoted to Assistant to the Owners, I ate with guests, picked them up at the airport and checked them in and out at the front desk. In September, a Navy Shipmates Reunion booked the entire ranch. One of my many jobs was tour guide, so I drove a few guys up to Yellowstone Park which happened to be my 27th birthday. It was so much fun, we had so much fun, all the shipmates presented me a bottle of scotch at their big reunion dinner.

Victoria had counseled me when I started having nightmares. I'd see two disfigured, scarred children. I had told her everything over those five months. She helped me to realize I had much to process after what Sev had done to me. She taught me to pick chamomile to drink as a tea before bed.

Eventually I realized that Joey and I were those scarred children, disfigured on the inside. Vic and I are friends for life. She visited me in Las Vegas that fall.

My Las Vegas rock singer promo-photo

Marty

Marty and I had dated a few times when I was singing in Will Sumner and Tropic Zone. Marty was Will's best friend. He called me regularly at the Heart Six Dude Ranch. Marty left Minnesota and moved to Las Vegas in 1983 and was offering me a place to live after my job in Jackson Hole. I'd share a house with him and his friends Jeff, Dickie and Emily.

Marty always reminded me of my Uncle Chet. Back in Minneapolis, Marty had invented the Pro-Fun tour. On Sundays, a bunch of us would tour sports bars and watch ballgames. Marty was the life of the party, spontaneous, always goofy. I wasn't sure how he felt about me or how I felt about him.

It was a gamble but I loaded my Chevy and headed to Vegas, ready to jumpstart my music-modeling career. I'd lost weight. I felt better. My throat felt better.

My first day, Marty and I drove hours to Los Angeles; he worked for a bottling company as a graphic designer. His little road trip had a purpose: Marty said we were not a couple or dating. Marty knew what Will had done to my confidence. Marty didn't say Vegas was his act of kindness but it was. I decided to stay anyway.

My third night, Emily took me to Caesars casino and we won a few hundred dollars playing craps. A Mormon guy from Utah hit on us, thinking we were hookers.

Our house on Gipsy Street in Vegas was party central with its own swimming pool. Marty and Jeff, my roommates, played semi-pro baseball; their team came over after their ballgames.

I grabbed the bull by the horns in Vegas. I got a new agent, dyed my hair blonde again, got tan by the pool, got publicity photos, met musicians and auditioned.

But this cowgirl never found the right man or rock band. My sex, drugs and rock and roll days were soon to be over.

Trophy Wife

Edie and Sev were aware of my travels, hinting to me every phone call I needed to settle down. That was parent code: get married.

They visited me at the Heart Six in Wyoming. Dad got to see the elk wildlife refuge he'd dreamed about and I drove them to the Rockefeller resorts and all around the Jackson Hole area.

They heard I was moving to Las Vegas to live with friends. When that didn't work out, I told them I was going to visit Joey, who was living in Florence, Oregon. That was daughter code: I was never moving back to Wisconsin.

Joey knew about my boyfriend Rickey, a southern rock musician. We'd met backstage in Yakima, Washington at one of his concerts when I was working for the Arts Council in 1979.

I'd never met anyone quite like Rickey. He flew me to Seattle when his band Blackfoot opened for The Who. I was backstage when a guy put a luggage tag on my wrist and said he was taking me back to New York, that I was a "10" like Bo Derek.

Blackfoot's picture was in *Rolling Stone* magazine. I watched their songs climb the Billboard charts. I was singing with Sardaukar when Rickey advised me about the music business, trying to discourage me. He said rock music was hard on women. He told me to pursue acting when I got to New York. He called me from the road or from Florida where they were based.

Rickey always knew where I was. We wrote long letters, and even talked love. I never gave up on my vision of a beautiful life with Rickey. Even in love, I never stopped working toward my own goals. In Minneapolis, I met Rickey before one of his shows; I had to miss his concert since I was playing with Tropic Zone that night.

When Blackfoot headlined in Green Bay, Wisconsin, I drove seven hours to see him in 1983, before I left for Wyoming.

Without warning, Rickey was distant. When we were alone on their tour bus, he said, "Take care of yourself."

That was boyfriend code: it was over. He'd obviously met someone else.

Being musicians, I thought our relationship worked. I didn't need anything from him. After New York, I was definitely more self-sufficient.

Now my "happily-ever-after with Rickie" (illusion) was dead and gone. Rick still called me but it was never the same.

I finally settled down in Florence, Oregon. I met David, a millionaire, a successful masonry contractor, a much older man. We met at his restaurant The Landing on Halloween. I actually worked for him; I was his cocktail waitress. David didn't like all the travel or my musician lifestyle so he moved me to his house in Lake Oswego, a wealthy suburb of Portland.

Eight months later we were married.

I became a trophy wife at 27.

Work, Work, Work

Dave kept me so busy I didn't have time to remember my old life. Dave was a workaholic and an entrepreneur, 18 years older than me. When he became a business broker, he persuaded me to buy a gift store in Portland, a few days before I turned 30. I was good at retail since it'd always been my back-up job between bands.

In September 1986, I opened my first store *I'quix fix*. Three years later I moved to a bigger location in the New Market Theatre building and renamed it *ZoolooZ in Old Town*. For seven days a week, 10 am to 6 pm, my life was nothing but work, work, work.

Over time, bad things happened as Dave's financial empire crumbled. I learned the more rich people have, the less they give.

After numerous lawsuits and mistakes, his fortune (a beach house, a restaurant, numerous properties and acres of land) slowly disappeared. He didn't ask me for advice since I was too young to know anything. Later he regretted it. His chapter 11 was converted to a Chapter 7. We lost everything.

Finally Dave accepted a job offer in Seattle, working as an estimator for another mason contractor. For six months in 1990, I worked my store alone. Then I liked living alone. Dave came home on weekends. We agreed I should move up to Seattle that winter. I kept my store open in Portland and hired a manager.

It took some time but I found an interesting full-time job. I was hired to be Antenna Theatre's manager of audio tours for the Smithsonian Museum's traveling art exhibit *Moscow: Treasures and Traditions*. This incredible collection had never left Russia before, until this exhibit. For ten months, I managed a staff of 20 and the mayor of Sausalito signed my Antenna paychecks. Antenna Theatre was a non-profit theatre company based in California, raising money by managing audio tours for museums. I saved enough to buy a Caribbean cruise for mom, Dave and me on the Song of Norway that Thanksgiving. Mom showed everyone her submarine certificate from her dive in Barbados. It was a fantastic week.

Since I'd left my own store, sales plunged. I called my manager but could not drive down that often. I had to close it so we liquidated the inventory and equipment. We rented then sold my first "new" house in Portland, mortgaged in my name since Dave had lost everything, including his good credit.

When the Moscow exhibit closed, I got back into music, this time the record business. I was hired to be Assistant to the President of Jerden Records, an indie-record label in grunge-crazed Seattle.

Jerry, my boss, was famous for producing the Kingsmen, whose biggest hit was "Louie, Louie." This was Jerry's third incarnation in the music business. He taught me everything. I hated the fact that musicians are at the bottom of the totem pole when it comes to making money.

Dave and I first lived in Redmond on Lake Sammamish, and then moved to Bellevue, east of Seattle. One summer I signed up for "Acting in Movies and Television," at Bellevue Community College. Our class studied with local acting professors and filmmakers. We auditioned for casting directors then we wrapped up by filming an original script.

I met interesting people in my West Coast jobs. If I signed on for this challenge, I might as well make the best of it, right?

Dave and I separated in 1993 so I moved back to Redmond and worked as buyer-manager for the Bellevue Art Museum store and we opened a holiday store location in the Bellevue Mall.

Naturally, I had no clue of my splitting sickness but it was still there.

Would I have been able to do all this without my illness? Not likely.

I'd done counseling when I was 22 and again in my 30s in Seattle, while I was married to Dave. A few close friends agreed I seemed broken but no one knew how to fix it. Those red blotches (nerve zits) on my skin were psychosomatic, a New York dermatologist cautioned.

My past was still showing up on my skin.

THE HARD WAY

Know Thyself

My friend Manidoogekek in Boston emailed me in 2008: In our modern world today, we may seem like drowning people because of the loss of much of our spiritual tradition. Our spiritual tradition shows us the way to live in harmony, balance and respect. The tradition taught us how to behave and how to conduct ourselves. The spiritual way taught us to pray and to purify ourselves. Handed down from generation to generation were the teachings about our way of life. Our relationship to Mother Earth and to each other was very clear. The Modern World does not relate to spirituality but to materialism. If we do not allow spirituality to guide our lives, we will be lost, unhappy and without direction. We are spiritual beings trying to be human, not human beings trying to be spiritual. It is said, "Know self. Pray to Great Spirit. Lead me to spirituality."

I always felt more at ease with my Indian friends. For many years I did my beadwork, mostly self-taught in my 20s. I learned the peyote stitch and took a beading class in Oregon. I designed quill and bead earrings but it didn't pay the bills. I'd take porcupine quills I cleaned (and bagged up in Ziplocs) to the American Indian Center in Minneapolis so I could trade quills for beads. They even sold a few of my earrings.

I knew all along I was an American Indian but had no clue what tribe. I didn't talk about it. There wasn't much to say.

In New York, I began my spiritual quest, after meeting amazing people: actors/models/ musicians who were into alternative medicine, parapsychology, spirituality and natural healing. They opened my eyes.

My boyfriend Dan (who practiced reflexology) told me to read Edgar Cayce, Ross Peterson, Catherine Ponder, Khalil Gibran, and took me to Manhattan bookstores. I needed to start someplace. My New York friends really lit a fire in me at age 23.

I morphed into a lifelong student of philosophy, quantum physics, healing and alchemy. Mystics like Cayce and early Greek philosophers all said, "Know Thyself" so I did. I'd have to know myself to heal myself, not just to survive but to thrive.

"Knowing" works like alchemy, turning a base metal into gold, turning fear into love, darkness into light.

While I was married to Dave, I was still numb, impatient over not finding my birth family. I had not even begun to scratch the surface in my 20s or 30s. I didn't know being adopted was the real culprit, even though I knew I was someone named Laura Jean Thrall.

The statistics say most adoptees get counseling for behavioral/emotional problems: 41% adopted as infants; 45% adopted from another country; 54% adopted from foster care. [Source: Illinois State University: A Comparative Study of Child Welfare Adoptions and Other Types of Adopted Children and Birth Children 2004]

Depending on where you live, information might appear in books, or on TV, with popular shows like Dr. Phil McGraw.

So far I haven't found any TV personality to be the least bit helpful in this experience of being adopted.

When I lived in Seattle, I wrote to Sally Jesse Raphael in 1993, when her talk show was a big daytime hit. Her people never contacted me. Sally and her husband Karl had adopted their kids. I wondered what they learned from this experience. I had not located my birthfather yet and hoped that Sally could help me find him.

It took me a long time to see adoptees are caught in webs of lies and secrets. The place we go inside our heads is like a prison. If all you have is a secret, then all you have is fear and that controls everything. That is no way to live. It is the hard way to live. It took me my whole life to see this.

Illegitimate

Before I did search for my birth family, I definitely wanted to meet another adoptee who successfully opened their adoption, or had a reunion with birth relatives. It didn't happen. It seemed there weren't that many adoptees, at least not in northern Wisconsin where I grew up.

Yes, adoptees (also known as orphans and bastards) were out there, droves of us divvied up across immense America. True, some kids didn't even know they were adopted. Sometimes our birthparents were our relatives, but most were strangers who lived yards or miles or days away.

Once I'd read my adoption file, it conveniently lacked history. There were no instructions on how to find my family. My birthfather obviously had a role in my becoming a person, yet he was name-less on my original birth certificate. Oh great, I was illegitimate. Disappointment may build character but it took me out, knocked me down. But I wasn't giving up.

Papers

In 2007, I found an amazing story about an adoptive parent who requested the right to read the adoption file in an effort to help their adoptive child find clues to their identity. I did not have this help when I was searching.

An adoptive parent does not need legal permission since he or she was a signer on the documents. The adoptive parents can request the adoption file. They can tell their adopted child pertinent details in their file. This was a great surprise to me and one bit of news I'm happy to share with adoptees *and* their understanding adoptive parents.

Sadly, this is a rare story but a strong possibility for those adoptees living in states with closed records. If an adoptee can ask their adoptive parent, please recommend these steps.

The other option: put your name on adoption registries, and pray to be found.

I get why adoptive parents might be afraid. Parents don't want to lose a child, especially an adopted child, after years of shared experiences and the bonds of love and time. Sev and Edie didn't offer me documentation on my adoption when I became an adult. I knew they had legal papers somewhere. It seems funny to say papers, like a pedigree dog has papers.

Clues to my identity were in those papers. Edie and Sev could not fathom how much I wanted to know. Asking seemed like an insult so I couldn't.

I did attempt to look for my file hidden somewhere in the house. Edie, even in her 80s, hid our papers, or maybe she destroyed them.

With respect to all my parents, I had to know. I had to know what I was feeling, what I knew as a child, was real. I knew I was different, not better or more special, just different. I knew this even as a child. Proof was important to me. I needed those papers.

My mannerisms, likes and dislikes, the way I pray, how I think, what was funny, even my choice in food, was coming from someplace very different. Solving my adoption mystery meant more to me than my grades, jobs, music or career. I had no grand ideas about life on a reservation or being with my people. I had no illusions that someone was looking for me. I just needed the truth. I didn't expect a reunion but I hoped for one, eventually. I never expected an apology, "We're sorry for what we've done, taken you from your people, your life, and your tribe." I never expected anything like that.

Late Discovery Adoptee (LDA)

Doing research for this book, I ran across a sad story about a 70-year-old man in Boston who was finally told he was adopted by his then 90-year-old mother. First he felt stunned, then utterly betrayed and devastated. Because she waited to tell him, he felt it was too late to find his biological parents. Even in his 70s, he was not able to open his adoption record, get answers or meet in his birth family. Massachusetts sealed their adoption records, too. This elderly man felt his entire life was based on deception and lies.

Some parents don't tell their child they're adopted or when asked, they'll deny it.

It's actually more harmful, more devastating, even more traumatic, when the child (or adult) learns they are living a lie.

Ask rapper Darryl McDaniel-Lovelace of rap group Run-DMC. He was 35 when he found out he was adopted—so he's a late discovery adoptee or LDA. He took VH1 television cameras with him as he took his journey to find his biological mother. For years he couldn't figure out the pain he felt, why he self-medicated with drugs and alcohol, and even made plans to kill himself. He didn't know why he struggled emotionally.

At the height of his music career, at the pinnacle of success, Daryl was a wreck. (I, too, was living as a wreck.) Finally his parents admitted he was adopted.

Daryl found his birth mom and made a music video "*Cats in the Cradle*" with another Grammy winner Sarah MacLachlan, who Darryl calls his angel. Her song *"Angel"* changed him, literally saving his life, he said in interviews.

I bought Sarah's haunting album, "*Surfacing*," in 1997. I didn't know back then Sarah was an adoptee. Her song *"Angel"* touched me, too; it was the sole reason I bought her album.

Sarah and Daryl are terrifically gifted musicians and both are speaking out about adoption issues and bringing their message to a wide audience. They serve a higher purpose in discussing their pain. They are strong role models for other adoptees.

Country music celebrity Faith Hill was able to open her adoption and meet her birthmother.

More adoptee celebs are popping up on the Internet.

Eric Clapton, born to an unmarried girl of 16 and a Canadian soldier, was adopted and raised by her parents. His mother left for a time so the family fiction became they were brother and sister. Clapton got his first guitar when he was 14 and went on to become one of the world's greatest rock musicians. In 1998, Clapton finally learned the truth and heard his birthfather's name. He went to meet his Canadian and American half-brothers and -sisters; since his father died in 1985, they never met.

Adoption doesn't destroy creativity, it actually stimulates it. Being adopted does not stifle talent, it magnifies it. Steve Jobs is a perfect example of this: utter brilliance mixed with emotional detachment.

Until we know the truth, we function half-alive. Every adoptee I know feels we must go full circle and meet our families to heal our heart, and to function emotionally well.

One of my adoptee friends told me he has yet to have a stable or lasting relationship with a woman, since he never met any of his relatives. It's been very hard on him.

Adoptee hurt affects our ability to love and be loved, and to trust. I did not know how to love my husband, or myself.

I see Dead People

Well, actually I do not see dead people but I know people who are living like they are dead.

Ok, imagine this. You are a child and you disappear. Not only are you upset, your entire family is crazy with despair and your parents are distraught. They might go on television and beg the people who took you to please bring you back. Your mom and dad might even divorce since they cannot forget you and they can't seem to heal since you are missing.

You (the child) on the other hand, might be too young to fight back, or even try and escape. But you want to.

That is child abduction and we all take this seriously in American and all over the world.

Now, change the word child to **adoptee**.

This is a life changing event: "adoption" does change you and your parents. American and the world do not think of adoption as abduction but I do. Why? It feels the same to the child. And to some mothers, it feels exactly like your child was abducted.

The trauma of being abducted or adopted is the same for the child. You are feeling you are not where you are supposed to be. Let's not get into the medical terms but those words do exist in medical journals.

So, I ask you, when will people who adopt children begin to understand that adoptees have feelings they cannot describe or display? Some adopters I know have taken this very personally and have tried to make the child feel better and assure them they will meet their natural parents someday. I have friends who have adopted and some are remarkable in their sensitivity. Some of them advocate for open adoption, so their adopted child meets their parent on a regular basis, if at all possible.

So, if you are adoptive parents and reading this, I need you to do something. Forget that there are laws preventing disclosure when it's a sealed adoption. I want you to request the adoption file —the legal proceedings. All of it! You signed the documents so you can request them.

Now you did it. When your adopted child asks, I want you to tell them you have the name of their natural mother and that you will help her/him find their natural parent(s) when they turn 18. It depends on the child and when they ask. If they don't ask, I want you to give them the file when they are 18 as a gift.

That is why I see dead people. If you are a mystery, it feels like you're dead.

Courage

I can't help anyone—or myself—owning a victim mentality. When you do find out which tribe, it may take years, and desire on both sides, to feel comfortable with each other, on or off the reservation. It's an adjustment that takes time. I've met many who were successful.

It took me 50 years to comprehend what's needed to heal this wound. I didn't know what I was getting myself into when I started.

I've met many more people who are shocked that an adoptee would want to know who they are. They reason that if your mother abandoned you, there had to be a pretty darn good reason. Their bad advice is enough to stall a search indefinitely.

"You might want to avoid that kind of drama, scandal, or potential disappointment," well-meaning friends would say to me, "It might be too much to handle."

No doubt there was risk, possibly pain or more disappointment. I chose to think I had a mother and a father, and grandparents and great-grandparents, maybe siblings and certainly cousins; thousands of strangers could be my relatives. I wanted to know them.

When I was figuring out how to search, it was worse than I'd ever imagined.

In my 20s or 30s, I had not met one adoptee who had opened their records. I prayed to St. Jude, the patron saint of hopeless cases. I was hopeless. Obviously, this was the test of all tests. The "mother lode" of courage was required.

When well-meaning friends would say, "Accept it, move on, let it go," I had to let them go. No way would this paradox of loss and lack of identity fit neatly in one tidy conversation or one simple explanation. There was no easy fix. Wild confusion raged inside me.

How would I know if I could handle the outcome of my search until I did it? I could not let it go. That also meant there was little I could say to them or to anyone, including my parents. Slowly, my brain fog cleared. (Thanks St. Jude). I realized there were no easy answers. There wasn't one place to look but several so I made a list, a plan, with no timeline. All of it felt dangerously wicked.

Little did I know...

I wasn't exactly ready to be pummeled, or hurt in some new way. Back then, honestly, I never expected to tell a reunion story or find my voice in this history but I did. I survived my guilt and eventually met my birthfather.

Laura Jean Thrall

After meeting with the (most incredible) judge in 1979 and opening my adoption, I felt a new sense of determination with the two small scraps of paper in my hand. I guarded them, memorizing every line. It was liberating to know my own name but it did seem strange to say my name: Laura Jean.

From that day on I checked every phone book in every state I lived in, or traveled through, looking up the name "Thrall." I walked to the library after I left the courthouse that day. I read phone books like a dictionary. My birthmother's hometown of Minocqua was east of Superior. I'd never been there.

After I graduated college, I moved to Washington, stopping in Idaho to visit Joey.

I told him what had happened, how I went to the judge and what I planned to do next. He listened but showed no interest in opening his adoption. He just couldn't reach that decision. Fear of the unknown and more pain can be terrifying. Even to me, it seemed like a lot of work. I offered to help Joey whenever he was ready.

During the adoption process Edie said she read secret papers on Joey. Mom promised herself she would never forget his real name, but she did. (Mom never wrote it down?) She thinks Joey's father owned a resort and had an affair with an employee who decided to give Joey up for adoption.

All Edie remembered about me was I was supposed to be named Helen. It's what the Catholic Charities nuns called me. Well, mom got that right. I might be named Helen, if my birth mom Helen had kept me.

Every state I visited, I looked up the name Thrall. It was an unusual name. There weren't that many in the phone books.

I wrote down phone numbers and addresses. At times I had the courage to call. I had a list of questions, names and dates running through my head. One call I made was to Seattle; a man answered and said his mother's name was Helen Thrall but nothing matched up. I thanked him for his time.

Every passing day my heart grew stronger. I wrote Helen's birthday (September 26) on my calendar and said prayers I would find her. I hoped that she was looking for me, and maybe she had a change of heart.

August 1982

What makes any adoption search difficult is that a woman usually marries and changes her name—undoubtedly I'd find relatives before I'd find her. I was always careful not to say too much. After two years of rereading my notes, calling up strangers, and hitting one dead-end after another, I finally found her—Helen. I was 26 then. She was 48. Without realizing it, I had called my grandmother, also named Helen on August 19, 1982. I must have sounded young.

My grandmother probably thought I was calling for her granddaughter, *also* named Helen, my half-sister. I simply said I was Helen's friend from school and needed her number. Without hesitation, my grandmother gave me my mother's phone number and told me my mother Helen's married name: Christie.

This was it, my big moment.

Much too nervous, and way too terrified, I waited a day and called the number. A woman answered. She said Helen wasn't home. I gave her my name, not Laura Jean Thrall, but Trace DeMeyer, and told Helen to call me, collect if necessary. I said I was looking for Helen Thrall, my birthmother. I said I was born on September 9, 1956.

Helen never called.

More time passed and I located another Thrall in Wisconsin; this time I reached my first cousin, and he was about my age. Bob Thrall Jr. knew my mother and he gave me the phone number of his dad, Robert (Bob) Sr., my uncle. I was thrilled to hear my cousin's voice and find someone who could help me. I asked Bob Jr. to leave a note on Helen's trailer door. He said he would. I gave him my name and phone number in Superior.

Again, Helen never called. Apparently she didn't want to be found.

Waiting

More time passed. I'd practically given up. Every single day I thought about the phone call that never came. Helen was the only birthparent I knew about then.

In 1984, I was married, living in Oregon and we had two homes and two phone numbers, both with answering machines. I'd changed my name to Seitzinger. Dave and I were married on August 4, 1984, shortly before I turned 28.

My husband Dave was very supportive of my search but *not* of my career, so I quit singing and became a business owner.

It helped to have a husband who would listen, then watch me try again. Dave seemed to understand the pain of my not knowing. He'd been raised by his grandparents and had a difficult relationship with his mother for many years.

I could never discuss my plans to find Helen with either of my parents. I tried to bring myself to tell Edie but there was never the right time or the right words. I knew mom couldn't handle it or deal with it.

Nine years passed after Bob Jr. left the note on her door but I didn't give up hope. I decided to write a letter to my mother, but I wasn't sure if she still lived in Minocqua. I decided to call her brother Bob who was very nice, and even happy to talk with me.

Bob warned me nicely — "don't expect much" and "be prepared to be disappointed." He gave me Helen's new married name. By now this was her third or fourth marriage. Bob didn't remember who Helen had lived with in Chicago and said even though she was his sister, they didn't talk anymore.

Bob explained Helen was the black sheep of the family and they were never close. He remembered when they were young; his parents would have to send one of the boys to get her, because Helen was always running off somewhere.

This is a sign of abuse. I would know, since I was molested. I don't know if a similar thing happened to Helen. I hope not.

After several drafts, on August 16, 1991, I mailed my Uncle Bob a letter and a separate letter for him to mail to my birthmother. Each letter was two pages and typed, with a set of medical questions for each of them to fill out. After years of knowing her name, maybe I could meet her. I was living in Seattle then.

For Helen, I sent three photos of me at different ages (young child, teenager and recent). I wrote that I wanted to meet her. I didn't want anything else. I did not blame her.

I waited again.

I was working at Jerden Records in downtown Seattle. Dave came to pick me up and had a letter in his hand. I could not believe it. I was too nervous so I sat there and Dave opened it and read it first. I could see by the look on his face it wasn't good. He just shook his head; I could tell he was disappointed.

It took months but Helen finally wrote me back. She wanted no contact with me. She didn't want to meet me. I didn't exist. She gave me the medical history I wanted. She returned my photos and wrote on the bottom and back of my letter. She didn't even mention my birthfather. "Sometimes life deals some pretty rough deals..." her words.

Since there wasn't a medical form or questionnaire to send to her, I created one. I am very glad I did.

Helen's note to me in 1991:

I KNOW you PROBABLY WON'T UNDERSTAND
BUT I AM MARRIED TO A WONDERFUL MAN WHO
DOESN'T KNOW OF you. THIS PROBABLY ISN'T
MUCH CONSOLATION BUT THE DECISION TO GIVE
you UP WAS MADE ENTIRELY FOR YOUR BENEFIT.
I DIDN'T CONTACT you BEFORE BECAUSE SOME
TIMES THE PAST IS BETTER LEFT THERE.
   I WON'T GET IN TOUCH WITH you FOR A
LOT OF REASONS. I HOPE you CAN UNDER-

STAND. SOMETIMES LIFE DEALS SOME
PRETTY ROUGH DEALS. You HAD A SET OF
PARENTS WHO WANTED you SO PLEASE TRY
+ UNDERSTAND WHY I HAVEN'T GOTTEN IN
TOUCH WITH you. MY BROTHER BOB DIDN'T
KNOW OF YOUR EXISTENCE UNTIL NOW
EITHER SO you NOW HAVE CAUSED
ME A FEW PROBLEMS.
   I HAVE MADE OUT THE MEDICAL
PAPER FOR you.
   PLEASE DON'T CONTACT MY
FAMILY AGAIN. THIS IS HARD FOR
ME BUT MY FUTURE LIFE WILL END IF
THIS HAS TO COME TO THE SURFACE.
GOD WILL FORGIVE ME SOMEDAY SO MAYBE
you SHOULD TURN TO HIM TOO. PLEASE
TRY + UNDERSTAND.
   I'LL CLOSE + HOPE you CAN
UNDERSTAND.

Helen just couldn't own up to what she did, and didn't sign her name. I was completely shocked and devastated.

Never Giving Up

Another year passed. I was more hurt than I cared to admit. I felt anger brewing inside me. I was in therapy, doing co-counseling in Seattle. I was mostly dealing with my childhood, remembering dad's alcoholism and abuse. (Edie would never admit we were hurt as children but I know we were.) I was getting stronger and wasn't going to quit therapy and planned to complete my adoption search.

My birthmother implied if her wonderful husband knew—it could possibly end her marriage. I decided that was her problem. How can any marriage work based on secrets, hiding a child who could pop up unexpectedly? Apparently she had not been telling anyone the truth. I could not accept this. I was alive. I deserved the truth.

Helen's need for anonymity was fine with me; I wouldn't bother her again. But I had one question only she could answer— who was my father? It appeared no one else knew but her. I would have to find out some other way.

I had called other Thrall family, including her mother.

I met my grandmother Helen but didn't explain who I really was. I drove to Minocqua the summer of 1993 and met my cousin Bob Jr. at the Thrall family boat business and he gave me directions to our grandmother's house in Boulder Junction.

Scared a little when I met Bob Jr., I said, "Hi, I'm Helen's daughter, the one she gave up for adoption; we're first cousins." Bob smiled and said I definitely looked like a Thrall.

What joy to meet a blood relative for the very first time!

I told Bob Jr. I'd been a musician and was raised in Superior. He told me he used to go to nightclubs to hear live music in Superior when they'd sell a boat and he had to deliver it. Bob might have heard me sing in a rock band.

All in all, this was turning out to be a great visit.

When I got to Boulder Junction, it was another miracle. I asked for directions in Edward Thrall's gift shop! This was my other uncle, Helen's brother. I didn't know Ed had his own business. Ed wasn't there but what a bizarre coincidence since I'd also owned a gift store, too. Ed's nice employee gave me directions to my grandmother's house, just a few blocks away.

I was very nervous, of course, but I had to meet her. My grandmother Helen lived alone and let me in when I said I was a Thrall from Seattle, which was true. I told her I was doing Thrall genealogy, which was also true.

We sat at her kitchen table and she told me all about her life. I was in awe when she brought out old photo albums. I saw my first photo of Helen, my birthmother, that day, sitting with my own grandmother. Helen's photos were not that recent but it was a shock. I didn't look like my mother at all; at least I didn't think so.

As my grandmother talked, I scribbled notes. She even showed me photos of my half-sister Kathy and her family. She didn't have one of my other sister, Helen— "the real beauty in the family," our grandmother bragged.

I have *two* sisters! Apparently we all had different fathers.

Ryan-Kilduff

My grandmother, Helen Kilduff Thrall was born in Ashland, Wisconsin in 1906, and she was a teacher. We both attended the University of Wisconsin in Superior; she told me she studied there in the 1920s. She earned her teaching degree and first taught at Odanah on the Bad River Ojibwe reservation.

She moved to Arbor Vitae in 1928 and married my grandfather Arnold in 1930. The Thrall family opened the Arbor Vitae Marine, their boat business in beautiful Minocqua, Woodruff and Arbor Vitae. This area is also the home of the Lac du Flambeau Ojibwe.

My grandmother said she was Irish, the daughter of Michael and Helen (Ryan) Kilduff. Obviously that Helen Kilduff was Helen #1 but everyone called Nellie. I wrote that my grandmother had five brothers and one sister (but three boys died as babies). Her dad Michael Kilduff was from Ottawa, Canada.

My great-grandmother "Nellie" lived in Wabasha, Minnesota. Nellie's grandparents had migrated from Limerick,

Ireland. Ryan ancestors are buried in Wabasha, Minnesota, in northern Wisconsin, and in Ironwood, Michigan.

My grandfather Arnold Thrall had family from Ontario, too, but his father George was born in Pennsylvania, according to census records. Arnold was born in Sugar Camp, near Crandon, Wisconsin. I am not sure of Indian ancestry but I wouldn't be surprised if there was some. I found an article about a Cyrus W. Thrall who testified in a 1911 newspaper that Menominee Chief Oshkosh was a great businessman, a good Injun, and not a drunkard.

Later I discovered a "Thrall" on the Brothertown (tribal) rolls in southern Wisconsin.

Even though this was the moment I had been waiting for, my grandmother didn't know anything about the man my mother lived with in Chicago. I asked her about it.

Maybe my grandmother had met him? Maybe she was sworn to secrecy? Maybe my question scared her? Maybe then she figured out I was her granddaughter?

I don't know. She didn't say.

I hit a new dead end. My heart sank.

I thanked my grandmother very much and returned to the Pacific Northwest. My marriage to Dave was unraveling and we separated. I stayed in Seattle and he moved back to Oregon.

I never regretted what I'd done. I'm glad I met my grandmother.

I kept in touch with Uncle Bob after we first talked. He wrote to me when my grandmother died. Helen Kilduff Thrall passed away at age 90 in 1996.

Finding Earl

There was time to summon more courage, even though hope was fading fast. I had no choice but to write my birthmother again, this time in 1994. I decided to mail her a card for her 60th birthday. She was Mrs. Becker by then. Grandma Thrall explained to me how Helen met Bob Becker and how happy they were.

In a few short sentences, I angrily demanded my birthmother send me the name of my father, or I'd go on the talk show circuit or hire a lawyer. I gave her 30 days. My patience was paper-thin.

It took two weeks for Helen to write me back: "Your father is Earl Bland." This time she signed her name.

Trace;
Your father and I never kept in touch - however I hope you can get the information you need. His name was Earl Bland of PANA-ILL. and any other facts have left my memory. I don't know if he's even alive anymore.

Helen Becker

HELEN BECKER
5835 COUNTY RD A
RHINELANDER WI 54501

TRACE SEITZINGER
P.O. Box 890
ROCKAWAY OR 97136-0890

That same day I called directory assistance, then the Pana Police Department. I asked the police to deliver an important message to Earl Bland since his phone number was unlisted.

That afternoon I got a call from one of my half-brothers, William, the oldest of Earl's five kids. He was calling from my father's phone. I could hardly believe it.

My birthfather was there and wanted to talk to me.

Earl William Bland

This was definitely the best phone call of my entire life. Earl and I talked a long time. It wasn't awkward on the phone. He was happy to hear from me, definitely surprised.

My first questions were about his past with Helen. Earl said yes, they lived together in Chicago but broke up. Earl didn't know about me and knew very little about her. He thought she'd moved back to Wisconsin.

Then I asked, "Are we (American) Indian?" Earl laughed, "Of course we are!" Then we both laughed. This was so important to me, more than he realized, perhaps more important than anything else I'd asked. I had proof, my suspicions were true. This was his greatest gift.

He also explained we are Irish, which is why I have his blue eyes.

Then Earl told me about his mother Lona and his grandmother, the Indian they called Granny. He said she was full-blood.

Granny, my great-grandmother, was Cherokee-Shawnee; she was tiny, not even 5 feet tall, and her dark hair was as long as she was tall. I could picture her when he talked. I needed this. Earl even described her smoking a small stone pipe.

I told Earl I'd write down everything I knew and send it to him right away. In my letter I explained when I was born, how I found him and other details from my adoption file.

Earl wanted to meet me. I wanted to meet him. He agreed to take a (very expensive) DNA test. (Dave, my soon-to-be ex, would help me pay for it).

I flew to Illinois in November 1994. Earl must have told everyone I was coming. I met his kids—my sister, my four brothers, aunts, uncles, nieces and nephews.

I had not read about reunions or how difficult they could be. I had no point of reference nor did I know what to expect. I had not heard any stories from friends who met a biological parent.

I just didn't know what I was getting myself into. No one really knows how to act during a reunion, or really knows what to say. It's hardly a normal experience. Adoption professionals claim it's easier for everyone if you use a mediator. I didn't know that.

My First Visit

Earl's oldest son William, nicknamed Butch, and his girlfriend (now wife) Brenda, picked me up at the St. Louis airport and drove me to Pana in Illinois. I was terrified of meeting so many new people.

Butch and Brenda were very sensitive and calmed my fears, telling me what they thought I'd needed to know before I met my dad. Both said they could not imagine what this felt like for me. I was too anxious for words. There was little for me to say. I let them cover a lot of information on the two hour drive.

I remember walking in the door like a terrified child, though I was 38. I was warned Earl's alcoholism and emphysema had nearly ruined his health by 1994. He was ill yet feisty and hanging on.

His first words were something like, "Yeah, you look like your mother," shaking his head. Then he mumbled some wisecrack about "big ass" or, "an ass like your mother."

His words hit like bricks. He was drunk. Of course I was embarrassed.

Earl introduced me to relatives as they arrived. Surely he wondered if I was really his.

So I sat at his kitchen table, listening, smiling, almost too weak to move. That was all I could manage.

That first night, I stayed with Earl and his third wife Sheryl in their mobile home in a Pana trailer park. They were nice and had a bed made for me and showed me where the towels were in their bathroom.

Sitting at his table that night, my father talked about his kids with Carolyn, his second wife, and offered little snippets of his past life. He mentioned a son he'd never met, a lawyer down in New Orleans, but he wasn't sure.

Earl didn't talk much at all about Helen my mother, maybe because Sheryl was hovering around. Developmentally disabled since birth, sweet Sheryl had the mind of a 13-year-old.

After one cockroach in the bathroom and another in the kitchen, I wanted out. This was not my first cockroach. New York

City has millions of them. Two was too much so my first night was sleepless. Some of this felt like my childhood. I didn't like it.

The next morning I woke first. Earl cracked open a beer. It was 7 am. I couldn't believe my eyes. It hit my gut. I got speechless again.

Butch called within minutes, thank God, to say he had already cleared it with the lab that Earl's beer would not affect our DNA test in Springfield, Illinois, that morning. Butch guessed I'd be concerned.

Butch drove us to breakfast, then took us to the lab. The lab technician took Polaroid photos of me and Earl and drew our blood.

Later, back at the kitchen table, Earl, breathing oxygen through a nose tube, hacking phlegm into a coffee can, finally told me his side of the Helen-Earl story. He called me his daughter many times.

As scary or strange as this experience was, I was experiencing new emotions. Even without the DNA result, I knew I'd found my father. I felt more peace after every conversation.

There was no way could I explain my life in just one sitting so I let everyone else tell me about their life. There was a lot of ground to cover. It was a quick week.

I was very self-conscious, having fought a losing battle with my weight since 1984. I could have blamed it on my pending divorce or how I quit smoking in 1983. I was feeding my pain, stuffing my body. Being fat and unattractive, men didn't even see me. I liked that—I liked being invisible.

Here I was, having my reunion and I wanted to feel something other than revulsion at myself. I wanted to feel better than this. I wanted my new dad and my new family to like me.

I could see this was too much to process all at once, a potentially toxic situation.

What was most pressing, Earl was dying. I was still reeling from this.

My Relatives

Earl and Carolyn had five kids. Butch, their oldest, took me to his house my second night in Pana. My brother Danny and his wife Kathy had me over for dinner. My brother Terry and his wife Sue came that weekend. Then my youngest brother Michael showed up. He was 18, graduating from high school and living in Alabama with Carolyn's relatives. Mike and his mom moved away when Carolyn divorced Earl. Mike didn't say much. Since I was 38, I'm sure my youngest brother thought, "She's old enough to be my mother!"

Three of my brothers had dark hair and brown eyes and looked more Indian than me, I thought. My sister Teresa had brown eyes, too. When Earl was young, he had black hair and blue eyes. My birthmother Helen had brown hair and blue eyes.

Earl's children were definitely affected by his alcoholism; much like Sev hurt me and Joey.

Did Earl molest his daughter? "No, he was a good dad, just drunk a lot," Teresa said.

Even in my 30s, I was still afraid of men. I was too old to be molested but that old fear was still in there. I thought I could handle any situation. I was getting divorced; I could no longer handle being a trophy wife.

Counseling in Seattle had changed me—profoundly.

That week Teresa took me to meet one of Earl's sisters, my Aunt Frankie. For the first time in my life, I really did look like someone. Frankie had an oval photo of my grandmother Lona Dell Harlow, Granny Morris' daughter. Lona and I had the exact same eyebrows and brow line, and bone structure. I couldn't stop staring at this photo.

So Granny was Shawnee-Cherokee, and Lona was, and my dad Earl was, and I am, too.

Seeing Lona's face, I absolutely knew I had found my family. Teresa said she knew, too, before the DNA results because I had their nose and ears. I do look like my brother Danny more than the rest of Earl's kids.

In December, the lab report came back. It was a 99.9 percent match. Earl is my biological father.

I was really happy. Earl called me in Oregon every week. I had moved to Rockaway Beach on the Oregon coast. My dad told me he loved me. I heard more about Earl's past from Butch, Danny and Teresa. Butch gave me a chart of the Bland ancestors dating back to Virginia in the 1700s. Teresa and I talked often.

I only met Earl that one time. I had regular updates on his health, and knew the day he was hospitalized. By then I was working as an editor at a busy newspaper in Wisconsin and couldn't leave my job.

On September 19, 1996, at 8 p.m., Earl died. I went to his funeral in Pana. I am listed as Earl's daughter in his obituary.

Sisters

I always wanted a sister. Now I have three.

The only one I've met is Teresa. She is an incredible mother of three girls, a devoted wife – really she is my hero. She's tremendously important to me; time and distance hasn't changed that. I spent Thanksgiving with her in 2005. In 2008, Teresa was diagnosed with ALS, Lou Gehrig's disease. We talk hours on the phone. I visited her again in 2009.

Even after my reunion, after Earl's funeral, I still had little connection to my Tsalgi culture. I found my dad, who I love very much and we bonded almost immediately. But it's not enough to simply meet someone. It takes years to really know someone.

I'd found Helen and hit a dead-end. More years passed before I found Earl. Earl's life wasn't about being an Indian but survival, jobs, wages, raising a family. He was assimilated, and had an alcohol addiction. I'm not pretending to have missed that life. I had one very much like it.

Granny's ancestors hailed from Cherokee territory: Georgia, the Carolinas, Indiana and Tennessee. Her parents were James Morris and Mary Frances Connor, and Granny was raised by a relative, a cousin Susan E. (Ward) Watson, another Cherokee family who had also migrated from Tennessee to Illinois. Granny was orphaned when her mother died but lived with Susan, her kin, which is our Cherokee tradition.

What I missed was my grandmother Lona and Granny, who would have made sure I knew how to navigate my life and know something about my culture. I'm sure each struggled as Indian women in this white world. If I'd met them, I would know their Cherokee history, how they lived with it and without it.

Earl's sisters Opal and Jane did help me understand Lona and Mary Frances (Granny). The Bland women are the keepers of our family history.

Eventually I researched online at the archives of the national Bland Heritage Foundation. It's a huge family; my ancestral roots do go back to the 1700s. It took more than a few years for me to piece together the story of Earl's ancestors. I'd like to do more research into the women and their family trees, since the Cherokee are a matriarchal society.

I expect more time will pass before I meet relatives who identify as Shawnee-Cherokee. What little I know about the Cherokee is from books. I learned to say *Osiyo,* Hello and *WaDo,* how you say thank you.

It seems many Cherokee and Shawnee people made a life in Illinois, and left behind an Indian identity to become farmers and raise families.

"You'd better hope you find the right relatives," my friend Rhonda told me years later. She is absolutely right. Lucky for her she met the right relatives in Bay Mills and now has her tribal enrollment.

I'd need documents since the Cherokee require an original birth certificate, which I will never have, unless the laws change. Original birth certificates are impossible to get in closed record states like Wisconsin and Minnesota.

There are many steps before an adoptee will get a CDIB, a certified degree of Indian Blood, or have their enrolled status in a tribe. I sincerely hope to meet more relatives who share my blood but I have no fantasy to be enrolled. Once I saw the difficult process, I no longer desired to be enrolled. It doesn't change who I am.

Of course there are things I would change. I'd love to have a copy of my original birth certificate from Minnesota. Even without it, it didn't stop my search. You can't stop what's in your heart.

Friends would say it isn't a piece of paper from the BIA that matters. "You are Cherokee and Shawnee. It's your identity. It sings to you." They're right.

Traveler

So I found my place as a journalist, writing about Native people. Call me well-traveled. I've lived in 12 states. I love packing my car and hitting the road.

Tucked inside my mother's womb, I was traveling before I was born.

Earl had been living with Helen in Chicago for a year or so. He was already divorced.

When he realized Helen was out all night barhopping, Earl said he told her family, "Come get her." He never said Helen was unfaithful. Earl got home at 2 am from his job at International Harvester and Helen wouldn't be there. He told me she worked days as a switchboard operator on the Loop.

When I was born, Helen was 22 and Earl was 28.

Helen's brother Tom did drive down to get her in Chicago— that's Earl's version—and apparently no one in either family ever knew I existed or knew what happened to me.

In my adoption file, Helen's version ran different: She claims she and Earl were engaged to be married. When he found out she was pregnant, he ran. She went looking for him and thought his family was hiding him. She told her version to the nuns, which was a terribly good reason to give up *his* baby.

Helen was raised Catholic. Keeping a baby as a single parent in 1956 just wasn't done. Even their living together wasn't an accepted practice. (I found a cousin Buddy who actually stayed with my parents in Chicago when he was a boy. I found this out in 2011.)

Some women did get pregnant on purpose, to entrap a boyfriend and force a marriage. Earl didn't fall into that trap.

Helen went to one of those places in Minnesota where you "wait out" your pregnancy. Catholic Charities ran homes for unwed pregnant girls and women; Catholic Charities handled my adoption. I was born in St. Joseph's hospital in downtown St. Paul. After the orphanage, I lived in two foster homes, arranged by Catholic Charities.

This may sound silly but I always wanted to know what time I was born and how much I weighed. My original birth certificate had real times and dates.

Nothing on my fake birth certificate would reveal my true identity.

Thrall

Helen was one of four children. Edward, Robert (Bob), Helen and Thomas – all grew up in northern Wisconsin. Tom, who served in the Navy, died in a horrible car accident in Milwaukee, at age 30. Uncle Bob said Tom was cut in two. Uncle Bob and I exchanged Christmas cards after our first phone call in the 1990s.

Shortly after I was born, Helen married Mr. Christie. Their baby Helen was born on our mother's birthday, September 26, 1957. Seven years later, my mother had another daughter, Kathy, but I never knew any details about her father.

I tried to contact Kathy. I wrote to her after I met our grandmother in Wisconsin and saw Kathy's photos in 1993. Grandma Helen gave me Kathy's married name and address in Illinois. Kathy never wrote me back.

By 2004, I asked Uncle Bob to put me in touch with my sisters, when he felt the time was right. Bob understood my mother didn't want anyone to know about me.

Eventually Bob told his daughter Mary about me. She read my letters and emailed me in January 2006. Mary decided to help. She'd put me in contact with my sister Helen, who never knew I existed.

I wrote my sister Helen a letter and sent her my photo. The first time we spoke was May 9, 2006. She had no hesitation in talking with me. Helen said both she and Kathy wanted to meet me and our mother didn't have to know.

Helen said her father (Mr. Christie) had abandoned them. Right after she was born, our mother moved to Madison, Wisconsin, leaving her (as a baby) with our grandparents.

Eventually Helen raised those two daughters together.

Lost Time

When I met Earl, he said if he'd known Helen was pregnant, he would have kept me and one of his sisters would have raised me. That would be a traditional Indian thing to do, I thought, so I believed him. It was comforting he wanted me.

Yet deep down, I wondered, "How could you not know? Wasn't Helen's pregnancy the reason you broke up?"

I wasn't sure what to believe. It wasn't easy making up lost time in phone conversations with Earl. Usually we talked a good half hour about our dogs.

At 68, Earl didn't reminisce as much as I needed. I sensed he regretted what happened but it was too late for apologies. He couldn't change anything. For him, some subjects were taboo, not worth discussing or even remembering. He never asked me about my childhood.

Once Earl said he vaguely remembered a call from someone saying Helen was pregnant, or she had a baby, or it was in a letter... he was fuzzy on this. It's sad when he can't remember something as important as his own baby. I didn't want to hear this.

When we met, Earl really wasn't sure I was his baby, which was why the DNA test was required. I understood that.

I wanted to know more about my dad but Earl drank sun-up to sun-down. I could not trust anything he told me. The real truth was somewhere between both versions. Earl died too soon after we met.

I made no plans to meet my birthmother but I really wanted to see her (just not meet her since she never wanted to meet me). I had found their phone number. I thought about ringing her doorbell to ask for directions when I was in Rhinelander in 1996, but I just could not bring myself to do it. I respected her desire for privacy.

My grandmother Helen Thrall had told me how my birthmother worked in a nursing home and how she met Bob Becker. They dated after his wife died. Bob and she lived in Wisconsin then retired to Florida.

After my 60th birthday card to her, my birthmother must have told Bob, her husband.

Butch told me he called Helen, after my first phone call with Earl. Butch said he spoke with Bob Becker who knew about me. I was puzzled: how did Butch know how to reach her—if my birthparents had not been in touch for 39 years? Did Butch need to verify what I'd said? None of it made sense. Butch claimed he spoke to both of them.

Regardless, Helen's current husband Bob didn't leave her when he found out about me. He stayed married to her. Her deep dark secret—me—did not destroy her marriage.

I accept I may never know what actually happened.

(PHOTO, next page) My birth certificate wasn't even signed until July 3, 1958. My fake with an official seal looks real enough.

Fake documents

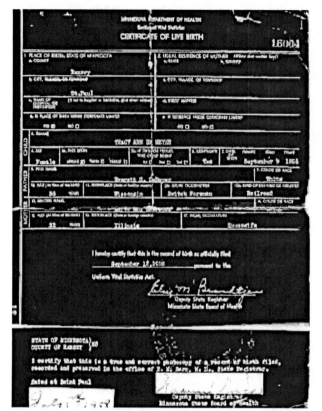

My fake birth certificate didn't say I was illegitimate. It didn't say my real name is Laura Jean Thrall, daughter of Helen Thrall and Earl Bland. It didn't list my time of birth, weight, inches or what hospital. If an adoptee has one like mine— missing information is the sign of a fake birth certificate from an adoption proceeding.

How did I ever get my passport with such an obvious fake?

Today I wonder lots of things. How did I feel being passed from one stranger to another? Who were they? Who were my foster parents? Why can't I know where I was the first year of my life? When did I stop crying? Did I have a bad experience? Was I sick?

So many thoughts. I thought Helen probably hated me while I was inside her. I thought about drugs they gave to expecting moms like her. Did Helen drink while she was pregnant? I'll never know.

Why didn't they keep me? It's obvious now. Just because she got pregnant didn't make them happy or ready to be parents. I wasn't sacred to Helen or Earl. Neither was in a position, nor sound mind, to raise me in Chicago. They weren't in love.

Both of them married someone else right after I was born. Each made new babies.

Granny Morris

I imagine for my Granny Morris, it was a necessity to marry outside her tribe, since she was living in Illinois in the 1890s. If she had children, she'd continue her ancestral lines. The Cherokee blood would flow.

In 2009, Aunt Jane told me how Granny was raped as a teenager in Missouri and people called her Dirty Nose. She kept the baby from that rape. If a Native woman had a baby outside of a marriage, she was called Dirty Nose. In some tribes, they actually cut the woman's nose.

Rape was a serious crime and if Granny had been white, the rapist would have been hung. If she was an Indian, her rapist would have been whipped.

Here is more of what I know: Granny's father (my great-great grandfather) James Morris was first married to Francis Baldwin, back in 1860 in Mercer County, Missouri. They had three kids, Jonathan, Mary A. and Martha J.

Something happened because James married my great-great-grandma, Mary Frances Connor, on April 13, 1876; apparently she died right after Granny (Mary Frances Morris) was born in 1877 or 1878. Granny was adopted by her relative Susan Ward, a well-documented, well-known Cherokee family. James found a new wife and married Sarah E. Throne on Oct. 31, 1878 in Montgomery County, Illinois. James obviously preferred to be married.

I've read about Cherokee bands that lived in Georgia, the Carolinas, Kentucky and Tennessee. Later they were found living in Indiana, Illinois, Missouri, Ohio and Arkansas. Not everyone moved to Indian Territory (Oklahoma) or wanted to go. Cherokee families who delayed leaving were forced by gun and many died on the Trails of Tears, which started in Chattanooga, Tennessee.

Some of my Cherokee-Shawnee ancestors traveled the Cumberland Gap like my other ancestors did. One of my great great-great grandfathers, Osborn "Aus" Bland started out in Virginia on the Cumberland Gap and headed to Kentucky, where he was captured by Shawnee-Cherokee fighting for the French in the French Indian War. After a year in Detroit, Aus walked out of captivity and settled with his family in Missouri, then Illinois. Most of my ancestors on the early census were farmers. (I located a document when Aus's son Jesse (my gg-grandpa) was released from captivity in the area now known as Detroit.)

If my ancestors passed as white, they could have bought land and owned a farm. Granny Morris' grandparents, Henderson and Olive (Carter) Connor were Cherokee-Shawnee, and their families migrated from the Carolinas to Tennessee then to Fayette County, Illinois.

Olive Carter was born in 1863 in Georgia and is Cherokee through her father John Martin Carter and mother Matilda C. Stephens. The Carters are Eastern Cherokee.

Henderson got very ill and was sent to a sanitarium after Olive died. Henderson then married Ellen Wright in 1877, according to the census. Henderson's son Miles Ira Connor left Illinois and relocated to Arkansas, and settled in a Cherokee community according to another census.

I did get a copy of the 1876 marriage certificate for my great-great grandparents James Morris and Mary Frances Connor. It's amazing to see such old documents. I also have the marriage certificate when Granny, Mary Frances Morris married James A. Harlow on January 1, 1897.

It's a mystery how Granny was listed as a widow on the 1900 census with two children Lily and Bessie (called the grandchildren of James Morris). Granny gave birth to my grandma, Lona Dell Harlow, on September 25, 1900. James Harlow is listed as Lona's father.

Then grandma Lona Dell married Hiram Bland in 1913 and they had 10 kids. My dad Earl was born in 1926.

A dear friend Paul Burke, a genealogist, helped me discover the intricacies of my Native ancestry and also found that one of my other great-great-great grandmothers, Naomi Oma, married a Paul Beck in Louden Co., Virginia in the 1750s. Her people were from the Delaware tribe, some of the first Indians to have contact with European Pilgrims in Virginia. I am still trying to piece together that part of my story.

My great-great granddad James Morris had Cherokee and Shawnee blood. Some of my Morris ancestors are buried in Oklahoma.

It does not mean you deny your tribal ancestry when you marry. It just means your children are Cherokee-Shawnee and something else, but no less Cherokee-Shawnee.

I admire Granny's tenacity to survive, even in a time when it wasn't safe to be Indian, when you were considered hostile and dangerous to American interests and Manifest Destiny.

By 1830 the U.S. government shifted its policy from butchering Indians to assimilating Indians, and relocating them, forcing 17,000+ Cherokee people to lands west of the Mississippi.

Many Cherokee relocated to eastern Oklahoma. Some of my Cherokee ancestors, who call themselves Tsalgi, "The Principle People," were in Tennessee when the Trail of Tears began.

Conquest in Indian Country

John Fire Lame Deer

One of my favorite memoirs is *John Fire Lame Deer, Seeker of Visions*. I've given away many copies of his book since it's the finest, most accurate book ever written about Indian life.

John describes a life and death situation for Native Americans in ways I cannot forget. To use his hypothesis, imagine it's right now and China comes in conquest to take over America. People die in great numbers, mostly with men fighting. We cannot understand at first but eventually it's explained that we can only speak Chinese. Our way of praying is wrong, our God is wrong, so that's changed. Families get separated. You die if you fight or get imprisoned if you don't adapt. New laws say children must learn this new culture and way of life. Diet is changed; food is served in rice bowls. Our clothing is burned, our hair cut off. Our old ceremonies are declared illegal and banned.

If you change the word Chinese to Christian, this is what happened to Indians, the people of the First Nations on this continent, from north to south and east to west.

Poverty
"It's hard to see the future with tears in your eyes..." – Mohawk proverb

Choosing to be a citizen of your tribe should be guaranteed, but closed adoptions like mine still prevent it. With identity erased and a fake new birth certificate, it is just as difficult to know who you are as it is to know your Indian people—if and when you find them.

There are real problems for the thousands of Native adoptees who want to connect with a culture that has its own tragedy to contend with, battling poverty, lost wars and broken treaties. Ethnic cleansing and conquest did happen from sea to shining sea.

As a journalist I was told Indian Country is a Third World surrounded by a much larger First World we now call America and Canada. Over a century ago Indians and their history took a backseat to Manifest Destiny.

I didn't learn much about Native Americans or European conquest at my parochial school. The truth is in the surviving Indian, hard to find in a book.

I did meet grieving Indian people though. Their hands are full. There is plenty to be sad about—contaminated by pain and loss, wounds still fresh, children still lost or missing. Indian culture is an inextricable blend of tribal and personal history. The Indian people in my life are the most beautiful and least arrogant. Indians don't complain, they simply tell their stories.

So in America's version of conquest, Indian people vanished. At one point, there were more of our bones in museum drawers than living breathing Indians. To understand the enormity of their treaty-making, some 3,120,069 square miles make up the lower 48 states... 86 percent was taken by the United States from 1775–1871. Poverty engulfed many reservations. Hunting was replaced with farming, which some did well, some did not.

When Lost Birds understand this, looking for relatives is like signing up for an episode of *Survivor* or *Amazing Race*. We ask ourselves, "How could I ever live in such a foreign place?"

I used to think adoptee pain couldn't possibly equal theirs on the reservation. After all, after adoption and assimilation, Lost Birds do become someone else.

Can our suffering equal theirs? Well, it does. It's the same suffering with different results, and clearly as successful in its intended goal, to **alienate** us from each other.

Poverty wasn't the only reason Indian children were taken. Social workers had long lists of people who wanted to adopt. Indian parents couldn't stop social workers from coming into their homes or hospitals, removing children. Every Indian reservation experienced this. Grandparents lost their children and grandchildren. Dismantling one tribe after another, left one grieving family after another.

So how did this happen?

Excerpt: 1974 TESTIMONY

HEARINGS BEFORE THE SUBCOMMITTEE ON INDIAN AFFAIRS OF THE COMMITTEE ON INTERIOR AND INSULAR AFFAIRS UNITED STATES SENATE NINETY-NINTH CONGRESS

SECOND SESSION ON PROBLEMS THAT AMERICAN INDIAN FAMILIES FACE IN RAISING THEIR CHILDREN AND HOW THESE PROBLEMS ARE AFFECTED BY FEDERAL ACTION OR INACTION. APRIL 8 & 9, 1974: STATEMENT OF WILLIAM BYLER, EXECUTIVE DIRECTOR, ASSOCIATION OF AMERICAN INDIAN AFFAIRS; ACCOMPANIED BY BERT HIRSCH, STAFF ATTORNEY

Mr. BYLER: Thank you, Senator Abourezk.

My name is William Byler, executive director of the Association on American Indian Affairs, a nonprofit citizens' organization whose policy is set by a board of directors, a majority of whom are Indian. We have been hoping to have such a hearing as this for 6 or 7 years and we thank you for your initiative in bringing this about. I have a rather extended statement which I'd like to have included in the record.

Senator ABOUREZK: That will be accepted for the record.

Mr. BYLER: Thank you.

The wholesale removal of Indian children from their homes, we believe, is perhaps the most tragic aspect of Indian life today. We would like to examine the extent of that tragedy, look at some of its causes and the impact that it has on Indian family and community life and make some recommendations for remedial action.

Surveys of States with large Indian populations, as you point out, show that about 25 percent of all American Indian children are taken away from their families. In some States this is getting worse. For example, in Minnesota, presently, approximately 1 out of every 8 Indian children is in an adoptive home, but as recently as 1971 and 1972, 1 out of every 4 Indian children born that year was placed into adoption.

The disparity in rates for Indian adoption and non-Indian adoption is truly shocking. I'd like to read some of the statistics. In

Minnesota, Indian children are placed in foster care or in adoptive homes at the rate of five times, or 500 percent greater than non-Indian children.

In South Dakota, 40 percent of all adoptions made by the State's department of public welfare since 1968 are of Indian children, yet Indian children make up only 7 percent of the total population.

The number of South Dakota Indian children living in foster homes is per capita nearly 1,600 percent greater than the rate of non-Indians. In the State of Washington, the Indian adoption rate is 19 times, or 1,900 percent greater and the foster care rate is 1,000 percent greater than it is for non-Indian children.

In Wisconsin, the risk of Indian children being separated from their parents is nearly 1,600 percent greater than it is for non-Indian children. Just as Indian children are exposed to these great hazards, their parents are, too.

The Federal boarding school program also accounts for enormous numbers of Indian children who are not living in their natural homes. The Bureau of Indian Affairs census, the school census, for children enrolled in the schools in 1971 indicated that there were approximately 35,000 Indian children living in boarding schools in grades kindergarten through 12.

This represents more than 17 percent of the Indian school-age population of federally-recognized reservations and 60 percent of the children enrolled in BIA schools. In some tribes this hits particularly hard, for example the Navajo where between 80 and 90 percent of all Navajo children from grades kindergarten through 12 attend boarding schools. That amounts to, in the case of the Navajo, about 20,000 children.

It has been argued that the Navajo youngsters, 5, 6 and 7 years old go to boarding schools because there are no roads available. If so, let's build roads. But the same children that are not able to get to kindergarten or first grade because there are no roads, travel roads to get to Head Start classes. Ninety percent of them are in Head Start classes.

It is argued, in the case of boarding schools, that Navajo children don't have adequate food and clothing. Let's bring the food and the clothing to the children and not the children to the food and clothing.

It is clear then that the Indian child welfare crisis is of massive proportions and affecting the people at a more severe rate than non-Indian people.

How do we account for these appalling statistics? I think one of the factors is the standards that are used in judging whether or not a family is fit.

A survey of a North Dakota tribe indicated that, of all the children that were removed from that tribe, only 1 percent were removed for physical abuse. About 99 percent were taken on the basis of such vague standards as deprivation, neglect, taken because their homes were thought to be too poverty-stricken to support the children.

The people who apply the standards very often lack the training, professional training, to judge accurately whether or not the children are, in fact, suffering emotional damage at home. They are not equipped sufficiently in the knowledge of Indian cultural values or social values, or norms, to know whether or not the behavior an Indian child or an Indian parent is exhibiting is, in fact, abnormal behavior in his own society.

For example, they may consider the children to be running wild. They assume neglect. In many cases, it may simply be another perspective on child-rearing, placing a great deal of responsibility on the child for his own behavior and, in fact, an effective way of raising children.

The use of alcohol is also advanced in the case of removing Indian children from their families. In some of the communities, as much as 50 to 60 percent of the people have drinking problems. This is acknowledged by the tribes themselves, studied by the tribes themselves and is of great concern to them. But that standard has not been applied as casually against non-Indian parents.

Once again, cultural factors come in here. The interpretation of the abuse of alcohol by non-Indian social workers, those that are not familiar with the dynamics of Indian society, is often based on the assumption that the pattern of drinking of an Indian person reveals the same kind of personality disorders that it does in a non-Indian person. There's been a good deal of evidence to show that the patterns, and what that says about the behavioral patterns and the abilities of Indian parents to raise their children are quite different than they are for non-Indians.

The discriminatory standards applied against Indian parents and against their children in removing them from their homes are also applied against Indian families in their attempts to obtain Indian foster or adoptive children. Nationally, about **85 percent** of Indian children are placed in either a white foster home or white adoptive homes.

In Minnesota, 90 percent of the adopted Indian children are in non-Indian homes.

I think one of the primary reasons for this extraordinary high rate of placing Indian children with non-Indian families rather than in Indian homes is that the standards are based upon middle-class values; the amount of floor space available in the home, plumbing; income levels. Most of the Indian families cannot meet these standards and the only people that can meet them are non-Indians.

We believe that there are other factors—such as the ability to grow up in the community where you have a number of relatives, where you're within your own culture—which are more important than indoor plumbing.

In addition to the failure of standards, we have a breakdown in due process. Few Indian parents, few Indian children are represented by counsel in custody cases. Removal of these children is so often the most casual kind of operation, with the Indian parents often not having any idea of what kind of legal recourse or administrative recourse is available to them.

The employment of voluntary waivers by many social workers means that many child welfare cases do not go through any kind of a judicatory process at all. The Indian person has to come to a welfare agency for help; that welfare agency is in the position to coerce that family into surrendering the children through a voluntary waiver.

The Indian family is also placed in jeopardy by the fact of going to a welfare department for help, just to get enough money to live on and money that they're entitled to under law. This exposes that family to the investigations of the welfare worker to see how that family conducts itself; and, welfare departments originate most of the complaints against Indian families and exercise a kind of police power. We think this is an inappropriate way of administering the laws.

There are certain economic incentives for removing Indian children. Agencies that are established to place Indian children have a vested interest in finding Indian children to place. It's interesting to note that in many cases, the rate of non-Indian people applying for Indian children for foster care, or especially adoptive care, raises dramatically when there is an Indian claims settlement.

It has been alleged by some tribal leaders that, especially in rural communities where non-Indian farm families may have a difficult time in making ends meet, some foster parents have an economic incentive, make a net gain by bringing Indian children into the family and using the foster care payments for general family support, and also have extra hands to help around the farm.

Finally, in the boarding school cases, there is a powerful economic interest. Not too long ago, in the Great Plains, a concerned Bureau of Indian Affairs welfare worker at rather a high level, thought it would be best to close down one of the boarding schools there, and, indeed, succeeded in reducing the enrollment of that school by 50 percent. That had the support of the congressional delegation.

During this process, however, the merchants began to complain and congressional intervention helped to halt the phasing out of the school and its full enrollment was restored. This, I believe, was in the 1950's. Its full enrollment was restored, and, indeed, it's operating today.

Senator ABOUREZK: Thank you very much, Mr. Byler, for some excellent testimony. Can you describe how removal of Indian children in adoption situation is accomplished?

Mr. BYLER: I can cite certain kinds of experiences that we have had. One case, not too long ago in North Dakota, Indian children were living with their grandparents. Their grandmother was off doing the shopping. The grandfather was 3 miles away with a bucket getting water. While they were away, the social worker happened by at that time and found the children scrapping. When grandfather returned, the children were gone, and I don't know whether, in that case, he was ever successful in finding where the children were. I think they were placed for adoption somewhere.

When that happens, Indian parents or grandparents are told this is confidential information. We cannot disclose to you where your children are. This makes is seem impossible for them to even try to do anything about it

Senator ABOUREZK: You mean the children were taken from the home and the grandparents never were allowed to see them again or to try to fight the actions?

Mr. BYLER: That is correct, and as far as they knew, they never received any notice that there were proceedings against them or against the parents.

This is very often the case, there is no notice given, or if notice is given, it is in such a form that the people who get the notice don't understand it; it does not constitute a real notice.

You'll hear testimony today, and tomorrow, from some of the Indian victims who will be able to describe much more pointedly the experiences that they have gone through.

Very often, children are taken simply by the welfare worker intervening when seeing a situation that she, personally, disapproves of out of her own value system, out of her own interpretation of behavior.

Senator ABOUREZK: Are there any States in which the State welfare workers are given training in Indian values or Indian culture?

Mr. BYLER: I don't know that they are given training in Indian values, Indian culture. I don't know of any that are. We can't believe that it is generally effective if it is given, because of the figures we see.

There are Indian communities, or tribes or individual BIA social workers who do a fantastic job. There's one community, an Apache community, in New Mexico that had a large number of Indian children out of the reservation. A BIA welfare worker was appointed and those children were brought back in, those that had not been placed for adoption, and few children there are placed off the reservation today. But then, there was a strong tribal input, a compassionate and concerned BIA welfare worker, and when you have that kind of combination, it works.

Senator ABOUREZK: Would you recommend that as one alternative, that the BIA, or some other agency, supervise a program that would, at least, make social workers aware that perhaps Indian people do have different standards and different values of their own?

Mr. BYLER: Yes. I would say, to train the welfare worker, to train the judges and to provide education for attorneys working in the community.

More importantly, if, for example, under title I of S. 1017, Indian tribes contract for and operate the whole child welfare apparatus themselves, if they have tribal welfare committees that function to determine whether or not a child should even be recommended for removal and then tribal court passes on this or some tribal agency passes on this question, that's the answer.

A part of the answer is not to orient non-Indian social workers, although that can be helpful and necessary, but to have far more Indian social workers.

Senator ABOUREZK: Did I understand you to say during your testimony that as far as reasons for removal of Indian children from the families are concerned, that alcohol problems in a family was given in only 1 percent of the removal?

Mr. BYLER: Physical abuse, the beating of a child, child battering, was cited in 1 percent of the cases. All the others were based upon somebody judging Indian behavior or the environment in the home.

For example, there is often the case that a welfare worker will see a father, let's say, or a mother every weekend going to the local bar, and maybe spending the night in jail for public intoxication. That is assumed to be grounds for removal, but there is never any need for proof, professionally demonstrated, that that mother or father's behavior is actually damaging the child. In fact, it could be argued in some cases that because the parent has enough problems in life and has found no better outlet for them, or for resolving the problems, getting drunk Friday night may be the best thing that can happen to him or his kids.

Another kind of thing that can be advanced for taking children away from their families is immoral conduct, and yet there's never any evidence to demonstrate in this case or that case that the behavior of the parent is damaging that child. Immoral conduct is often judged by the wildest stretches of the imagination.

For example, on one reservation more than 50 percent of the people live in common-law situations. These unions have lasted 5, 10, 15 years. The people don't have enough money to afford divorces and they want a family life, so they live with a person for 5, 10, 15 years. Police will sometimes, then, make a sweep of a whole reservation and arrest the people that are living in illicit cohabitation. People living in illicit cohabitation are subject to having their kids taken away from them.

Senator ABOUREZK: I wonder if this may not be a question better reserved for some of the professional psychologists that we have coming up, but I will ask you. You don't have to answer it if you cannot. If you know, what is the effect on the Indian family of this kind of removal?

Mr. BYLER: I think they will, in fact, give documentation on that, but what we have observed is that by taking the child away from the parents, you remove the main incentive for those parents to fight to try to overcome the difficult circumstances they have. Taking children away does not cure alcoholism. It may aggravate alcoholism. Taking children away does not encourage somebody to take a job, but discourages him. He may see no point in having a job.

Senator ABOUREZK. One more question, Mr. Byler. Since Health, Education, and Welfare supports foster home placements, have you received any encouragement at all from that agency with regard to revised criteria for grants that they make to States, which might eliminate some of the abuses that you cited in your testimony?

Mr. BYLER. We have not. They may well be contemplating that, and I hope they would revise their standards. We would hope, under S. 1017, it would be possible for Indian tribes to gain those foster care moneys directly so they would not have to go through the State.

Senator ABOUREZK. Most of the money that goes to the State and county welfare agency comes from HEW at this point. Do you think if they did revise their criteria for adoption in foster home placement and so on, with a lever that the money would be withheld if the regulations are not carried out, do you think that would be a beneficial thing?

Mr. BYLER. Yes; a dramatic impact.

[SOURCE: www.narf.org/icwa/federal/lh/hear040874/hear040874title.pdf or www.liftingtheveil.org/byler.htm]

The result: Indian Child Welfare Act, 1978

Recognizing the special relationship between the United States and the Indian tribes and their members and the Federal responsibility to Indian people, the Congress finds:

Congress, through statutes, treaties, and the general course of dealing with Indian tribes, has assumed the responsibility for the protection and preservation of Indian tribes and their resources; that there is no resource that is more vital to the continued existence and integrity of Indian tribes than their children and that the United States has a direct interest, as trustee, in protecting Indian children who are members of or are eligible for membership in an Indian tribe; that an alarmingly high percentage of Indian families are broken up by the removal, often unwarranted, of their children from them by nontribal public and private agencies and that an alarmingly high percentage of such children are placed in non-Indian foster and adoptive homes and institutions; and that the States, exercising their recognized jurisdiction over Indian child custody proceedings through administrative and judicial bodies, have often failed to recognize the essential tribal relations of Indian people and the cultural and social standards prevailing in Indian communities and families.

§ 1902. Congressional declaration of policy

The Congress hereby declares that it is the policy of this Nation to protect the best interests of Indian children and to promote the stability and security of Indian tribes and families by the establishment of minimum Federal standards for the removal of Indian children from their families and the placement of such children in foster or adoptive homes which will reflect the unique values of Indian culture, and by providing for assistance to Indian tribes in the operation of child and family service programs.

§ 1911. Indian tribe jurisdiction over Indian child custody proceedings

(a) Exclusive jurisdiction

An Indian tribe shall have jurisdiction exclusive to any State over any child custody proceeding involving an Indian child who resides or is domiciled within the reservation of such tribe, except where such jurisdiction is otherwise vested in the State by existing Federal law. Where an Indian child is a ward of a tribal court, the Indian tribe shall retain exclusive jurisdiction, notwithstanding the residence or domicile of the child. . . .

§ 1915. Placement of Indian children

(a) Adoptive placements; preferences

In any adoptive placement of an Indian child under State law, a preference shall be given, in the absence of good cause to the contrary, to a placement with (1) a member of the child's extended family; (2) other members of the Indian child's tribe; or (3) other Indian families. . . .

(d) Social and cultural standards applicable

The standards to be applied in meeting the preference requirements of this section shall be the prevailing social and cultural standards of the Indian community in which the parent or extended family resides or with which the parent or extended family members maintain social and cultural ties.

[Source: ttp://www.uoregon.edu/~adoption/archive/ICWAexcerpt]

Laws Protect Full-Bloods

To protect Indian children from adoption agencies, tribal leaders pushed for the much-needed Indian Child Welfare Act (ICWA), made law in 1978. Since its passage, full blood Indian children are protected and kept in their tribal community.

But the Multi-Ethnic Placement Act of 1994, (amended by the Interethnic Adoption Provisions of 1996) decided: "If it turns out that a child is of mixed ancestry, including some Indian heritage, but is not an "Indian child" under ICWA, then the child's placement is not subject to ICWA and the child is entitled to the MEPA-IEP protections against discriminatory placement decisions. If a caseworker has reason to know that a child may have some Indian heritage, it is essential to determine whether the child is a member of a <u>federally recognized</u> Indian tribe, or may be eligible for membership by virtue of being the biological child of a member. Delays in determining a child's status as an "Indian child" can have the unfortunate consequence, years later, of disrupting stable placements with non-Indian foster or adoptive parents to rectify an earlier failure to abide by ICWA."

I'm a mixed blood, meaning my blood was somehow tainted or ruined. The ax cuts both ways. Tribes might lose children if one parent was white and doesn't disclose the child's Indian ancestry. Some tribes exclude mixed bloods based on blood quantum. Some tribes dis-enroll members who move off their reservation.

Entire tribes were terminated by the 1950s, when the U.S. government ended its federal trusteeship of roughly three percent of the Native population through a process called termination. Of the 109 tribes and bands terminated, 62 were in Oregon and 41 were in California. Others were in Minnesota, Nebraska, Utah, and Wisconsin. (Many adoptions happened in those states, too, before the ICWA.)

Termination caused cultural, political and economic devastation for those tribes. Some did reestablish the trust relationship but for others, their lawsuits lasted years.

Lost Birds I've met want to find their families, even if not federally recognized. Mixed blood children now can certainly fall into these loopholes. Caseworkers might determine your Indian status based on how you look, which is ridiculous.

Really, it's a mess. There are 250 tribes on a list of non-recognized tribes, with 150 of them petitioning for federal recognition. State-recognized tribes like the Abenaki in Vermont, who receive no federal benefits, are currently petitioning the federal government. The idea that a tribe doesn't exist is troubling. If there are tribal members, there is a tribe.

Not long ago, Vermont decided to apologize for sterilizing Abenaki Indian women and children, after a deliberate attempt to make sure there would be no more Vermont Indians. Vermont's apology took the form of teaching Abenaki tribal history in all its schools. For many years, the Abenaki were so afraid of the government militia called Roger's Rangers; they did not teach their children the Abenaki culture, language or ceremony.

Some history I wish wasn't true.

The Removal Movement
"What is tradition, what is culture? It all depends on what we do as a people. We make history today."

—American Indian Elder on the National Indian Child Welfare Act website

Affected tribal nations, grappling with poverty and oppression, could not defeat the new enemy called America. What happened to Indigenous children prior to 1978, removed from tribal rolls (and official membership), can now acknowledged for what it was: Ethnic Cleansing. These are strong words but genocide was a strong act, as was putting children in boarding schools and adoptive homes. The basic premise for removal was obviously Native people were not good enough, or American enough, or Canadian enough. Judgment.

If you want to destroy a culture, destroy its future. You don't make treaty with dead Indians or prison Indians or pay for Indian kids adopted by whites.

Removing Indians from tribal rolls was a clever move by the federal government, eliminating the need to pay them again for promises. Even now you must be a card-carrying Indian to be eligible for treaty rights.

In 2011, some tribal nations do offer education, but not all. Some offer casino royalties in "per cap" payments, but not all. Some offer housing, but not all. Tribes usually have some form of Indian Health Services and food commodity programs, but not all. Poverty is like a wobbly wheel with spokes and spikes digging new holes for new people to fall in, generation upon generation. A life in poverty is a life riddled with bullet holes, run by gangs, street crime and drug thugs. The end result is the same everywhere: violence, despair and disappointment. Nearly half the planet lives in poverty but Americans don't see it or hear about it. Major media networks are owned by fewer and fewer people who cleverly control what we watch, hear or read. Occasionally *The History Channel* shows a good documentary about Indians, some are even written by American Indians. America rarely sees life on desolate Indian reservations.

How Indian Mothers Lost their Children

I read from excerpt at the University of Wisconsin in Platteville in 2008 by author/historian Renee Ransom-Flood about her experiences as a Social Worker, which explains how American Indian Mothers lost their children:

"...But prejudice in its blatant form wasn't the main reason I was concerned about continuing in my job. I had watched while many Indian children were placed in foster and adoptive care away from their tribes. Due to ignorance and lack of funds there were inadequate services offered to Indian children in foster care, and some were lost for years in the legal system, lobbed from one foster home to another like battered tennis balls. Many had been taken from their families because the social worker, lawyer or judge did not understand Indian ways.

One day I went to a local hospital with another social worker. On the maternity ward, we found a young Lakota mother holding her baby boy. She had him wrapped up tightly in a warm blanket, and he was asleep. When the social worker barged in on the mother, she didn't look up. A nurse came and pulled the curtain around us.

"Are you having trouble finding a place to stay?" The worker began sympathetically. She gave me a knowing look and she thought the Indian girl hadn't noticed.

The girl was scared. Without looking, Indians can read body language like radar. "We just need a ride back to Rosebud," she said softly, still without looking up.

Now began the barrage of questions, each unconsciously calculated to destroy the young woman's self-esteem. "How will you raise your child without money?" the worker asked. "What kind of life can you provide for him on the reservation? If you really love your boy, you'd give him a chance in life. We have a long list of good people who can never have children of their own. They have money, beautiful homes. Your baby would have everything; a good education, nice clothes, loving parents, opportunities you can never give him..."

When we got to the state car in the parking lot, I looked back up at the hospital window. There stood the young Lakota mother, her open palms on the window above her head. The worker handed me the baby, and I held him, still looking up at the Lakota girl watching us helplessly as we drove away with her precious child."

Pathways to Prosperity: "We are working from a cultural and spiritual foundation that recognizes poverty as much more than simply a lack of money," states United Indians of All Tribes Foundation (UIATF) CEO Phil Lane, Jr. (Yankton Dakota/Chickasaw). "...Poverty is many things braided together. It's an interdependent

web of social, cultural, political, economic and personal factors that
combine to trap families, and whole communities in patterns of ill
health, deprivation, and dependency. The only way out of the trap is
to truly engage these same families and communities in a journey of
learning, healing and building."
[Source: U.S. Newswire, October 10, 2007]

Dawes Rolls

Reading the Final (Dawes) Rolls, I see many Cherokee names—including mine: Connor, Carter, Beck, Morris and Bland. I do not know if Granny Morris was ever officially enrolled. We do think she was born in 1877 (or 1878) in Fayette County, Illinois. I checked with that county and there is no birth certificate for her. Maybe some of her relatives did move to eastern Oklahoma in the early 19th century. I do not know.

I do know that the federal government's confusion and mishandling of people with biracial identities denied many who were African and Native American, or what is known as Black Indians. The Dawes census people were disrespectful to many in the Five Civilized Tribes, since a mother's ancestry was often used to determine tribal rolls. Some Cherokee are not happy that the Freedmen, former slaves, are on their rolls, despite the Cherokee Supreme Court decision to grant them membership in 2006. Their expulsion of Freedmen (and women) came in 2007 in a vote that was later appealed.

I believe once blood is drawn and DNA tested, skin color will have nothing to do with Cherokee membership. Many Black Indians will be enrolled. (The Seminole did the same thing to exclude their Freedmen.)

Dawes Commissioners, like many others, used their eyes to determine who was Indian. Census takers would eliminate tribal identity based on how one looked. Their counts remain flawed by such flagrant racism. Many of my ancestors are listed as white when they are Indians.

No wonder Native Americans don't trust census takers, even today. This construct of blood quantum and blood degrees was not the invention of Indian people. Measuring Indian blood meant eventually there would be no full-blood Indian people left, so those tribes would become extinct on paper. Their way, Indians disappear.

Without full-bloods, it would no longer be necessary to honor treaties or sovereignty.

Most tribes maintain, "One drop of blood makes you an Indian." This way they'll never run out of citizens.

One friend used to ask me, "Which part of you is Indian, your right arm or your left foot? The government says you are part. What part do they mean?"

His point was you are Indian, not part anything.

QUOTE: Historian Patricia Nelson Limerick summarized in The Legacy of Conquest: The Unbroken Past of the American West, "Set the blood quantum one-quarter, hold to it as a rigid definition of Indians, let intermarriage proceed as it had for centuries, eventually Indians will defined out of existence. When that happens, the federal government will be freed of its persistent 'Indian problem.'"

Hopi Men Imprisoned at Alcatraz

Nineteen Hopi men from Arizona were imprisoned at Alcatraz in 1895, simply because they refused to let the state take their children away for boarding school and assimilation. Brenda Norrell at Censored News (November 2009) reported: "John Martini described the prisoner's cells at Alcatraz as 'tiny wooden cells ... worlds removed from the western desert and plains.' Indeed, a description of Alcatraz in 1902, just seven years after the Hopi prisoners were jailed there, suggests that the cells were in poor condition: 'The old cell blocks were rotten and unsafe; the sanitary condition very dangerous to health.'" There were rumors that some of Hopi men had died. Rumors circulated that they were "poorly fed, clothed, worked hard, some were perhaps killed.

[Source: PHOTO COURTESY of Hopi Cultural Preservation Office, STORY: http://www.bsnorrell.blogspot.com]

Many Moons...

I've lived all this time, and know I would not have been able to write this 20 or 30 years ago. It took many moons. I did the work.

I had therapy twice, but not for adoption issues—no one ever said being adopted was an issue. I had no idea doctors were studying birth trauma in adoptees.

I had to dig, read and process whatever I could find, and learn for myself. Of course I discussed it with other adoptees.

For days I could only think about adoption, not write about it. Processing was slow; then reading, phone calls, and eventually more writing. I've met several adoptees who are more "ok" than others. Not all my adoptee friends are Native American; some are biracial, multi-ethnic, or a mystery. Not all react the same about our apparent trauma. Most had never heard of the Indian Adoption Projects or the history.

A few adoptees said they love their adoptive parents even more for supporting them through their search, allowing them to reconnect with their tribe. Not every Native adoptee had a bad childhood. Some are extremely fortunate to have two families to love. Some lost their adoptive parents when they did locate their Indian parents.

Many adoptees admit their pain. Some handle it better than others. Some did resort to drugs or alcohol, or self-abuse. Some said reunions with birthparents went worse than expected. Sometimes birthparents don't live up to the fantasies we concoct for them.

Some claim their reunion with siblings was the most incredible experience of their life.

I surprised myself at times, scribbling and writing memories at 4 a.m., tapping what I call my buried ugly stuff. Some memories were blocked. I found it was better if I didn't try so hard. I took a yoga class and learned to exhale anxiety in every breath. In the daytime I'd work on this book as a journalist, reading adoption history or news. I try to read everything first then compare.

As I was writing, it hit me. Secrecy didn't work, not for *any* of us. By us, I mean me, my adopted brother Joey, my adoptee friends Kim, Larry, Dan, Rhonda, Anecia, Thomas, Susan, Suzie, Bridget, Garnet, Bill, Adrian, Mary Ann, Jeff, Sandy, Mary Liz, Gail, Carol, Aaron, Forrest, Ted, Drew, Lisa, Mark, Linda, Phyllis, Alice, Nathan, Janey, Diane, Joan, Von and countless other adoptees I know.

Regardless of our growing years, our loving (or not-so-loving) adoptive parents, whether we are Native American or not, we need to know who we are. No more pretending. We need our birth records, no matter how old we get, despite what anyone else thinks.

If we're Indians, we need to know which tribe, what clan, what nation. We need our past to regain our momentum, to stand tall and face the future.

Time Machine

There is no time machine to transport you back to the moment you were abandoned. You can't erase how you felt or how it feels now. Or how it controls your life. Or how it breaks your heart into a million pieces. You don't know how to stop feeling this way. You pray you'll find your family, someone like you, who gets you, who looks like you. You want to put the pieces of your life back together, but you don't know how.

These were thoughts I had—as I was processing.

Yes, there are adoptees that also feel this but never get to say it. I do see pain on their face.

No matter how much love and care we are given, the truth is —we are (and will always be) someone else's children. We're just not able to say it, not usually.

No doctor diagnosed me with birth trauma or splitting sickness. Therapists would recommend drugs which would only deaden my senses, missing the whole point. I didn't want to feel *more* dead. I was already dead, or at least part of me was. I wanted to feel alive! Instead I had just shut down: Power off.

My sickness was a dead zone, a black hole. It was not visible on my skin, nor did it raise its ugly head in one outburst or one tantrum.

I heard a story about another adoptee, a doctor with an Ivy League education, who was unable to meet his birthmother before she died. His wife told me he was never able to get the information he needed to find his birthfather, or know his identity. Regardless of this man's expensive education and medical training, the pain wounded him so badly he just couldn't function, feel love or have a successful relationship. The pain was so deep, he couldn't see it.

His wife told their therapist about his adoption, how he reacted, and how he seemed cold, heartless. Even marriage counseling didn't save their marriage. Their therapist thought his adoption trauma was too much for him to handle; trying to work on it might kill what was left of him.

I'm not sure where I got my strength.

Birth Psychology

I was surprised at how much scientists have explored birth and babies in recent years. It's just not making headlines.

When closed adoptions began, judges, social workers, ministers, church officials and lawyers, apparently weren't able to scientifically test or measure trauma and pain in an orphaned baby. Today scientists can. Birth psychologists can prove a mom's importance to a growing baby's health and brains. Yes, babies have feelings, too; separation causes trauma which can (literally) be life-changing, even life-threatening.

It is a primal pain. Orphans don't get to know our mothers, our creator and source of unconditional love. Orphans don't get to know our fathers, a key in our emotional development, a mentor of life skills and conditional love. Orphans don't know their grand-parents who pass along history and family traditions from the "Old Country."

To make matters worse, adoptees don't get the breast milk we need, which will impair our immune systems in a multitude of ways, for the rest of our lives.

That didn't seem to matter when they instituted adoption or developed, packaged and promoted baby formula. Even now, they'll discourage mothers about breastfeeding, which is utterly ridiculous but a clever marketing strategy which has earned those companies millions, if not billions, of dollars.

Breastfeeding in those first 24 hours can save literally a child's life and immune system. Breast milk gives babies *colostrum*, a nutrient in mother's first breast milk. Colostrum, often called the "perfect food for every newborn," is rich in antibodies and essential nutrients.

In birth psychology, breast milk is known to increase a child's intelligence and lifespan. It's known that much of who we are today is created in the womb. It's also known that a mother and her child are a single entity, profoundly connected physiologically, emotionally and spiritually. A baby does not even understand that he or she is an individual until at least nine months after birth.

Adoption ads would never admit this.

Not All It's Cracked Up to Be

I fell in love in 1999 and married Herb in 2004. My husband works in college admissions. Teaching a course in diversity, Herb believes sexism is the all-time "ism," even more deadly than racism. Herb has Cherokee blood like me.

He and I talked about adoption often and he was kind to remind me, "You can say some, you can say many, you can even say most on occasion, but you can never say all."

I accept that. Not all adoptees feel as I do. Not all feel rejected or think they're split. Some, like my brother, don't want to open their adoption. Not all want to know what happened. Not all want their medical history. Not all want a reunion.

When Americans do think about us—possibly 10 million adoptees (of every race, creed or color) across America—many people will still say we're lucky. We had "happily-ever-after" lives.

This belief will only perpetuate how good adoption is. Myths do not help. Closed adoption is not perfect, far from it. Open adoption is also not working. Kinship and legal guardianship are working solutions.

Adoption in this century has been a Band-Aid for a "poor people" problem. Poverty is spreading to more areas, affecting more women and families, hitting already stressed-out Indian reservations or urban ghettos. I could not find one story about rich people abandoning their babies; they'd hire nannies.

Poor children and their poor children are still cycled into a pool of adoptees. Indian Country was never poor until America happened. Indians never willfully abandon their babies, ever.

So, no, adoption is not all it's cracked up to be. America is deadly silent or reluctant to admit poor folks (and Indians) will ever break free of poverty.

The poor are forced to give up their children, when they can't afford essentials like food, medicine, clothes or a roof over their heads. Poor people can't afford birth control. It's low on their list of priorities. Some impoverished countries like Mexico are experiencing critically dangerous population levels, following strict adherence to the Catholic rule, "no birth control."

I remember in high school, our social studies teacher Steve discussed poverty and over-population. I asked why people would continue to have babies when things were so bad, and oppressive, and he said that a man and a woman would find comfort in each other, with intimacy. It probably was their only happiness.

This idea never escaped my mind, now years later.

Poisoned Gas

"After the experiences of totalitarian regimes, after the brutal way in which they trampled on men, mocked, enslaved and beat the weak, we understand anew those who hunger and thirst for justice," Pope Benedict XVI, writes in his book "*Jesus of*

Nazareth," criticizing the "cruelty" of capitalism's exploitation of the poor.

"Confronted with the abuse of economic power, with the cruelty of capitalism that degrades man into merchandise, we have begun to see more clearly the dangers of wealth...," Pope Benedict decries how the rich and wealthy have "plundered" Africa and the Third World, both materially and spiritually, through colonialism.

In 2009, according to www.globalissues.org, there are 2.2 billion children in the world and one billion live in poverty, without shelter, safe water and health services.

Guess where they live? Third World countries and Indian Country.

How might we react being detribalized and colonized for centuries? Spain, France and England didn't discover Turtle Island or our tribal nations; they just colonized every human being they found in North America. If that didn't work, they used genocide. British Prime Minister Winston Churchill said, "I am strongly in favor of using poisoned gas against uncivilized tribes." Nothing stands in their way.

Few people have heard about the Massacre at Sand Creek in Colorado, where Methodist minister Colonel Chivington massacred between 200-400 Cheyenne and Arapaho, most of them women, children, and elderly men. Chivington specifically ordered the killing of children. When he was asked why, he said, "Kill and scalp all, big and little; nits make lice."

If America was so great, or an indication of equality, liberty, justice and freedom, then why did they condone the bad treatment and genocide of Native people, or the Indian Adoption Projects and boarding schools, or forced sterilizations and internment camps they call Indian reservations? I can't answer. I just don't know.

It was the prophet Gandhi from India who once said, "Poverty is the worst form of violence." Clearly, poverty breeds more poverty and the conditions of living in poverty consume any energy we have left. Without essentials like food and water, hope starves, too.

Americans like Madonna and Angelina adopt Third World children but barely notice how colonization created such intolerable living conditions for these families, or note how their baby's mother suffered.

Before they rush in to take a Third World child, don't they need to ask why? Why not ask, "What can we do to help her raise her child?"

We do not help all children equally. Not every child will receive an education. Not all men feel women are created equal.

Like any experiment, "adoption" is a knee-jerk reaction and based on judgment. Those poor kids are lucky to go to prosperous American families, some say. But I know those kids will never forget they're adopted.

Guatemala

At this moment, the adoption experiment has spread to more impoverished people; Guatemala is the new supplier of fresh infants, free to adopt in America but I really don't mean free. I read the State Department warnings online in 2009 and found new international guidelines preventing Third World adoptions. I've met a few adoptees from Guatemala. They say Americans began shopping and adopting Mayan children over 20 years ago. Some of them were sold to Americans by unscrupulous lawyers and government officials.

Guatemala is the size of Tennessee but has 24 Indigenous languages, principally Kiche, Kaqchikel, Q'eqchi and Mam. More than half in their country are descendants of indigenous Mayan people. The Mayan people were colonized by Spain in 1523–24.

Now 80 percent of the population lives in poverty; two-thirds of them—7.6 million—live in extreme poverty. In addition to earning low incomes, the Mayan have limited economic opportunities for jobs and advancement, no social services, and very limited access or influence on their government's policymaking.

Sound familiar?

Arrogance

If they witness reservation poverty firsthand, government leaders will say Indian people are better off in cities or urban areas and just need to find work. What arrogance to suggest a job and three meals a day are all an Indian family needs.

Our neighbors in rural Wisconsin were Finnish-Ojibwe (who we called Finndian). They lacked indoor plumbing and used an outhouse but Joey and I didn't care. We practically lived there and grew up with their five kids, our best friends. Something essential, vital to my being, was there with them. Their kids had less material stuff but no one cared. We were all cared for by their Ojibwe mom who was so beautiful. She fed Joey and me with her kids. We ran barefoot all summer. We played baseball. We rode our bikes. We were constantly laughing. I don't know which meant more to me, but I know I was happier there. Adoptees are still American Indians. Our friends keep us company while we wait, knowing someday, someone will show us the way back home.

Biracial

I know my biracial identity makes me unique—I am, after all, Tsalgi, Shawnee, Delaware (from the Beck ancestors in 1700s), Celtic-Irish, and who knows what else. And I'm a woman.

I pray I bring out the best qualities of each. That's not to say I don't exhibit their worst qualities, too. Sometimes I hear how stubborn and how hard headed I can be.

Like Mount St. Helens—I blow off steam once in a while. I was living with my band Sardaukar in Kennewick, Washington when Mount St. Helens erupted on May 18, 1980. I lived close enough to see the heavy weird clouds that haunt me to this day. I woke up late that morning, thinking it must be night already since it was so dark outside. I thought maybe I'd slept an entire day! My bandmates weren't home. Very quiet outside, it looked like the world had come to an end, ash falling everywhere. If a Hanford nuclear reactor had exploded, it occurred to me I'd be dead.

My life was like a volcanic eruption in many ways. I steamed if the pressure got to be too much. When I'd erupt, I'd pack my car and leave. I left situations all the time.

All through my journey, my grandmother's spirit never left my side.

I understand my transracial identity now. Indian people intermarried for good reason—survival. Consciously or unconsciously, all Native Americans had to choose. Either you evolve, have babies, live on despite hardships, or die.

Despite the Trails of Tears death march they were forced to walk, my family were as determined to live as the Americans were determined to see them die off or disappear.

The "land grab" affected every Indian in its path; many tribes were walked to the Indian Territory, what is now Oklahoma. This was as devastating to the Cherokee as it was to all Indian people living during Andrew Jackson's time as president. Wars cost lives on both sides. There isn't a tribe in North America without some devastating tragedy or trail of tears.

Those early historians, mostly educated white men, were clever just to tell the conqueror's side of the story, elevating American leaders to hero status, not calling them slave owners or mass murderers.

Never doubt that tribes know their own story and pass it down, even if it isn't published in a book.

Mythistory

"We are called to become hollow bones for our people and anyone else we can help, and we are not supposed to seek power for our personal use and honor." – Fools Crow, LAKOTA

Regardless of my strength, or grit, whatever it is, I still grieve over Helen and Earl. I appear strong but there are still days I can barely stand up. I try to balance the good with bad. I accept what's happened in my life and accept there will be more challenges ahead. I'll face those disappointments with the same hope and love. Strength doesn't come cheap. It has a price.

Adoptees eventually understand: as one door closes, another door opens. Grief is like a mountain, built on repressed feelings, towering, forbidding and enormously scary to scale.

I head this more than once, "You're not completely well until you grieve all of it."

For some of us adoptees, that process may never be completed. Answers may not come. One reunion may lead to another and another, with more to process or grieve or celebrate.

I've shared my story and tell adoptees, "Never give up. Stop and catch your breath. Climb at your own pace. Healing this isn't always obvious. The brain fog will burn off then you'll know what to do. Trust your instincts, your blood. Trust yourself." America can never admit its complicity in ethnic cleansing, using the Indian Adoption Projects. It's hard to fathom America has not connected the dots.

This is the case for adoption. Whoever is perpetuating the myths of perfect outcomes is using what I call Mythistory.

Myths are hard to break. But when I meet Indian people who were adopted, I see how assimilation failed. Adoption gave us the strength and the will to survive as Indian people.

The System

I feel it's important to add that many Native adoptees I know have become parents. Despite their trauma, many are doing an amazing job. Some have not met their birth family. Of course, being adopted makes you value family and tribal culture even more. Many tell me their children are their greatest accomplishment. Their kids keep them strong. They teach their children everything they can about culture.

For years, Edie made very sure we understood she sacrificed a lot to give us a home and a good life. I know they loved us. I know they supported us. But it hurt I could not talk about my adoption or be truthful about how I felt or how I grieved. How could they not notice my pain? I don't know.

I kept my plan secret, like an innocent kid running into a minefield.

There wasn't an internet when I began my search in the 1970s. It was done the old fashioned way, going to a library and reading. I clipped news articles about adoptees for years.

What I learned and what surprised me most of all is the adoption industry was created for the adoptive parents by the adoption agencies. The system was actually designed to grow and to recruit potential parents. Churches handled immorality so there were plenty of babies to distribute. States opened and operated secret places called maternity homes and facilities for girls and women to wait out their pregnancy until they deliver. Babies were farmed out like fresh produce. Over time it became a booming billion dollar business for someone.

I tried to imagine how it must feel to give up a child. I watched a few television movies about birthmothers who would change their minds, then fight in courtrooms to regain custody using lawyers. People on both sides would argue who was more deserving, which mother had bonded more with the baby.

America finally instituted a six month waiting period for a birthmother to change her mind, before the adoption decree was final. This made adopting a baby more difficult and scary, since a birthparent might want their baby back.

Recent movies like *Juno* don't mention the orphan who lives with pain, trauma and sadness, nor do the movies relate what it's like for the adoptee that grew up in a closed adoption.

The system of closed adoption needs to change.

Foster Parents

"Let's put our minds together and see what kind of life we can build for our children..." – Sitting Bull

Since my adoption in 1958, couples who wish to adopt a baby still fill out paperwork, give references and have two or more home inspections and rounds of interviews. There are still caseworkers in the state-governed adoption systems. Now prospective parents are finger-printed. Most states, not all, perform extensive background checks on potential adoptive parents. In recent years, more and more adoptions are open.

Couples today take classes before adopting; first they must become foster parents. I know this because I became a certified foster parent in Oregon in the 1994. Single and divorced people do adopt. Most important was income, if I could afford to raise a child. (My divorce from David was final in January of 1995.)

It's inconceivable to me that periodic checkups on adoptees are not mandatory, especially for children who come from a different culture or country prior to their adoption. After my adoption was final, all investigation stopped. No one came back to check on Joey or me. Since my original birth certificate was sealed by a court of law, I might never have found out I was adopted.

Again, it's not about the adopted child.

Social Workers

Who is looking out for the orphans? They are the social workers. There are thousands of them.

In my twelve weeks of pre-adoption training in Oregon in 1994, I learned that all children over *age three* are considered special needs because they have been abused sexually, emotionally or physically, or neglected in some way.

In America? Yes. They weren't kidding. It's true. One would think this would make adopting a child less attractive. Well, older kids are usually fostered and not adopted. People prefer cute cuddly babies.

With older kids, slap on a Band-Aid, write a prescription and it's going to be alright. Place these special children with foster families, and move on to the next case, which they do every day.

We know social workers have hundreds of cases, and foster kids slip through the cracks; this makes the news from time to time. There was one story in Florida where children were caged like animals and their foster mother collected money on each caged foster child every month. Eventually she was convicted and sent to prison.

During my foster care training, one class debated if drugs and medication are best when it comes to behaviors in young adoptees and foster children, like those who have bonding problems, or they act out, get aggressive, or have the newly-discovered Attention Deficit Hyperactivity Disorder (ADHD).

My class heard medicating "troubled children" was the preferred option. To my astonishment (and horror), this is common in every state. Apparently bad behavior is just not tolerated—so at the first sign of trouble, special children are medicated.

I thank God I wasn't medicated. I'd either be dead or drug-addicted, and definitely not sitting here right now.

Sometimes ideas are just plain scary. It's easy to see why the pharmaceutical companies (and drug cartels) are so successful, with television campaigns on various drugs. We know what drug we need and tell our doctor. They are creating a new breed of addicts.

Really, I use herbal medicine and natural healing and only their western medicine and first aid when absolutely necessary.

Social workers admit but seriously underscore behavior problems in adoptees. In many states, they'll pay for psychiatric care *and* prescription drugs until the foster child or adoptee becomes an adult.

You won't see a TV commercial about this.

Abandonment

No drug can ease this primal pain; no drug can erase your mother, or that feeling of being abandoned, or rejected. Drugs can numb you (or dumb you) but only delay the inevitable.

Children want parameters, stability, permanence, and rules to feel safe. Our grief can be healed. But abandonment, that must be understood.

On a few occasions, I told my Oregon classmates how it feels to be an adoptee, though I didn't understand it as I do now. I was still naïve, still grieving my loss and I still needed answers then. I had not met my birthfather yet.

Not every adoptee I know was mistreated, but I know many who were.

I told my class how the social workers never came back to see how my brother or I were doing, or managing, or coping with the mystery of who we were.

As my class neared its completion, I looked through numerous three-ring binders of adoptee profiles. These children were victims of poverty or were born to parents who did not wish to be parents, lost in a cycle of failure. The children "legally free" and available to adopt were not babies; the majority was siblings seeking one permanent home. There were at least six binders of children legally free, each hoping for a family in Oregon or Washington. Thousands were in need in 1994. I could hardly believe it.

Unconsciously perhaps, I took the training because I wanted to understand adoption and how it relates to children in the system now, and how it affected me.

There is so much the system doesn't tell adoptive parents and adult adoptees. I've met many Native American adults who still suffer the effects of emotional, physical and sexual abuse by their adoptive parents, relatives, or priests, or boarding school officials or other kids.

I find it hard to believe more people don't know about this.

No Children

Sure, I was taught about Jesus. He was crucified for our sins. He suffered as the Son of God. I believe I am a child of God, who I call the Great Spirit and Great Mystery.

Years ago, I decided if I could live through this (my childhood), I could live through anything.

Believe me, because of Christ, I loved my adoptive parents, despite what Joey and I experienced. I forgave them. I even forgave myself for hating them at times.

In my 20s, I decided not to have children. The more I thought about it, the more afraid I became. I didn't know who I was. I sensed rage inside me and anger I didn't trust myself to control. I didn't know if I could control it so I made my decision: no children. I'd live with it.

Knowing what I know now, I am not surprised. I couldn't parent anyone. I was emotionally barren and disturbed. I trusted my own instinct on my ability then to parent.

There are days when I wish this had never happened to me. I wish that I could have been normal. I wish I could have raised a flock of children, biological or adopted.

I had good reason to be concerned, carrying around such deep emotional scars. I couldn't parent anyone. I was abused and could have abused my own child.

Child abuse is a vicious cycle, proven over and over, again and again.

I never adopted a child in Oregon. I could not afford child care if I had been a foster parent.

If I could have a baby now, I would, but it's too late, biologically speaking.

Herb married me when I was 48. This is my first healthy relationship, what I consider healthy. Herb found me at the right time. He could have taught me how to parent.

Because of Herb, I have a lovely granddaughter Cameron. I will not tolerate abuse from anyone. I've had enough. My sense of being and self-worth finally did recover. I got my answers. I grew my strength. I cannot lie about anything anymore. I don't pretend. I don't have illusions. I live my truth.

Opening

Each of us was put here for a reason. Each of us has a gift. We chose to be here. It's our job to find our purpose and fulfill it.

Of course, this is true for all people, not just adoptees.

It will take a mind-altering experience, what I call an opening. Maybe some adoptees were too young to handle the pain when it happened so we buried it. First we have to acknowledge something happened and accept that the wound exists.

It's not like I can go back and change the past. It's not like I can reach into my body and remove it.

It was not easy for me. I had to rewire myself. I had to stop the tape running in my head, "Be grateful, be grateful, be grateful. Bury the rest."

I didn't realize how much emotional damage I had. I was lucky because I had good friends praying and holding good thoughts for me.

My friend Black Bear told me that in many tribes, the medicine person would travel back to a time before the injury, before a sick person was sick or hurt. Sometimes pain is too hard to remember, so they do it for you. By removing the pain, they restore good health. That is how they did it, how they cured a sick spirit.

His story made me cry. I want to do this for all my adoptee friends. I want to invent a time machine. I want to ease their pain and travel back for them. It would be good if we could do it for ourselves.

What is good is finding out *why* you were abandoned or stolen. This knowledge brings great emotional relief. It's a big step. Knowing something, anything, will help ease pain, and start to erase the trauma. The wound reopens so it can be healed.

I tell others what I experienced. "Once you get your name, you open up. You may remember things you forgot. Then you can be a parent to yourself. No one but you can make your life better."

I was someone who traveled the darkest journey imaginable and came out into the light. Once I healed, my emotional paralysis was gone. I was never a cruel person but I was without feeling— good *and* bad. I was not able to function emotionally for many years. I was lost in a fog but I walked out of it.

When the fog finally lifted, I was like a newborn, aware I had a body, aware of sensation. I was a new person, literally reborn into this body.

Healing of Nations

Black Bear (my uncle Stephen LaBoueff) is a member of the Blackfeet tribe in Idaho. My uncle agreed adoptees should know more about healing themselves.

He wrote the following about his work in suicide prevention:

"Several years ago, I was asked to attend a community meeting on a small reservation in one of the western states. Two young men took their lives within a four-month period and the community was scared. They came together for comfort, for information, and to discuss what they could do to prevent further suicide attempts. They wanted to save their young people and achieve some sort of healing.

I had been invited because of my research in suicide prevention among Native young people; however, they did not specify what topic they wanted me to present.

I was struck by the size of the crowd. The total population of the community was only about 400 and nearly 175 were in attendance. I noticed immediately the lack of any young people – all in attendance were adults. Since I was the last presenter, I sat back to listen.

The first presenter was a Catholic priest in his 70s. He was gentle and kindly. He told the people they must have faith. They must pray. He said, "God loves us. Only *He* knows why these things have to happen."

The second presenter was a psychologist from the Indian Health Service. He spent all of his time answering questions. "Why did this young person kill himself?" "Why did this have to happen?" "Why……..?" At first I was a little irked. I thought, "If you want to know why this is going on, why don't you ask the kids, they will tell you."

I began to think about my role. I remembered watching grandmothers, aunties, or older ladies, and that whenever there was a death in the family, or some other trauma, they would always get busy doing something. They would begin to cook, for they knew the people would need to be fed, or they would begin to clean— sweeping, dusting, picking up. It didn't seem to matter—only that they were doing something.

Trauma, especially the loss of your children or other loved ones, creates a confusion, a depression, a swirl of negative energy that frequently prevents rational thinking. It looks and acts like a "**black cloud**" that hangs over you —it blocks the light and keeps you in a state of hopelessness. If one is allowed to remain in this state, our elders tell us "that one too will become ill."

The grandmothers intuitively understood this and began to work, to do something—they undertook a task that would get them moving and out of their head.

Now it was my turn. I thought, yes, the people needed to have their faith reaffirmed and be told to pray. The apparent randomness and sudden violence needed to be put in some "universal or cosmic" order. The people also needed for someone to explain "why" to them. There was, however, one critical element missing. No one had told them how to deal with the intense pain, fear and loss, no one had helped them formulate a plan of action, and no one had given them tasks to do."

[Black Bear's website: www.healingofnations.org.]

My Cherokee blood

I submitted the following to the *Cherokee Phoenix* newspaper in March 2007 (I never heard from them and do not know if they published it)

Are we Cherokee by blood or by culture? Can we even remember our great-grandparents names anymore? I know most Cherokee can. Our history and language make us Cherokee.

I unfortunately am an adoptee – so obviously I want to be an enrolled member, but because I was not raised in Cherokee culture, in ancestral territories, what should be the criteria for me?

Because my father Earl was assimilated, he did not speak the language but my aunts remember rituals of digging roots and drying plants under the watchful eyes of Mary Frances, who they called Granny. She smoked a stone pipe, whispering her prayers.

Adoptees aren't private investigators. As a matter of fact, we are Split Feathers with two identities from two worlds. Very few of us ever return to our tribe, perhaps because no one is looking for us.

I couldn't afford an expensive search back in 1979 when I opened my adoption. I always knew I was different and felt more comfortable with other Native people. I was careful never to say which tribe, because I honestly didn't know.

Then I heard about all these people claiming to be Cherokee, so I was even more reluctant to talk about any ideas I had.

When I finally met my father, Earl Bland, he was dying in 1994. After a DNA test, it was definite, a 99.9 percent match. This stranger who I now called Dad had one year to catch me up on a lifetime. Alcoholism and emphysema had already destroyed his health. My new siblings were curious about our Cherokee ancestry but never really cared much about it, other than in conversations with me. I was raised in Anishinabe territory in Wisconsin, so I had the rich experience of family and friendships there with them. Adoptees are starving for culture, believe me, so it was essential for me to know what tribe and get as many particulars that my new birthfamily could provide.

Aunt Jane told me recently she remembers helping shampoo Granny's hair in a washtub outside. Her hair was as long as she was tall – barely 5 feet! Granny would roll and wrap her hair into a tiny neat little bun, which seemed impossible to do, but Jane watched her do it repeatedly.

I don't know how Mary made her trek to Illinois from Missouri, but I'm hoping that perhaps someone will read this and know the Connor-Morris families. I am always careful to say I have Cherokee ancestors with the greatest respect.

Granny's daughter, my grandmother Lona Dell Harlow, was the first person I ever looked like – we have the exact same eyebrows! Every single year I am on this earth, I strive to make Mary's family proud of me. I hope to meet relatives and hear their stories.

As an adoptee I will never have the right to own a copy of my original birth certificate, unless laws change; now it is illegal in many states. When I did see the certificate in a sympathetic judge's office in Wisconsin, I was illegitimate so my father's name wasn't even there. I never gave up looking for him, trying 17 long years.

I understand every tribe had casualties on their Trails of Tears and lost many children to the Indian Adoption Project and *boarding schools, in the past century. I understand the trauma of removal, since I was raised by non-Natives myself.*

Does a piece of paper, a name on a roll, or our blood make us Cherokee? All I have of my Cherokee culture are questions, and the voices I feel in my bones.

My birthmother named me Laura Jean Thrall. My birthfather's name is Earl Bland. I became a member of the Native American Journalist Association, after I found my father and knew my ancestry. I have spent the last 11 years writing about Native people and issues; because it is the only thing I care to write about. Enrollment is not possible without papers, I accept that reality, but it doesn't make me any less Cherokee."

From the Cherokee Nation website: In order to obtain a CDIB, applicants must formally apply and provide acceptable legal documents which connect them to an ancestor who is listed with a roll number and a blood degree from the final rolls of citizens of the Cherokee Nation, commonly called the Dawes Final Rolls. These rolls were compiled between the years 1899–1906. Quantum of Indian Blood is computed from the nearest paternal and/or maternal direct ancestor(s) of Indian blood listed on the Final Rolls. Many descendants of Cherokee Indians can neither be certified nor qualify for tribal citizenship in the Cherokee Nation because their ancestors were not enrolled during the final enrollment. Unfortunately, these ancestors did not meet the requirements for the final enrollment. The requirements at that time were (1) applying between 1899–1906, (2) appearing on previous tribal rolls of 1880 or 1896 and (3) having a permanent residence within the Cherokee Nation (now the 14 northeastern counties of Oklahoma). If the ancestors had separated from the Cherokee Nation and settled in states such as Arkansas, Kansas, Missouri or Texas during that period, they lost their citizenship with the Cherokee Nation. Only enrolled citizens of the Cherokee Nation named on the Final Rolls and/or their descendants are eligible for Certificates of Degree of Indian Blood and tribal citizenship.

[SOURCE: http://www.cherokee.org/NewsRoom/FullStory/2748/Page]

Harm

In my world, I am becoming more complete as I find out more about my history. My early experience taught me to trust no one. It's a hard thing to admit but it's true. My young mind was not formatted to trust. It's an adoptee mindset.

At my birthfather's funeral, I heard stories about crazy dangerous fools and treacherous alcoholics. These men didn't set out to be scary—they were just born that way, I guess.

I descend from James Bland, born in 1708 in Virginia. My other Bland grandfathers are John, Osborn Sr., Jesse, Osborn and Hiram. Great-great-granddaddy Osborne beat the tar out of his son Jesse who beat the tar out of his grandson Hiram who beat the tar out of his own kids, like my dad Earl. One of my uncles got hit by a falling tree, cut down on purpose by Hiram (pronounced Harm) who was an old tyrant; another uncle lost fingers and his tongue. All true.

My great-grandfathers (not exactly great men) had owned slaves in Kentucky and in Virginia. I found numerous slave records in the Bland census records. I found one letter detailing how Osborn's wife Lettice Hambrick-Bland inherited her husband's slaves then sold them as her property. Family history can be embarrassing, but not uncommon in America. These were some of the stories I found out when I opened my adoption. Not quite the rosy picture you'd expect, right? There were too many stories I didn't know.

Think Tank

I developed a deep sensitivity when I healed. Sometimes I call this my super-sensitivity wound. One science fiction movie, *Code 46,* calls it the empathy virus.

In her book *Primal Wound*, Nancy Verrier, an adoptive mother, maintains that no matter how early or smoothly an adoption occurs, every adopted child interprets being separated from its biological mother as rejection.

Now I consider it a challenge, a test, even a gift. It was meant to make me strong.

Adoptee friends, who I call my Think Tank, believe the truth, the official story, even a letter from our birthparent to us, would have cured our pain almost completely, if the letter had our history, what tribe, an explanation and an invitation to meet eventually.

My Think Tank believes all adoptees need access to birth records by age 18, definitely by age 21.

We know any personality can be greatly influenced by disruption. In this way, our adoption trained us to be warriors, which is good. Traditional Elders recognize our gifts when we're still children; after time they give us our spirit name that reflects who we truly are. Sitting Bull had three names. Our spirit name is the one we use when we pray.

As adults we may take a new name, when we become what we are born to be.

Survivor Stories

We rarely hear survivor stories. Despite thousands of books and memoirs, I found just three rather recent ones about Lost Birds/adoptees.

The adoption story of Paul LaRoche, now the famous recording artist known as Brule, is told in the 2006 book *Hidden Heritage* by Barbara Marshak. Paul was a late discovery adoptee or LDA. He was 38 when he learned his ancestors are from a South Dakota tribe. Paul's reunion with his Lower Brule (Lakota) family is told in Marshak's book.

I met Paul in 2007 when he performed at Foxwoods during Schemitzun, the Mashantucket Pequot's powwow. It was incredible to hear Paul describe his journey onstage, done with remarkably gentle storytelling between his songs.

It struck me when Paul said it was *reverse assimilation* when he returned to his South Dakota reservation and his people. Overwhelmed at first, he channeled those emotions into music. He quit his engineering job and launched an amazing musical career. Paul's two children perform with him. Like their dad, they also returned to their tribe as lost birds, knowing very little about their tribal identity.

Adoptee Yvette Melanson's memoir, *"Looking for Lost Bird: A Jewish Woman Discovers her Navajo Roots"* became a Hallmark movie, shown on primetime television.

There is author-historian-social worker Renee Ransom-Flood's book, *"Lost Bird of Wounded Knee: Spirit of the Lakota."*

In Connecticut, I met Ojibwe playwright Drew Hayden Taylor who wrote *"Only Drunks and Indians tell the Truth,"* the story of a Canadian woman who reconnects with her Ojibwe birth family in Ontario as an adult, long after her adoption. On the same topic, Drew published *"Someday"* and *"400 Kilometers,"* both powerful award-winning plays, well-known and performed in Canada.

Colorado scholar Susan Harness, a Salish-Kootenai adoptee, did her master's thesis, *After the Indian Adoption Project: A Search for Identity*. Susan and I read in 2008 at the University of Wisconsin in Platteville and our program was recorded on DVD as a fundraiser for their Inter-Tribal Council. The audience's reaction to our talk *"Stolen Generations"* ranged from horror to outrage.

In 2009, Susan published *"Mixing Cultural Identities Through Transracial Adoption*: *Outcomes of the Indian Adoption Project (1958-1967"* with Edwin Mellen Press.

A very moving movie, *"Rabbit Proof Fence,"* is about Australia's cruel removal of Indigenous half-caste children; it's an unforgettable story of three little Aboriginal girls who try to escape their captors at a government-run boarding school. Their government finally shut down those prison schools and apologized to Australia's "Stolen Generations."

The 2000 Sundance Film Festival premier, *The Return of Navajo Boy*, is a sad documentary of one Navajo boy placed with non-Indian foster parents. He grew up about a four hour drive from Monument Valley, Utah where his Navajo family lived; his relative's photos were used on tourist postcards; some even worked as extras in movies. Due to an extraordinary sequence of events, the Navajo boy (now a man) and his family were reunited after 40 years, brilliantly recorded on film.

"Outsiders Within: Writing on Transracial Adoption," edited by Jane Jeong Trenka, included a relevant chapter on American Indian history by Sandy White Hawk, an adoptee from the Rosebud Tribal Nation in South Dakota. [South End Press, ©2006, paperback, ISBN: 0-89608-764-4.]

Studies on American Indians adoptees include *Split Feathers... Adult American Indians who were placed in Non-Indian Families as Children*, a study of 20 adoptees, done by Carol Locust (Cherokee) in the 1990s.

Professor Rita J. Simon and Sarah Hernandez (Rosebud Lakota) published their 2008 study with 20 adoptees in "*Native American Transracial Adoptees Tell Their Stories*." I know a few of the adoptees who participated in this book.

Haskell

In 1818, the House Committee on Indian Affairs put colonization this way, "put in the hands of Indian children a hoe, a primer and a Bible."

One aunt in my Catholic adoptive family refused to believe governments and various churches in the US and Canada—Catholic, Presbyterian, Anglican and United Churches —built and ran boarding schools just for Indian kids.

Apparently this history wasn't taught at her school either. Indians know this all too well. It was hard describing to her the horrific abuses that happened to these kids at the hands of missionary and clergy, even by nuns and priests.

Aunt Mary, in her 80s and a devout Catholic, never heard any of "this crap" and didn't believe me. She wasn't with me in 1998 when I visited the graves behind Haskell Indian Boarding School, seeing row after row of nameless children, only their age and tribal affiliation etched on their tombstones. Many tribes have yet to reclaim them.

Because of great distance, some parents never saw their child again or knew what actually happened, even when or how (or if) their child died.

"*The Only Good Indian*" tells the story on film. The movie revisits 1905 when Native children were forced to attend Haskell Boarding School in Kansas. Though it is fiction, it is based on actual accounts of the Kickapoo tribe's resistance, written by Tom Carmody, and released in theatres in 2009.

Rich Heape Films also released, *"Our Spirits Don't Speak English: Indian Boarding School"* in 2008. From the Circle of Life series, this documentary is "told from the Native American perspective and uncovers the dark history of the U.S. Government policy, giving a voice to the countless Indian children forced through the system." Grace Thorpe, a dear friend of mine who passed away in 2008, is featured along with Dr. Henrietta Mann, Dr. Daniel Wildcat and author Gayle Ross, renowned Native leaders and teachers. [To order: www.richheape.com.]

Former students of South Dakota boarding schools filed a federal lawsuit in 2003, seeking millions from the federal government for mental, physical and sexual abuse, even though most of these religious boarding schools were permanently closed in the 1970s. Lawyers for the various churches (including monks, bishops, priests and sisters) claim the victims waited too long to sue. Some government-run boarding schools opened in the 1800s; some were operated by religious organizations in America and Canada. Too often school records disappeared. Some victims and perpetrators died years ago.

Unfortunately, there is no statute of limitation on suffering, for a victim or their family. Who knows if a survivor will have the will or strength or money to file a lawsuit that could drag on for decades? The Church has much deeper pockets to pay for expensive lawyers. Many Indian children did lose everything—family, language and sometimes sanity, enduring sexual and physical abuse, while realizing thousands more died in these schools. Some survivors say they heard, "God didn't want them to talk about it."

Anyone who survived a boarding school has a legitimate case, and this troubling story is still unfolding.

My dear aunt, who passed away in 2001, has certainly met those Haskell children in her heaven.

My Lakota Relatives

Before I started working as a journalist, I traveled alone to the Pine Ridge and Rosebud reservations. My first trip was in 1992. It really began when I met Merle Locke, a Lakota painter who specializes in Ledger art. I met Merle at an Oregon art show. Finding him was like finding a lost brother. We talked and I bought a print of his artwork, then Merle said, "You need to meet my sister."

I planned to attend the Running Sundance in Rosebud that year. I was living in Seattle and had already called the Running family to get their permission to attend.

When I finally arrived at the Sundance grounds, everyone was given jobs. I made hundreds of prayer ties with other women. For four days, we sweat once or more a day; some men were there to purify by sweating before they did the ceremony.

Steven (a friend who is Northern Cheyenne) explained to me in Seattle, "Do not pray for you in the sweat lodge." He told me about the Running Sundance and told me what to expect. I learned we enter on hands and knees and where and how we'd sit. Men might wear a towel or shorts and women would wear a skirt and t-shirt. I kept a towel near my face in case the air got too hot to breathe. There were rounds of prayers and the passing of the pipe. We prayed for the sick, we sang and gave thanks in our prayers.

I felt so much better after I sweat, and slept so much better. Unfortunately, my period started so I had to leave. I would not have been able to participate in the ceremony on my moon cycle.

So I left Rosebud and drove to Pine Ridge. I looked for Merle's family home in Porcupine. There were no street signs or numbers on the houses. I stopped for directions, and even went inside the wrong house. Finally I found it. I finally met Ellowyn, Merle's very shy older sister.

Getting past shyness after a full day of conversation, we wasted no time. I'm sure the rez buzzed, "Whose car is that?" Ellowyn and I drove from one end of her reservation to the other, meeting her friends and family along the way. We shopped for groceries in White Clay and Gordon, Nebraska. She took me to their powwow and parade.

Ellowyn's family, 13 brothers and sisters, became my extended family. After my first visit, I returned nearly every summer. We'd sit at her kitchen table, listen to KILI radio, I'd repeat

Lakota words and, of course, we laughed. There were times when we didn't know how we'd eat, or what we'd eat. Food, or people with food, always seemed to show up.

Ellowyn was unmarried and 40 when we met. She'd lost her job teaching the Lakota language. For money, she sewed star quilts on an old fashioned Singer Sewing Machine, with a push-pedal. Ellowyn also made clothes and traditional Lakota dolls. She sold to German tourists who flock to Kyle every year to buy quilts and crafts.

Over time and in her way, Ellowyn adopted me. That is in their culture, making relatives. Ellowyn knows what's in my heart after all these years. After many visits, she gave me my name, Winyan Ohmanisa Waste La Ke (She loves to travel).

The courage I needed to find my relatives grew after my trips to Pine Ridge.

My skin problem (those nasty red welts) disappeared, after I did sweats in Rosebud.

Mary and Elizabeth

Ellowyn told me she knew another adoptee named Mary, who was not able to open her adoption, though she tried. I also learned that Mary was horribly abused and raped by her adoptive father.

When Ellowyn knew her, Mary lived in Provincetown on Cape Cod (Massachusetts) where she was a very well-known artist. After Mary met Ellowyn and Merle, she made regular trips to Pine Ridge. Mary told Ellowyn how when she was a teenager she was forced to give her own baby up for adoption.

This killed Mary, Ellowyn said, because she could not stop mourning for her daughter. (That dark fog of the mind.) Mary's lost child Elizabeth is also an adoptee, and she found Ellowyn. Elizabeth opened her adoption to find out her birthmother had already died of a brain tumor. When Elizabeth read her deceased mother's letters, she read about Ellowyn, her mother's closest friend in South Dakota.

I am grateful that Ellowyn is very close to Elizabeth, and treats her like a daughter. We both pray Elizabeth heals her pain and solves her mystery.

Even though Mary was never able to open her own adoption or meet the baby she lost, Elizabeth did have a reunion with her mother's best friend and it was healing for her to hear stories about her mother and know about the close friendship Ellowyn had with Mary.

Everywhere I've lived, Ellowyn and I would write long letters. When Bill Clinton was president, Ellowyn finally got a phone. Now we can talk as often as we like.

Ellowyn is my sister and my best friend. She watched me take small steps in discovering my new family. She said I did not have to rush. She said I did not have to accept any bad treatment, even if they are my blood. We may never have a right relationship, she said.

It was good Ellowyn told me about the Janus, her French great-grandfathers. I told her about my Ryan-Kilduff ancestors from Ottawa and Quebec and Ireland.

Their blood doesn't make us any less Indian.

Leonard Peltier

In the summer of 1998, I drove to Kansas to interview political prisoner Leonard Peltier, a Lakota-Ojibwe warrior serving two life sentences for the murder of two FBI agents. At that time, Peltier was incarcerated in the federal penitentiary Leavenworth.

Earlier that year in February, I'd met two Peltier volunteers, Mary and Retta, respectively Creek and Lakota Elders, who were also in South Dakota. Hundreds of Indian people from across the country drove through blizzard conditions to commemorate the 25th anniversary of the takeover of Wounded Knee by the American Indian Movement (AIM) in 1973 and the Massacre of Wounded Knee in 1890.

Mary, Retta, and several of us got stranded together in a Martin, South Dakota motel. We eventually caravanned to the

Little Wound School in Kyle for the final day of the memorial. That night the elders stayed with me at Ellowyn's home in Porcupine.

To my delight and surprise, the Elders invited me to visit them in Kansas in warmer weather. They arranged for me to interview Leonard Peltier (by phone) through the Peltier Defense Committee office, which I did. I also met and interviewed Bobby Castillo who ran Peltier's office and campaign for clemency.

During my week in Kansas, I wanted to know more about my elders. I stayed with Mary and she told stories about her Creek tribe and how Cherokee use tobacco medicine. I still have the quilted towel and little beaded medicine bottle Mary gave me. An old photo of Mary and Peltier still hangs on my refrigerator.

Mary and Retta drove me out to the Haskell campus and graveyard so I could take pictures. Retta shared her boarding school experiences and explained her participation in the 1973 AIM takeover, walking in supplies. My interview with her was in *News From Indian Country* (NFIC) where I worked.

In 1998, NFIC published my interview with Peltier and others I'd interviewed at the Wounded Knee Memorial.

Peltier, still in federal prison in 2011, has become a world-renown symbol of injustice toward Indians. The story was told in *Incident at Oglala*, a documentary by Robert Redford. I went to the Jumping Bull Compound in Oglala where Peltier's bullets allegedly executed two FBI agents; and where Joe Kills Straight Stuntz, a warrior, was killed in crossfire. (Peltier wrote to me that he has read this book, sent to him in federal prison in Pennsylvania from his friend Harvey Arden.)

I've also paid my respects at the grave of murdered AIM member Annie Mae Pictou-Aquash, before her remains were moved home to Mi'qmaw territory in Nova Scotia. Her death is still being investigated and three suspects were on trial in 2009.

Peltier, Aquash, and others were involved in the AIM movement; many Indians took a stand at Wounded Knee, responding to numerous unsolved murders happening all across Indian Country, then exposing the brutality of the Lakota tribal government (under Dick Wilson's GOONS) in Pine Ridge.

Before I became a journalist, Ellowyn took me to Wounded Knee and showed me the bullet holes in the church, which I photographed. She taught me her tribe's history, and at home in Seattle I watched the Redford documentary on Peltier and read Mary Crow Dog's book *Lakota Woman* and other books Ellowyn recommended. I also read books about the Cherokee, Anishinabe and other tribes during the 1990s. I was never afraid to travel alone to Pine Ridge. It felt like home.

I did get nervous when Leonard Peltier asked me to write a good story about him. (That story became front page news back in 1998. I asked Leonard what he would do once he is free.)

Ellowyn taught me very important history at her kitchen table, stories I would be hard-pressed to find in any book. That is how Indian people learn, from each other.

My Lakota sister-friend taught me the most important thing I know: we are all related.

New Myths, New Moms

Wonder why is it called splitting sickness or soul sickness?

Some, like my aunt, had a hard time believing this horrific treatment happened to Indian people. No wonder so few people try to understand.

It's obvious to me adopted kids took the backseat in history, strapped in by new myths and new moms. It's not explained that Indian kids were part of an experiment meant to change us and our future and our tribe's future. Adoptees suffer from this. It alters consciousness. One expert calls the outcome a disorganized personality.

It's hard enough being orphaned, quite another to think priests and politicians still defend the practice and deem it appropriate, or good.

I've met elders in Indian Country who don't like to talk about it. The past is still too painful. Children are still missing.

Even Indians don't learn about Lost Birds like me in school. Many have no idea what happened to us or how we were lost by this government order of adoption and to be changed by assimilation.

The challenge for all adoptees is to know what really happened. Living on your rez, it's no problem. There you live your history. Relatives teach you every day in the way they live.

For Lost Birds, finding your tribe is like finding a key to a lost world. Sometimes friends take us to their reservation first. They give an introduction or beginners course in tribal culture. No one wants to do anything inappropriate or stupid when go back to your own reservation. Unfortunately, assimilation by non-Indians taught us to talk and not listen. We learn this when we meet other Indians.

To go back, you have to find relatives, the right relatives. That's hard but many adoptees do. You find the key or it finds you—eventually.

An unusually high number of Native adoptees are quite well-known—medicine man Pipe Mustache, authors Sundancer Peter Catches and Dr. Charles A. Eastman (Ohiyesa); and journalists Paul DeMain and Deborah Locke. Each is strong, spirited, and well-known. They are adoptees who found their way, their identity, and their relatives. I'd like to think all made peace with their past.

I call my early years in training to be a journalist in Indian Country, "the college of Paul DeMain." In four years, doing intense newspaper work, living under constant pressure of news deadlines, Paul taught me most of what I know about being a journalist.

Paul founded the oldest independent national Native newspaper, News from Indian Country. He and I co-founded Ojibwe Akiing in 1996.

Paul is one of the few adoptees I know who has two mothers (biological and adoptive) who talk to each other and each has bragging rights. Paul plans to write his memoir someday. I call him a Full Circle Adoptee, one who knows and loves both families.

For the first time in history, White Earth adoptees were invited to a Welcome Home Gathering in October 2007, at the Shooting Star Casino in Mahnomen, Minnesota. They held three days of workshops and activities. Their press release said, "The White Earth Band of Ojibwe recognizes the importance of acknowledging all its relatives and wishes to provide a time of healing. Our community has been deeply impacted by systematic child removal, especially prior to the passage of the Indian Child Welfare Act. It is time to welcome our adoptees back home, to come together and provide healing and reconnecting. White Earth offers a community forum and healing, including spiritual teachings, education, and the opportunity to learn more about your history."

Native America Calling aired a special program about this. The Elders say it's time to call adoptees home.

Acceptance

But will our tribes accept us? It is much more complicated than I ever imagined. There's the "American" definition of who is Indian and how much blood makes you an Indian. This invention narrows us down using blood quantum. Indians even use it to determine their rolls.

What choice did Lost Birds have in all this? None—since we were adopted as babies or young children. Can we learn our language, and traditions? Many do. Can we move back? Yes, sometimes, but many don't. Do tribes discriminate over blood quantum? Yes, some do. Some tribes have taken steps to close their rolls or remove people they feel don't meet their blood requirements.

It's up to the individual adoptee how they proceed; each journey is sacred and unique.

Sometimes our parents are dead or don't want to be found. The reunion could be harder and longer than the search. The triad—adoptee, adoptive parent and birthparent—may express anger or hurt. I've met adoptees who forgave their birthparents before knowing all the circumstances of how or why. This is not about blame.

In the past few years, I published a few feature articles on the subject as an adoptee, and I gave an interview to a newspaper in Wisconsin.

It became clear to me there was much more about adoption than was being told in books or newspapers. Academic friends questioned me intensely, since little is known or compiled about Native adoptees or the adoptions that came before, during and after the Indian boarding school era.

After you read this book, I believe that you'll never look at adoption in the same way again.

Thank you, World Wide (Sacred) Web, for helping me to find so many others, do research, read such riveting stories, and figure out how all this happened.

The Apology

"Next to the death penalty, the most absolute thing a government can do to an individual is to take a child away. But these were acts against individual immigrant families, and no European national group was singled out for these removals to the point of being imperiled. One ethnic group, however—American Indians and Alaskan Natives—a people of many cultures and governments, and the original citizens of this land— was singled out for treatment that ranged over the decades from outright massacre to arrogant and paternalistic "improvement." CWLA (Child Welfare League of America) played a role in that attempt. We must face this truth. No matter how well intentioned and how squarely in the mainstream this was at the time, it was wrong; it was hurtful; and it reflected a kind of bias that surfaces feelings of shame, as we look back with the 20/20 vision of hindsight. I am not here today to deny or minimize that role, but to put it on the table and to acknowledge it as truth." – CWLA director Shay Bilchik apology given to adoptees on the Menominee Reservation

I heard Bilchik's words in 2001 at the first Wiping the Tears Orphan Ceremony, an inclusive Inter-Tribal ceremony for adoptees and grieving families. Attendees were there to begin a healing process, honoring more than one generation torn apart by removals and relocations. News spread quickly by mouth and email—the new moccasin telegraph. Hundreds of people showed up in Wisconsin, including me. I wrote an article and editorial afterwards.

That November day, for the first time, the Drum played the Orphan Honor Song, thanks to Sandy White Hawk (Rosebud), a military veteran and Lost Bird with a vision that Split Feathers are warriors who need to be honored.

White Hawk worked with Chris Leith, an advisor to the National Indian Child Welfare Association, and together they started First Nations Orphans Association who organized this first gathering.

The formal apology given by the CWLA official Shay Bilchik was a historic moment. Later one adoptee whispered, "His apology was ruined when he said it was people who had those jobs before the workers now."

The orphan ceremony in Wisconsin was led by the most sacred Lakota Holy man, Chief Arvol Looking Horse, Keeper of the Sacred White Buffalo Calf Pipe and Dakota Elder Chris Leith.

Looking Horse is respected by many of the western tribes as their most sacred, like the Tibetan Buddhist's Dalai Lama. All tribes were welcome to attend, though the ceremony was clearly a Plains ritual.

One apology was the tip of the proverbial iceberg. I was 45 then, and many adoptees were my age or older. We needed our information and fast. Time is running out. The majority of Tribal Nations are not set up or prepared to help us make reconnections or have reunions.

First Nations Orphans Association decided to help adoptees make those connections and hold ceremonies.

Initially, I was surprised at how many Lost Bird/Split Feathers there are—not a handful but thousands; unsealing states records would be the only way to know exactly how many children were removed. Canadian adoptees call this their repatriation, being allowed to return to their tribe and meet relatives; Canada is helping some of them. America has done nothing for us.

At least ten other adoptees I met at the ceremony were shocked, too. We'd been isolated. No one told us. None of us had realized the immensity or tragedy of all this, and that we were a part of it. We'd been lost from each other and from our tribe. More than a few were still unable to find out which tribe.

Some of us didn't even know how to act, adults standing in the circle for the very first time. It was new, overwhelming, yet certainly beautiful. It was alright to shed our difficulties in tears; it was expected.

Dr. Patty Loew filmed a special news segment of the ceremony for a local PBS affiliate in Madison, Wisconsin. (I went back to Wisconsin to watch her mini-documentary when it premiered on television. I was one of the Split Feathers she filmed.)

Split Feathers do have one thing in common—emotional trauma, whether we realize it or not. We need our place in the circle to heal this, to find our relatives, to be liberated from exile and grief. At the ceremony we heard we were taken as babies, or children; it wasn't our fault or under our control.

Even after the ceremony and the loving generosity of the Menominee tribe who hosted the powwow portion for adoptees, there were still too many of us living without proof, without documentation or a real connection to our own tribe.

We Are All Related

The earth is our mother. We believe that. I've met Indigenous people from around the world and I've yet to find a difference of opinion on that... —Chief Oren Lyons (Onondaga), Surviving in Two Worlds

North American Indians are connected like tree roots, different but the same. The Lakota say *Mitakuye Oyasin* which means "We are all related."

The Cherokee say, *Ea Nigada Qusdi Idadadvhn* which means "All my relations in creation." It's an honor for me to share these important words. All Indigenous people have the saying "we are all related" or "all our relations" across the globe.

Where an adoptee grows up is relevant. Lost Birds I know say they found great comfort outside, alone, in the wild, under the sky, in dreams, and in time spent with other Indian people. Our spirit is the same in the birds, bears, buffalo, in the natural world around us.

How we live builds character, personality and humility.

Elders say gratitude to Great Spirit is the basis of all prayer, grateful for our time and place, and for others who walk with us. "Don't carry hatred in your hearts. Don't remedy hardship with hatred." I heard their words. Indian people listen and remember this way. Humor is important, too. The Hopi say, "Now is the time. We are the ones we've been waiting for…"

Split Feathers may not necessarily feel wanted or needed, but we truly are—even if no one has said this to you. For many, it seemed a painful way to learn through adoption.

Perhaps you need to look at it this way: good medicine was healthy loving adoptive parents who shared their world, their food and their generosity. Even though it seemed a hard (or easy) way to live, we can take our new knowledge back to our tribe, after we heal ourselves. Adoptees need to hear this. It is our medicine. We can learn to heal others. Lost Birds can live in two worlds successfully.

Now is the time, we are the ones we've been waiting for…

Generation After Generation, We Are Coming Home

[The *Talking Stick* article published in 2005]

Native musicians Buffy Sainte-Marie, Brule, Star Nayea; filmmaker Chris Eyre; and newspaper publisher Paul DeMain - what do they have in common?

They are all adoptees, raised by white families, each well known for their gifts and talent, and all are unquestionably Indigenous or Native Americans.

"Unci, our Grandmothers, prayed to the Great Spirit for us to return," Sandy White Hawk said when we met in 2001. We are both orphans, adoptees with Native American ancestry. Sandy is Sicangu Dakota, from the Rosebud reservation in South Dakota. Her mother enrolled her before she was taken at age three and raised by missionaries.

We met at Wicoicage Ake Un-Ku-Pi, a ceremony Sandy organized for the First Nations Orphans Association, held on the

Menominee Reservation in Wisconsin in 2001. It was the first ceremony to wipe the tears of the lost ones and the found ones.

"The vision of a song for adoptees came to me, an honor song that would help those looking to find their way back. I shared this vision with Chris Leith, a Prairie Island Dakota Elder and Spiritual Advisor to the National Indian Child Welfare Association," Sandy White Hawk said. "Chris asked Jerry Dearly, an Oglala Lakota, to make the song. I hoped the song would also help heal family members who have lost children to the system."

There were thousands of Native American children taken from their families and tribes across North America. In the 1950s and 1960s, the Indian Adoption Project placed hundreds of Native American children with white parents, the first national effort to place an entire child population transracially and transculturally.

This was the White man's way of assimilating the Indian, to break their spirit, by building Indian boarding schools away from the reservation, and removing babies and children to be raised by non-Native families.

Missionaries and Christians abhorred the savagery of these child pagans so much that they scrubbed their tongues with lye soap for speaking a word of their language, forced them to speak English, wiped out their customs by erasing any trace of their identity, cut off their hair and burned their clothing. Children were not allowed contact with their families.

Tribes bent on saving themselves could do little to stop the theft of these future generations. Their grieving never stopped—it was yet another brutal disappointment, another form of genocide.

For adoptees like me, we look in a mirror and know something is wrong, yet we're helpless to change it. No one can discuss identity issues with you. You're troubled by that. The feeling of being lost and abandoned never leaves you alone or gives you peace.

Some of my friends, who are also Native American adoptees, are opening up and talking about their childhoods—the suffering from being abused mentally or physically. Not all were abused, but we all felt a loss of identity. We agree that our identity is not mirrored back to us. You hate your own skin because you're different, because you don't look like mom and dad. You don't look like anybody.

Sandy White Hawk told me that in one study, they found that taking a First Nations child from their family is more traumatic than being a prisoner of war. There is more psychological trauma and damage to that child than to a soldier imprisoned by enemies during wartime.

Non-Indian parents weren't made aware or told about this beforehand. It could have soured the federal government's deal. Indian children weren't studied for how they were damaged by removal but how well they adapted and assimilated. How well did adoption agencies discuss or prepare parents to deal with the culture or traditions of your tribe? Displacing these children came with a heavy price, which eventually lead to the passage of the Indian Child Welfare Act of 1978. The system failed in a big way. It's a mess that few are willing to talk or write about; it's still too painful.

I can't speak for the others, but there are ancestors who keep you company while you are away from your tradition and culture. The ancestors never abandon you. You see them in dreams; they wake you with ideas. There are signs as you wake up to the natural world around you and feel the connection to your brothers, the four-legged and winged ones. Your Indian friends, if you are lucky enough to have them growing up, talk in terms your heart can feel.

Every child has a gift. Tribes respect their children; they never laugh at them. They teach children to be honorable, respectful, courageous, and generous. Our white parents don't know this.

What is remarkable about Buffy and so many others is their spirit was strong enough to overcome. They followed their heart, vision, and the call to be an artist, musician or writer. Being creative is an effective outlet for a grief this enormous. We reconnect to our tribal identity when we are ready.

In June 2001, Child Welfare League Executive Director Shay Bilchik legitimated Native concerns, formally apologizing for the Indian Adoption Project at a meeting of the National Indian Child Welfare Association in Alaska. He put the Child Welfare League of America on record in support of the Indian Child Welfare Act. "No matter how well intentioned and how squarely in the mainstream this was at the time," he said, "it was wrong; it was hurtful; and it reflected a kind of bias that surfaces feelings of shame."

[The Washington Post, October 7, 2001: Mr. Bilchik acknowledges CWLA's wrongful involvement in the Indian Adoption Project, a 1950s–1960s effort to facilitate the adoption of Indian children into white homes for the purpose of "saving" these children from their own culture and language. In the summer of 2001, after a careful analysis of the history of the League's involvement with the Adoption Project, Mr. Bilchik made a public apology on the League's behalf.]

What disturbed me, it took Bilchik and his colleagues until 2001 to apologize for what happened between 1941 to1978 [dates of one Indian Adoption Project]. Twenty-five to 35 percent of Indian children were taken from their parents by the federal government.

Bilchik became Executive Director of the Child Welfare League of America in February 2000, and assumed leadership of the nation's oldest and largest association of agencies that directly help abused, neglected, abandoned and otherwise vulnerable children and their families. CWLA has more than 1,100 public and private, voluntary member agencies nationwide. The Washington, DC-based organization has offices in Boston, Chicago, Denver and Los Angeles. Bilchik came to CWLA from the Office of Juvenile Justice and Delinquency Prevention (OJJDP) in the U.S. Department of Justice.

Bilchik gave his public apology again in October 2001 at that first healing ceremony for First Nation adoptees that I attended.

"Orphans be strong, listen to our traditions, they will give you strength, hear the Drums' voice, it will tell you things," this is sung at each ceremony. It is the Wablencia Honor Song for First Nation orphans, translated from Lakota to English.

Dakota spiritual elder Chris Leith knew a ceremony was needed. Leith brought in Jerry Dearly, Ojibwe, who wrote the "honor song."

"It's a healing," Leith said, of the song and ceremony, "to bring back that sense of belonging, of dignity, of identity, and that love and tender care that everyone is searching for."

Historically, American Indians struggled to maintain their cultural and traditional ways since contact with Europeans. Physical discipline and sexual abuse experienced by the children at the boarding schools filtered into the culture when they later returned to their tribal families as adults.

In the 1950s, many American Indians were moved from reservations into cities through the Relocation Program initiated by the Federal Government. However, they were given no assistance in adjusting to the stresses of urban life. Some felt loss with the move to urban areas. The combination of the Boarding School experience, as well as urban life adjustment difficulties, contributed to the breakup of many Indian families, on and off the reservation. It's a cycle that perpetuates itself, even today.

To make matters worse, tribes are exactly prepared for adult adoptees who return. There is no tribal reunion office. For some adoptees, the return home is just more pain. Parents may have already passed on or don't want contact; or on some reservations there is stifling oppression; or tribal rolls are closed.

Some tribes are more concerned with economic opportunity than they are with reclaiming lost ones, who need to connect with their relatives, attend ceremonies and be allowed time, maybe even years, to heal.

I have a friend Daniel. He's Lakota. He knows this because he opened his adoption and located an uncle who told him his name. The uncle contacted Dan's birthmother but she wanted no contact with Dan. The door to answers about his life slammed closed again. Dan was abandoned again. He has no information as to where to find his relatives or cousins, or even what band of Lakota or what reservation. You won't find an instruction manual for this. Dan is lucky he learned his name. A friend told him about the first ceremony in Wisconsin where he met Sandy White Hawk and other adoptees. I pray that he finds his answers.

*[*Update: I was able to locate Dan's mother and uncle for him. I do not know if Dan has been in touch with the Sisseton Wahpeton Oyate, but he certainly belongs to their tribal nation. I wrote a letter to their tribal chairman on Dan's behalf. I also sent a copy of this article to his mother and his uncle. I do not know if they have made contact with Dan since I wrote the letters. Dan hoped for a reunion and find his relatives in Sisseton. He looks like just one of the hereditary chiefs.]*

In one study on Indian adoptees done in the 1980s, it barely scratched the surface of what adoptees felt or endured; the questions weren't exactly culturally appropriate since they were posed by non-Indian social workers. Those adoptees admitted they were depressed, suicidal, jobless or drug-dependent.

I cried at the first ceremony like a baby. The Menominee people graciously greeted each of us, welcomed us home and let us cry. I attended another ceremony, held at Indian Summer in Milwaukee, and White Hawk said many more are planned.

She said any tribe can call out to its lost ones and create a welcome ceremony for them. First Nations Orphans Association, based in Minnesota, now advises social workers and government agencies and hold workshops. They will travel and conduct the ceremony, when it can be arranged. White Hawk recently testified at a child custody case in South Dakota. With a clear victory, the courts are in favor of keeping Native children within the tribal family.

Sandy White Hawk was first accepted by the Menominee people who gave her a sense of culture and identity—in a way they fostered her. After that, she had the strength to find and meet her relatives in Rosebud.

It was a happy ending, for her, but it's not over. By the time she found them, her birthmother had died and she needs to find more siblings. I wish her the best on her journey.

To learn more about the efforts of one Minnesota Indian tribe to reconnect adopted children with their relatives, go to www.startribune.com/a1475. For more about the White Earth Band of Ojibwe efforts to locate their lost children, go to: www.whiteearth.com.

Famous Lost Birds

Born on a Cree reservation in Qu'Appelle Valley, Saskatchewan, Buffy Sainte-Marie was adopted and raised in Maine and Boston, Massachusetts. Her adoptive mother was Mi'kmaq. By age 24, Buffy Sainte-Marie had appeared all over Europe, Canada, Australia and Asia, receiving honors, medals and awards which continue to this day. Her song *"Until It's Time for You to Go,"* was recorded by Elvis and Cher, and her *"Universal Soldier"* became the anthem of the peace movement. For her very first album she was voted Billboard's Best New Artist. She disappeared suddenly from the mainstream American airwaves during the Lyndon Johnson years. In Indian country and abroad, however, her fame only grew. She continued to appear at countless grassroots concerts, AIM events and other activist benefits. She made 17 albums of her music, three of her own television specials, spent five years on *Sesame Street,* scored movies, helped to found Canada's 'Music of Aboriginal Canada' JUNO category, raised a son, earned a Ph.D. in Fine Arts, taught Digital Music as adjunct professor at several colleges, and won an Academy Award Oscar for the song *"Up Where We Belong."* Buffy invented the role of Native American international activist pop star. Her concern for protecting indigenous intellectual property and her distaste for the exploitation of Native American artists and performers has kept her in the forefront of activism in the arts for over forty years. Presently she operates the Nihewan Foundation for Native American Education whose Cradleboard Teaching Project serves children and teachers in eighteen states. She lives in Hawaii.

Star Nayea, raised in Detroit, Michigan, has often been described as the "little lady with a big voice," who launched her career in Austin, Texas, then moved to New York City. In New York, several years ago, Star fully developed her unique contemporary edge of bluesy rock with hints of folk and traditional Native American vocals. Star, possibly Ojibwe-Potowatomi, adopted by a white family as an infant, is seeking her own birth family. Star currently lives with her son in Seattle.

Brulé, aka Paul LaRoche, has a unique story to tell. Along with the amazing music, theatrics, and traditional dance troupe, Paul tells the story of how he came to realize his Native American heritage after nearly 38 years of separation from his biological family, who resides on the Lower Brule Sioux Indian Reservation in central South Dakota. Paul, adopted at birth off the reservation, discovered his Lakota heritage in 1993 after the death of both adoptive parents. He was reunited on Thanksgiving Day 1993 with a brother, sister, aunts, uncles, nieces and nephews. The discovery of his true heritage has greatly affected Paul's life and those around him.

Chris Eyre was born in 1969 on the Warm Spring reservation in Oregon. He grew up in Klamath Falls, Oregon, adopted by a non-Native family. "I'm Cheyenne and Arapahoe. I went to school in Portland, Oregon. I pursued an associate's degree in television, in directing; I earned my bachelor's degree in media arts at the University of Arizona, and my master's at New York University in filmmaking." Chris Eyre attempts to display portraits of contemporary Native Americans as individuals who are plagued by problems common to all people, but who react within the confines of their own particular circumstances. He founded Riverhead Entertainment, a production company that for several years produced commercials, films, and documentaries.

Paul DeMain is a member of the Oneida (Wisconsin) and Ojibwe tribes, and was raised by a non-Native family in Wausau, Wisconsin. "I grew up with some compassionate liberals who never tried to hide my identity and encouraged me to inquire about it," DeMain says. In the early 1970s, he made contact with the Oneida tribe, where he is enrolled. He has met his biological family. In 1986 he launched *News from Indian Country*, an independent newspaper that covers tribal politics, with a circulation of 9,000 readers worldwide.

Eric Schweig was born to an Inuit mother and a Chippewa-Dene father in Inuvik, the Northwest Territories. At six months, he was adopted by a German-Canadian family. During his childhood in Inuvik, Bermuda and Toronto, he was systematically and physically abused by his adoptive parents then he ran away from home when he was 16, and became a laborer on construction sites. In 1987 he was "discovered" while walking down a Toronto street and cast in the movie *The Shaman's Source*. At least 16 films followed, most notably as Uncas in *The Last of the Mohicans*. During this time period he endured a "roller coaster of alcohol, drugs, violence, failed relationships, despair and confusion" [Schweig said] due to the abuse and racism and ethnic identity deprivation of his childhood. In 1996 he began to regain his cultural identity and is now primarily a carver, especially Inuit spirit masks, living on Vancouver Island, and he continues to act in films. He is a passionate opponent of the adoption of Aboriginal Native People by Europeans.

Mary Youngblood, Chugach Aleut/Seminole, is a Grammy award winning flutist, who was adopted and raised by a non-Native couple. Mary opened her adoption at age 26.

FACT: In 1984, 80% of American Indian infant adoptions into non-Indian homes were made without notification to the child's tribe or the Secretary of the Interior. Six years since its development, the ICWA still was not understood, was not being implemented correctly or was simply ignored. The problem exists today; and with the time-frame of child adoption procedures being accelerated under President Clinton's new adoption policies, the risk of Indian children being permanently removed from their families, their tribes, and their culture continues to increase. – From the American Indian Child Resource Center

Wiping the Tears

Joining the Native American Journalists Association (NAJA) in 1996, I made close friends across Indian Country.

I became editor of the *Pequot Times,* and my employers were famous. The Mashantucket Pequot Tribal Nation own

Foxwoods, the world's largest resort casino. Their public relations department recruited me in 1999.

When I first heard about First Nations Orphan Association, I called Sandy and she officially invited me to attend as an adoptee. The Wiping the Tears ceremony was so important, something that opened my heart with more impact than I expected. I was flooded with tears, both happy and sad: Happy to be reunited with the spirit of my ancestors and my relatives. Sad because I feel I've spent so much of my life without them.

After I attended two ceremonies, I still encourage other Lost Birds-adoptees to attend. But it is only one step. Each tribe has its own ceremonies and language.

The pain of being lost is indescribable yet each of us knew what it felt like. As I stood there crying, I knew we were all related in this pain. I heard it when I talked to others after the ceremonies.

What surprised me most was when I turned slightly during the ceremony to see how many people there were. I was stunned. Hundreds of people were there, not all were adoptees, but families who had lost children.

It made me realize how big this is—how many of us were denied our birthright.

There is Hope

Several adoptees now connect on Facebook, thanks to Diane Tell His Name (Lakota), another Lost Bird/adoptee. Lost Birds chat on the internet, some helping others find their way home.

Adoptees don't have to travel far with a computer at their house or at the library. This is a good and hopeful sign.

Many Native people come out of adoption even more adamant, more creative, and more determined to be the person they are born to be, with or without a tribal identification card, or Certificate of Degree of Indian blood, or a reservation to call home.

Other Native people can make us more comfortable, and foster us on this journey, very typical of Native generosity.

I tell others to first register with a reunion registry, if you know which state. The non-identifying birth information will be appalling, and possibly untrue, but live with it as best you can. Keep trying other avenues. Follow your instincts. Register your birth date online and give your contact information if you are in a closed adoption state. Siblings with computers may find you on a registry. Some older adoptees I've met hired private investigators.

What happened before and after the Indian Adoption Projects was many Indian people were sent to boarding schools. Our parents may have endured this so they are suffering.

Canada made a formal apology and promised restitution to boarding school survivors. Canadian churches are going to pay Indians restitution for boarding school abuses.

America has yet to openly admit what it did to Indian children.

Kinship Adoption

There is no saying more appropriate to the Hopi way of life than the African saying that it takes a village to raise a child. —Hopi Tutuveni newspaper, June 8, 1999

We truly can't fix adoption until we end human suffering and help all parents to care for their offspring. Family, community, tribe and nation must step up to help heal the parent and help raise the child.

What works best? Kinship adoption. A child who is raised by birth family, grandparents or cousins or Native American foster parents is less traumatized than a hasty removal to strangers and non-Indian foster care.

What is clearly missing with a closed adoption—recognizing the adoptee and foster child's trauma and abandonment issues. This should be of great concern to those who participate in an adoption. The way it is now, adoptees are handed off, job done.

History is a great teacher. America's welfare system was created to ease the suffering of poor families, to keep them functioning and intact. The Great Depression of the 1930s changed how Americans care for each other. President Franklin D. Roosevelt's New Deal established Social Security in 1935 and inaugurated the modern day federal welfare program with a modest small program called Aid to Dependent Children (ADC).

The next great expansion came during the Lyndon B. Johnson administration in the 1960s, when Medicare, Medicaid, public housing, and other programs were established. America's human safety net for the poor expanded dramatically over the past 100 years. Families, local communities, and charities (often religiously based) provided the backbone.

Regardless, humans do have an emotional (mental) body, a spiritual body and a physical body, and all are interrelated and react to the concern of the other.

My Northern Cheyenne friend Steven taught me that each of us has four souls. We each possess a Spiritual Intelligence. If we share DNA, we share the blood of our ancestors. Removed from family and tribal contact is doubly traumatic and disruptive.

In a perfect world, a family unit, tribe and extended family raise their own, in a culturally-appropriate, sensitive, familiar atmosphere, across the planet.

Has the American government succeeded in destroying Indian culture and family? No.

This story doesn't end or begin here. It's still being lived.

Spiritual Genocide

I needed to understand how to survive spiritually. One of the most prophetic Indian people alive today is John Trudell (Santee). It was a "dream come true" when I interviewed him.

A founder of the American Indian Movement, a respected actor and recording artist, Trudell made a concert stop with his band Bad Dog at the Mashantucket Pequot Museum in 2000. I wrote about our conversation for the *Pequot Times*.

It hit me that Trudell uses words as medicine, in a "quantum" way, meaning it's understood on more than one level.

During his performance, Trudell explained, "I called this album *Blue Indians* because there is a kind of spiritual and cultural genocide perpetrated on everyone that is poor in this country... The advance of technology has put all of us on a kind of reservation.

These are the people who can't educate their children, or afford health care. They've been robbed of life, which is what happened to Native people; so in that context, we're all Indians."

Trudell referred to humans as being mined, like minerals, since we are composed of earth's organic materials. Explaining the effects of mining humans, he said, "The feeling of powerlessness that this society has is the result of mining humans, because the people do feel powerless. I think no clear, coherent thinking people, would accept as normal the conditions that they have to accept. So, the only reason I can see that people would accept the inequities, are because they feel powerless to deal with them. The powerlessness may disguise itself as rage, or racial hatred, or sexism; it may disguise itself in many ways, but basically the common thread is a feeling of powerlessness among people.

"...All the aggressive attitudes basically get internalized. I think that's the obvious result of being mined as an individual. If they are being real with themselves, no pretending, no justification or rationalization, how many people do feel that they have any real power? How many people feel powerless to deal with situations put in their life? It's got to do with perceptional reality. If we use our intelligence as clearly and coherently as we can, I think we'd understand that we are not necessarily powerless. But we don't know how to relate to power or recognize it; therefore we don't know how to exercise it."

Trudell believes, "We're not taught about our personal relationship to power. We're not taught about our relationship to the Great Spirit. Recognizing power is what you have to do. When you recognize it, you exercise it. You can't take back what they have already taken but you can stop the taking of your power, once you recognize it.

"Responsibility is the way to fulfillment, so when one recognizes and exercises their responsibility, this is how one is to be free. It's a way of reconnecting with power for us as humans," he explained.

Trudell deals with his own life in this way. "I see as clearly as I can. The objective is for me to be as real to myself as I can possibly be. The more real I can be to myself, the more real—maybe I can be to other people. It's a challenge. I look at anger as healthy. It's like sadness. There's a reason we're given certain feelings. I think anger is necessary to our survival and reality, but now we live in a technology reality where people are programmed not to accept their anger. I think we can use it as fuel for clarity, focus and accomplishment. Anger doesn't have to be a distorting experience."

"Medicine People are spiritual beings who have made a decision to seek the Red Road. They sacrifice and seek the way of the Creator. After many years of dedication, the Grandfathers teach them about power and about laws and about how to use the medicine. The Medicine People develop tremendous faith in their medicine and the Creator. When we go to the Medicine People, we too must have faith so they can help us. We can only be helped if we want to be helped. Because the Medicine People know how to help—that is only one half of it. The other half is up to us. We must have faith that the medicine has powers to help."

—Don Coyhis, Mohican, **www.WhiteBison.org**

Knowledge

"The power of a name...that's old magic." —Doctor Who ("The Shakespeare Code")

I get it now. "Knowledge" is power. Before quantum physics, Indians called it medicine. Professor Ron Welburn, a Cherokee friend, once said, "Indian people didn't need the String Theory or quantum physics because we have The Theory of Everything."

For those who maintain disbelief in the possibility of distance healing and Indian medicine, take a look at quantum physics. It's still a new science for scientists but it's old news to Indians. New science points to the realism of distance healing and using thoughts (and/or mind meditation, prayer, miracles) which explains why people are able to get so many stunning results and heal using it.

In a new book, "Reality Begins with Consciousness," author-neuro-psychiatrist Dr. Vernon Neppe suggests in the Theory of Everything, proposed by Einstein and Hawking, has major failings because they didn't factor consciousness in to their equation. Neppe describes three levels of consciousness—neurological, psychological, and a kind of meta-consciousness which pulls in information from all sources, and "technically would not require a brain...and implies infinity."

Meta-consciousness suggests that life-after-death is a reality, as consciousness can exist outside the brain. Neppe believes, "In our model, we cogently argue that time is not just one linear dimension that goes past, present, future, but that there are several different dimensions of time, and all of existence could be said to exist at the same time because we have an extended amount of time that always is, was, and will exist." Neppe was interviewed on Coast to Coast with George Noory in 2011.

Medicine to heal is not complicated. Adoptees need our name and identity to settle confusion and discord. Like me, I always knew I was adopted so I made the decision to solve this mystery. I felt better after I opened my adoption and others adoptees have also.

Everyone wants to learn about their roots, another reason why so many people are having their DNA tested. We don't just inherit our looks and perhaps our personalities—our susceptibility to disease is also inherited, and if we find out what genes we have, we'll deal with those problems before they get too serious. University of Wisconsin researchers say that you will be able to receive information about your family's genetic history (by 2012) for less than $100.

The Power of a Name

As is held in folktales and legends, there is great power in a person's name. Madeleine L'Engle brought this up in her Wrinkle in Time series: to Name is to create, to Un-name is to destroy. The practice of unnaming and renaming adoptees is an attempt to assert control over us. It's said that if you know someone's true name, you have absolute power over them. The very fact that adoptees' true names are sequestered by the state is evidence of this ancient law stretching into our modern society. For if we adoptees knew our true names, we could reclaim the power that has been taken from us, the power to access our records without restriction.

  — Triona Gundry (Illinois adoptee) blog, www.73adoptee.com

Emotionally Impaired

  I do believe adoptees can help other adoptees. It can be a perilous journey. There is plenty to stall an adoptee or prevent them from trying. They need a friend, someone who knows this pain, a friend who has lived as that secret—or perhaps as that scandal.

  Adoptive parents or non-adopted people, even doctors can only guess what this pain feels like. They don't live it as we do, and they can't live it for us.

  Creativity, music and the arts do help. Adoptees become actors, athletes, artists, musicians, writers, some very well-known for their gifts. Being emotionally impaired can be a challenge but once we begin the journey, hearts do heal.

  I realize a powerful link exists between what I'm feeling and what happens in my body. Years ago I'd use emotional binging, working more than one job, just to numb my emotional pain. By 18, I was a complete workaholic. There may be some adoptees who do not wish to heal their pain and go on as they are, holding on to self-pity, rather than jump in and do the work.

  Recognizing a pattern of belief is tough, partly because you gain sympathy by stealing (or sucking) energy from others when we act sick. That is no way to live. Adoptees need to be their own person, self-energizing, and not steal energy from anyone.

  Adoptees are meant to survive this, no matter how traumatized we are. It's a test. Can we heal our own minds? Yes. Can we love two families? Yes. Can we recover and go back to our reservation or community? Definitely, yes.

Some adoptees believe that when we meet our mother or father, all pain will disappear. That's just hope. That is not the way it works. A reunion is just one step on the journey and a reunion helps, but there are many more steps just as difficult.

It truly is a test. Regardless of ancestry, adoptees can heal this. The only one who can fix it is the adoptee.

I'm uneasy around new people, very shy and reserved at times. I've lived through many disappointments. It's very upsetting to find out about orphan trauma now, years later, knowing no one bothered to tell me or help me while I was experiencing it.

I came to terms with all of it, eventually.

Damaged Kids

Rhonda and I talk almost every week. One day she joked, "You can't raise a polar bear in the tropics." Then she said something that hit me like a ton of bricks. "We (Native adoptees) are so different we do lose touch with reality."

After I was married in 1984, I actually did want to have a child. Dave and I were unable to because of his vasectomy, done years before we met. He was reluctant to adopt a child with me even though I hoped we would.

After an adoption lecture in Washington State that I made him attend with me, Dave blurted out in the car, "These kids are damaged and I don't want to deal with that shit. I don't want to adopt someone else's problem..."

His words were loud, angry, "Damaged kids!" I could not repeat his words out loud and shuttered when he said it. I felt so humiliated. I never knew people felt this way.

What struck me most—I was one of those kids. What hurt as much—this was my husband who I thought I knew. What did he really think of me? I thought he understood.

Well, I thought wrong. This wasn't the first time I'd lost touch with reality.

Dave only said we'd have a family when he proposed to me on Friday the 13th, a sign I missed. I did agree to marry him. He didn't really mean it about our having a baby.

The day before our vows, August 3, 1984, I cornered Dave, demanding his answer, "Will we have a family?" He'd been evasive since we met, changing the subject or making up an excuse. He had no intention of having a child with me ever—he lied. He said "yes."

No one in my family really knew him. I didn't know he was lying. It was wrong. We did get married.

I didn't know how to be this much-younger trophy wife. It took me a long to see reality and how I was made a fool.

I drove to Wisconsin to plan our wedding after Dave proposed.

When I got there, Dad was so sick, I became the ambulance driver, taking him from doctor to doctor, trying to find out what was wrong. Within a week, Sev was hospitalized with colon cancer. Dad had surgery the day before the wedding so Joey walked me down the sidewalk instead of Sev.

The wedding was held at my parent's house on a Wisconsin lake. Dad wasn't there.

After the reception, Mom, Joey, Dave and I went to see dad in a Duluth hospital, still wearing our wedding clothes. That entire day is a blur and doesn't seem real to me. It's like a bad dream.

A Good (Trophy) Wife

Mom and Dad hardly knew Dave, my rich husband, who had two grown sons, Mitch and Del. Dave and I stayed a few days after the wedding and headed back to Lake Oswego.

How did Dave handle me lugging emotional baggage back to Oregon after our wedding? Driving through Montana on our honeymoon, Dave complained I was moody. Dad's doctor had said he had six months to live. I didn't know trophy wives are not supposed to worry about the cancer diagnosis of a parent.

Dave got so angry, he told me to get out of the car somewhere in Montana. He used threats to lift me out of my moods. I switched on the smile and pretended to be OK, and held my tongue. I knew how to pretend; I'd done it my entire life.

Was I sicker than I realized? I believe I was.

I was not expecting to be abused by every man I knew. No. My life was a bad script, line after line. It didn't take me long to realize this. I was not equipped to be married. I was not prepared to live in fear, this time in fear of my husband.

So I tried to love. For 10 years I tried. I was committed to our marriage. I tried to feel love and give love. All my effort was in trying, trying to be someone like a good wife, trying to do something meaningful. Trying was—well—trying!

Finally I got counseling in Seattle. It worked. Like magic, the puzzle started to form a picture, piece by piece. I knew I'd see a pattern eventually, how everything was connected. Finally it hit me, I was experiencing abuse. Dave was controlling me, every mood and every move I made. This was damaging me and I was allowing it. I drew the exact same experience I'd hoped to avoid. I was very afraid of Dave and that wasn't love. I was deceiving myself again. This marriage was not what I needed. I'd gone from one controlling man to another, Sev to Dave. Both abused me.

How did this happen? Why did I choose to say, "'til death do us part"?

Dave was so controlling I did not see it at first. I had no idea. He controlled the money, what I bought, who I could see, even when I could speak. I wasn't allowed to find a job the first three years we were married. I found a list of what constitutes marital abuse - out of seven, I scored five.

A few days before the marriage, I did a tarot card reading with a friend. The cards described me as being trapped like a bird in a cage. From this experience I would grow in awareness of my own power. Even trapped, I could fly. The tarot reading said I would be financially secure. How true.

Bankrupt

Dave was very good at making money but a very insecure person, deeply terrified of abandonment. Dave's mother had abandoned him so he was raised by her parents. He was defined by this experience so he constantly talked about it.

When Kathy, a first cousin, met Dave, she told my aunt Betty I was being abused. She'd only guessed. I never told anyone David had hit me in the face twice.

Dave and I argued about his money. He had millions tied up in real estate. Eventually all was lost to bankruptcy. Our lives were bankrupt, too.

As it unraveled, I could not confide in mom; I didn't tell her any of the bad stuff. Plus she didn't believe in divorce. It was obvious Edie liked Dave's money. He had money. She told me if we broke up, it would be my fault. I'd heard Edie say women should marry money—which was her era's belief. That is akin to prostitution.

Dave and I finally separated in 1993. I stayed with friends until I got a job and my own apartment in Seattle. Dave's wealth was gone. I didn't want money. I wanted my car, my computer and a few pieces of furniture.

Later mom said I wasted all those years when I should have had a baby. She was more outraged I never saw a dime of alimony. It would have been nice to know what she was thinking while it was happening when I really needed her opinion. I knew mom and I would never talk about what was really important until it was too late.

I'd changed after counseling. I was a different person. I couldn't live with Dave anymore. We stayed friends. That was all I could manage.

After we separated, Dave changed. I became stronger and he actually softened. I liked the new Dave. I told him he was swimming against the current, trying to swim upstream when all he had to do was let go.

Hurt

I'd moved to the Oregon coast in 1994 and explained to the social workers my future ex-husband was 18 years older than me and had refused to reverse his vasectomy. I wanted to adopt an older child in Oregon since I was already in my late 30s.

I didn't tell the social workers how Dave said these children were someone else's rejects or damaged goods.

What a bastard, I thought. His words hurt me more than a slap to the face. His words hurt a long time.

Dave is not the only person who feels that way—many people see orphans as rejects, as bad decisions or products of a bad environment, or bad seed from bad parents.

Some siblings tease each other with "you're adopted, you're a bastard" because it hurts to hear it. Adoption definitely has a stigma attached.

I know how these words hurt.

The Opening

For years my mind was out of sync with my body. Rhonda calls this "out of balance."

Even when I was the perfect weight, I was uncomfortable in my own skin. I ate sparingly at times. I didn't trust my eyes or the image in my mirror.

Beginning in high school, I'd get heart palpitations and couldn't catch my breath. Even when I was smiling, I wasn't really feeling it or living inside my body. I suffered numerous panic attacks.

In Seattle in the 1990s, I did co-counseling. This worked for me. I relived and remembered everything I could from my childhood, all the abuse, feeling very powerless. With co-counseling, you tell your *whole* life story with complete and total honesty, which was the first time I had ever done it. It took a few years. Then it was like a powder keg exploded.

Before we separated, Dave and I were in Sedona, Arizona in 1993, thinking about relocating there. While I prayed on a hill in the red rocks, something happened. The sound I heard was deafening, like a vibration, or a million crickets singing. Dave didn't hear it!

I was taught you do not pray for yourself. I didn't pray for myself in Sedona that day. Almost too much to comprehend, I felt something had happened to me, what I called an "opening." It truly felt like I walked out of a dark fog into a clearing. Something had kept me dead or dreaming, safe from reality.

For a few days, I could not stop crying. Dave thought I was having a nervous breakdown instead of a breakthrough. I had started to feel again.

All that darkness that surrounded me was gone. I could actually feel light inside my body— that's why I called what happened an opening.

I tried to put my experience into words but it was indescribable. I felt connected to Great Spirit in creation, in sound, in a vibration.

I wasn't completely aware of what had happened to me until later. There is great power in this opening, when the heart opens. It's the power of all love and all creation, when I felt all life and all living things are related and connected. I felt compassion and empathy and saw beauty all around me. It's like everything was sparkling. My old life was gone. I could let it go.

I was never the same.

Addiction to a Thought Pattern

I am not a medical doctor but I do know what I did and what happened to me. The majority of adoptees have difficulty with foggy thoughts, like there is a black cloud or fog around them, or they're not feeling much of anything, even as adults.

Taking control of thought and creating new feelings is difficult.

Once I did see clearly what happened to me, without blocking it, without drugs and medication, big changes did occur.

I tried the Emotional Freedom Technique called EFT, which I did by myself. Emotions trapped in the body are released. (Google: EFT for adoptees)

There was a workshop in Vermont that explained about a person's destructive emotions. These destructive emotions are thought of as an "auto-immune" disease of the mind. Tibetan Buddhists, who are like the Navajo in many ways, call them "obscuring emotions" because they cloud the healthy, luminous quality of the natural mind.

They explain the intensity of the dark emotions will arise as if in response to a survival threat, when it is actually an addiction to a thought pattern.

Using mental images as antidotes, what I call rewiring my brain, it was possible to retrain my mind out of suffering and end these obscuring emotional habits or thought patterns. For centuries, medicine people have studied the true nature of the mind over body. In Buddhist teachings, neuroscience, and Native American medicine, each is more alike than different.

One who faces their trauma and dark cloud faces the enemy. The cure is available to all adoptees. Train the mind out of suffering. Let it go slowly. Be courageous.

I don't regret one second of this experience. My life is far from perfect but I can feel everything now. Good or bad, I'll deal with both.

Where Do We Go From Here?

One thing I heard from other adoptees is return to your tribe well, in a good way, with a good heart and a strong mind. I know this is easier said than done—believe me, and I know it can take years.

With an epidemic of alcoholism and diabetes, there are already enough victims and broken souls on reservations and in our tribal families. They need us whether they realize it or not. Once our tribal relatives get to know us, and become familiar with us, and know who we truly are, adoptees are welcome. My Lakota relatives say this may take a long time. We might be a grey hair before it happens.

Be patient. Good things take time. I know this is hard to read for adoptees not close to a reunion. Some might harbor deep resentment, sadness and anger. That is not what your tribe needs.

Adoptees must grieve alone, like a vision quest you do alone.

With my recovery, I wear my scars. The joke is, "just don't let your scars wear you."

Adoptees should make friends with other adoptees. There is truly something great in making relatives. New relatives become your new life.

Even if you don't know your tribe yet, or haven't gone to visit, I was told, "don't isolate yourself." Use a computer and read tribal news–many tribes still make history.

Teach your adoptive moms and dads tribal history so they can appreciate it, respect it and understand its importance.

Tribes need their Lost Birds to return well.

Manifest Destiny

One part of Manifest Destiny meant making Indian kids white, American, civilized and assimilated.

Many children did not adapt well to the loss of identity and loss of family. The Indian Adoption Projects records are sealed so it's impossible to know how many families were affected. Both parent and child in Indian Country suffered. Some children were so distressed and depressed; some tried to run away from their adopters. In 2011, most states have sealed adoption records, making it impossible for these adoptees to find the information.

How did government accomplish Manifest Destiny? Their real intent was getting the land by getting Indian people out of their way. If you get rid of Indians, you'd disrupt or stop future generations. It was a three-part system: residential schools, foster-care/orphanages and permanent adoption of Indian children with sealed records, using churches, religious conversions and non-Indian adoptive parents to change the child.

Lost Children were disinherited from the rolls and their sovereign tribal rights.

Birthright

In the first decade of the 21st Century, census figures attest that more and more Americans are identifying themselves as Native American. With the populace claiming Native ancestry growing

three times as fast as the population as a whole, Native people are
one of the fastest-growing minority groups in the United States.
[Source: US Census 2000]

If you are an adoptee with Native American ancestry or mixed ancestry, I know exactly your frustration of sealed records and hitting one wall after another when you begin your search. Our information could be buried in filing cabinets in adoption agencies, court houses, or tribal offices, or in church records, like Catholic Charities who handled my adoption. Churches and states may not allow you to open your file, even as an adult. Sometimes our tribal identities are erased in their records.

You may have a birth date and birth place but no family name. You may have a name but are unsure which state, or which tribal nation, or even which country. You may only have the fact that you were given up for adoption.

Where do you start? I gave you my solution; I went to a judge privately. Other adoptees can try this. I offer no guarantee. I also recommend adoptees write their senator or congressman in their state and ask for immediate help. Letters can't hurt. Go to an adoptee rights website and join their work.

I found contacting hospitals not to be helpful since they abide by the state laws concerning adoption records. One woman said her file was in front of her at a hospital when she went searching for her ancestry yet she was not allowed to read it.

If you can afford it, hire a lawyer who understands the law in the state where you were adopted. Adoptees may eventually discover a birthparent enrolled you in your tribe, before you were taken and adopted. Sometimes finding answers involves finding the right paperwork. Lawyers can do this.

Adoptees can ask their adoptive parent to request the complete adoption file since they signed it, then they can tell you your name and pertinent details.

Also get on every reunion registry for adoptees and birthparents, by mail or email. And definitely use search angels—many are available and work for free or modest fees—Soaring Angels is one excellent group I found on Yahoo.

For me, meeting relatives took several years. For Rhonda, in her early 40s, it took her under a year to find her tribe and relatives in Michigan, and she was officially enrolled on March 19, 2007. After a few more legal formalities, on May 20, 2007, she received her official Tribal identification card and paperwork from the Bureau of Indian Affairs.

I recommend, "*Birthright, the Guide to Search and Reunion for Adoptees, Birthparents and Adoptive parents*," published in 1994, by adoptee-filmmaker Jean S. Strauss. It's among the best ever written for adoptees. I wish I'd had a copy of her book when I began my search in 1978. It shows an adoptee how to be methodical, how to find records like an investigator. Her book offers lists, addresses and solid suggestions.

Because of her adoptive mother, Jean Strauss had her adoption file to answer many of her early questions. I didn't. Strauss still had to search, and was successful using her own methods. Strauss wrote a beautiful memoir, "*Beneath a Tall Tree*" and has made two award-winning short films in 2005: "*Vital Records*" on the debate about access to original birth records for adoptees in New Hampshire, and "*The Triumvirate*" which documents the reunion with her birthmother and birth-grandmother. Check out her books and films at your local library or Google: Jean Strauss.

Hopefully this book will find its way to tribal government offices where they can make immediate changes on how to find, handle and help adult-adoptees returning to their tribes. There is no specific place for adoptees to go for tribal information in the US. There is no repatriation counseling yet.

The way it is now—heartbreaking.

Contact the Bureau of Indian Affairs. They have regional offices which you can find on the internet. Call them and ask them to steer you to information if you know your tribal affiliation. It is their job! They can help with your tribal status, if you need a CDIB - the certificate of degree of Indian blood. In Wisconsin, for example, the adoption record has your tribal information in the non-identifying information. If that is the case, you call the BIA.

Once you are enrolled, you are entitled to what your tribe offers—housing, college scholarships and medical care. If you haven't already done so, contact the enrollment office at tribal headquarters for a tribal identification card.

One Hopi called his ID card his Indian passport.

Be Creative

Virtually every family I've read about who lost an adopted family member to suicide, has said, "I thought if I loved him (or her) enough, I could fix it." Their love wasn't enough to fix the damage done by adoption, the separation anxiety and psychic wounds. Watch the movie *"Unlocking the Heart of Adoption,"* available on Amazon. One of the adoptees in the movie did commit suicide. It was so hard to watch this film.

Just remember it takes creativity, truth and time to heal. If Lost Birds follow their instincts, they are already creative in some way. That is a good place to start. We all have gifts.

I offer these suggestions: Meet other Lost Birds (online or in person). Go to socials and powwows. Watch the dancing, hear the drums. Let things happen. Take a class on Native American studies, taught by Native professors.

Modern Indians are doing amazing things. Tribes have tribal colleges. In many states, there are casino jobs. Not all casinos are successful, but every tribe wants to become economically self-sufficient. If you get an education, share it with your tribe in a humble way; be very helpful.

Despite this horrible history, there is much laughter and happiness on the rez, not always apparent to outsiders. I am amazed at the humor of my Indian relatives.

Just remember, go back to them well. Do not expect instant acceptance. Listen and watch. Volunteer to work with kids or elders and attend ceremonies when invited. Each day will require sensitivity and patience. It's a test.

Nothing happens in Indian Country without some sort of initiation or ritual.

Two Worlds

Split Feathers can live in two worlds.

Lakota Pipe Carrier Dave Chief told me that I would never need a weapon because the animals in my neighborhood would warn me of danger. I should pay close attention to them at all times so I do.

I count hawks because Sara, an Oglala Lakota elder, told me the more I see, the better the day. I counted 14 hawks when I was driving to Connecticut a few years ago.

I pray every morning when I wake up. I pray to the four directions.

History is an interpretation. Native Americans do not and cannot rely on history told by white men isolated in their institutions. Many scholars have never visited a reservation or even know an Indian. It is their interpretation of who they think we are. That is very dangerous so I was warned, "be careful what you read."

Quote: Thomas Littlewood stated in his book on the politics of population control, "non-white Americans are not unaware of how the American Indian came to be called the vanishing American . . . this country's starkest example of genocide in practice."

Prayers

After my divorce, I gave "my will, my ego," to Creator, Great Spirit. I'd experienced enough ego and drama for ten lifetimes. My life now is synchronicity. I go with the flow.

Great Spirit answered my prayers often, for sanity in my insane world. I did what I had to do. I didn't magically change. I kept good thoughts and many prayed for me.

I'd multiplied myself as a child. I was the strong girl who could stand the alcoholism and fighting in my house; a polite girl who could greet the priests and fool the nuns who taught me in school. I could fool everyone, please everyone and not let anyone know what was happening at home or in my head. I could sing in front of large crowds, not a bit self-conscious.

I just know my grandmothers never stopped praying for me.

Forgiveness

It's never easy to forgive. I had to forgive everything and everyone to improve my physical health. I had to replace my hostility. If I tried too hard, my brain seemed to go completely haywire. Parts of my memory were missing and logic went out the window many times. Opening up is not easy. I did manage slowly to be myself.

Two scientific tests are being done now on the power of forgiveness. One survey found that people (age 45 and older) who forgave others were more likely to have better overall mental and physical health than those who did not.

When Edie would scream day after day, "You're a slut, a no-good whore," she hurt me deeply. She hoped to prevent me from heading down the wrong path. I forgave her those words. Her cruelty enlightened my future. She saw me as a threat. I get that now. Hurting me was not intentional.

Forgiveness is one of the benefits of opening a closed adoption. Knowing the situation for your birthparents, knowing this history, is like taking your first breath again. It frees you, and opens your eyes.

I had a long time to think about Helen and Earl. I accept they did what they felt was necessary. They thought leaving me was for the best. Understanding and forgiving birthparents is beneficial in a myriad of ways. I made time to feel my anger, shock and grief, then made time to forgive.

Still, in 2009, the Catholic Church and lawyers from large adoption agencies, remain unwilling to open adoptions, saying our birthparent should be afforded privacy, since they were guaranteed secrecy when they gave up their child.

On the internet, many of our birthparents say they never wanted or expected privacy or secrecy.

This discussion is far from over, obviously.

Shift

After the opening was my shift, and I changed so much, I hardly recognized myself—again. I felt I was inside my body. I could feel things. I could never stand up on a stage and sing like I used to; I'd be much too self-conscious. Shyness returned in a big way.

Grief never completely goes away so I learn to live with it and laugh at it.

After "my shift," I walked away from the fog that surrounded me. I faced being an orphan, a victim of incest, and a whore with little or no self-esteem. That no longer controls me. I am no longer my own worst enemy.

It was hard to love myself so I let men do that for me. I did prostitute myself. I was reckless and did not think of myself as sacred. Later as a trophy wife, I imprisoned myself. I did not treat myself very well. I didn't need attention to my outer beauty. I needed love for my inner beauty. No one could give that to me. I had to give it to myself.

It hurts to write that I was a whore who got burned in my relationships with men. I was about as promiscuous as the men were. I could have worn a t-shirt that said, "Low Self-Esteem: Come Get Me." Or, "Watch Out, I'm Going to Leave You."

I made bad choices and drew the wrong men and women into my circle. I could not manage a healthy relationship.

Being a rock musician didn't help; it's a very rough business. Unsafe sex is really about control. Musicians use sex as power and entice others to fill their egos.

I do ache over all my mistakes. I do regret a lot. It helps to have a perspective, to look back and see why.

In the late 1980s, I went to a Face Reader, a Sihk gentleman. I had a reading with him in Seattle. He told wonderful stories. He read my face and explained my spirit was like a pretzel that had finally untwisted. I chose to be here. My life here was about dharma—reliving every past life, mistakes finally realized and undone. My soul wanted to see it all again, experience it all again. I chose this!!

Am I crazy? Apparently not.

Different Elders believe adoptees chose their path, to learn from it, so we'd practice healing ourselves, to eventually heal others. Our choice was to sacrifice to be closer to Great Spirit, God. My soul chose this. My life is one small sacrifice.

Enough
"I am still learning…" – Michelangelo, age 85

So my life has been hard enough, long enough, absurd enough, destructive enough, and even foolish enough, to have earned my Grey Hairs.

As a rule, I try and treat people as I wish to be treated.

I feel beauty and ugly at the same time. I am humbled by what I learned, not arrogant.

Research for this book would never been available to me, if not for the Internet. I am grateful to its inventors and profoundly grateful to all the people who were honest about adoption. I thank my Think Tank for their help, good words and thoughts. I thank Great Spirit most of all.

I am useful as a speaker on adoption culture now. I will be more of an activist now. I'm Cameron's grandmother. I don't regret the lessons. I realize how little I know. I have more to learn.

Don, a dear Ojibwe friend sent me this: "Thirty years ago I knew everything; now I know nothing; education is a progressive discovery of our own ignorance. Spirituality is the art of knowing that we do not know. It is waking up in the morning with our eyes fully opened and awaiting the adventure of the new day. New things, new theories, new facts are being discovered every day and it makes for a glorious, confusing and exciting world. There was a time when I could not say this; a time when knowledge and facts were collected and regurgitated. I used knowledge to protect myself from the challenge and inconsistencies of life. The Creator had to be not only a proven fact but evidenced in theories and dogmas—the mystery was lost. Today I believe that the Creator cannot be contained by dogma and rules. The doubts have become part of my faith. The state of "not knowing" becomes creative and stimulating. My relationship with the Creator today is real. To "not know" is the beginning of wisdom."

I could not have said it better myself.

Happy Girl

I met my second husband in October 1999 at a friend's birthday party in Connecticut. He had been married before like me. Herb was born and raised in Harlem, a culturally diverse community in New York City. He is one of the best people I have ever met. We were married in September 2004. My days here in Massachusetts are my happy days. I count each day as blessed. Our New York City friends call me Happy Girl.

Herb calls me Woodstock, his little yellow bird. I always wanted a good nickname.

It's good to feel things. I never thought it would be possible for me to fall in love, ever, but I did, finally.

Uncle Bob

In 2006, driving solo across Ontario to Wisconsin, I decided to call my Uncle Bob Thrall. We'd talked on the phone a few times but never met face to face. He agreed to meet me for coffee the next morning, 9 a.m., August 27 in Minocqua.

I hardly slept. I didn't know what to expect but wasn't afraid.

For me, this was my first real reunion with my Thrall family. Sure, I had met my grandmother but she didn't know who I was. Since the 1990s, Uncle Bob and I exchanged letters. Mary, his daughter, helped me to contact my half-sister Helen, living in Florida since 2003.

Bob knew from my letters that I was resigned to the fact that I would never meet my mother, his sister. But I still had questions.

Sitting at the table, uncle Bob looked as anxious as I was, when I walked in. I had no idea what he looked like, though I parked next to his landscape business truck. My uncle had a perfectly wonderful smile. But he seemed nervous. He said Mary was on her way and was bringing some family photos.

Mary got there so we ordered breakfast and we volleyed questions back and forth. Both said I look just like a Thrall. I was glad to hear this. I can see how I have my grandmother's double chin!

This conversation was astounding. I not only found out why Bob and my mother had a falling out years before, but why they were never close. Bob said Helen had abandoned her baby at his house, while he and his wife were raising their four children. To make it easier, Uncle Bob calls my half-sister Helen, "Peanut."

Bob explained years earlier, he went to a local bar, furious enough he knocked down the door. He wanted to bring Helen back to his house because Peanut really missed her. That was the last straw. Apparently Helen, my mother, never forgave him.

Mary showed me photos of Peanut. Mary also had photos of her three brothers (my first cousins) and our grandparents.

I was blown away when Uncle Bob shared stories of his younger days with his grandfather (my great-grandfather) George Thrall and his wife Lottie (Angle). An ox took them to town in a cart. Their entire trip would last a whole day. Bob loved those early memories, I could tell. He filled in many blanks I had about my Thrall family history and ancestry.

Mary had a recent photo of Peanut and it made me cry. She and I look so much alike.

I cried often during our four hours together that Sunday. They cried, too.

Bob asked why I needed to know about them, what made me persist for so long. All I could say was I couldn't live without knowing them so I never gave up.

I wasn't expecting to hear that my mother Helen had a baby before me, a child born in 1952. Bob thought maybe I was that child.

I still can't believe it. My mother was 18 then. There is another child out there, another child she abandoned, another child she will never meet.

Bob remembered in 1952, his mother drove Helen to Illinois in the family station wagon and came back alone. Months later, his mother brought Helen back.

Bob definitely didn't know I existed until I called him in the 1990s. I reminded him I was born in 1956, not 1952. I explained I was 22 when I opened my adoption and looked for them for over 14 years.

Bob and Mary took me to the cemetery in Minocqua so I could pray over the graves of George, Lottie, Arnold, Helen Sr. and Uncle Thomas.

I left my tears on their grave markers, so they would know I found my way home.

Helen's Death

Quite unexpectedly, Helen, my birthmother, died from complications of diabetes on May 17, 2007. She never changed her mind about meeting me. She got her wish. I remained a secret, at least to her.

My birthmother Helen obviously had pain and trauma in her life—something hurt her. Something difficult had happened.

I decided in Minocqua to try and find my brother or sister, this child born in 1952.

At the Wounded Knee Memorial in 2005, a Lakota friend asked me if I had a sister named Julie. I said no, I didn't think so. This was before my uncle Bob told me I had another sibling, another child lost to adoption.

Through my Navajo friend Sara, I contact a Lakota lady who can dream for others. I asked her to dream about Helen's first child. She dreamt for me and said my sister died as a child.

I call this sister Julie. The dreamer said Julie was the light of her parent's lives. She even dreamt about mud pies Julie made for her dad.

I don't have to look—she's already gone to Great Spirit.

Personal Victory

In September 2010, I mentioned I still didn't have my adoption file to Jackie, who I visited on my Wisconsin book-tour. Jackie helped Ben get his adoption file so she gave me the email for the state office in Madison, Wisconsin. I'd write an email!

Wisconsin, by law, allows adoptees in a closed adoption (like mine) to request and receive their non-identifying information. You simply fill out their form and request it (and pay them $75 an hour). Let me clarify: your non-identifying information is a bit of history with no names. It will not help you locate your tribe or your missing natural parent(s). In fact, it's so vague it's really no help at all!

I decided to request my identifying information (aka the real deal, my sealed adoption file.) They emailed me that I would need a court order. I needed to fill out their form, have it notarized and mail it back to them so I did. Within a month, I spoke to a woman on the phone, and she proceeded to fill out the paperwork for a court order. She would present it to the judge and I didn't need to be there. Now this was weird. She asked me why I wanted my file.

Why was this so hard for me? I have a million reasons. But I didn't know what the judge wanted me to say. What was a good reason?

I said I wanted my adoption file to help me understand my early history and where I was the first months of my life: that is what I think she wrote down. (I told her I was nervous).

Ok, I'm sure the most used reason for such a request is the need for family medical history. There are many good reasons, yes. But what did the judge want to hear? I didn't know.

If the judge read my form, he'd see I already knew the names of both my natural parents. (Remember I read my adoption file when I was 22.) Heck, I knew their birthdays and when each of them died.

So like all adoptees, I waited and prayed. The un-named judge would review my request. He or she could deny me. But the judge didn't.

Because I wrote my birth parents are deceased—that is why I believe the judge granted my request. It's only a guess. And if they considered my age—54, I'm no kid. Maybe that is why.

So this white envelope arrived the day after Thanksgiving and I was too emotional to open it. Yes, I was a wreck! I knew it would hit me like a ton of bricks. It did.

My friend Anecia met me for breakfast on Sunday morning and since she is an adoptee, she said she would read it to me. That was better, we thought. It was best to do this with a friend who was also adopted. So she read and I cried (in a restaurant!).

The worst part was not my crying. There was family history on one page and a small post-it note that said the next part was not on microfilm. I did not receive the entire context and testimony my natural mother Helen gave to the social workers.

So I am processing that I am the daughter of Helen—who, by the way, did want to keep me. This broke me up so hard—my emotions are still ragged and raw. It was 1956 and she was not able to keep me, no way. If someone in Wisconsin does want to do this - and if they need tribal information, it is on the form and the only way an adoptee can do this is through a court order. And pay $75 per hour.

When I was 22, I'd asked a judge to read my file but the one I have now (this file) is different than the one he let me read. He had more legal paperwork in his file. The effect on me now is greater, plus my father's version was different than my mothers.

One of the reasons I didn't mention: I was in a foster home. Who were they? Now I have their name and address. That was huge for me. Now I know where I was the first days and months of my life. I feel so fortunate, so blessed I was able to get my adoption file when so many are still in the dark about their identity and name. Every adoptee on the planet deserves this information, absolutely. It's criminal that we can't in all but 6 states in the USA.

I do not have a copy of my OBC—original birth certificate. Wisconsin said I'd have to get it from Minnesota where I was born. Minnesota is a sealed record state so I may never see it.

There are only three states assisting birth/natural parents in their search: Illinois, Tennessee and Georgia. (2008)

My Adoption File

In September 2011, writing on my *American Indian Adoptees* blog on how to open an adoption; it hit me that there are adoptees who will face the same situation I did. When I found my natural mother Helen, she refused to talk with me or meet me. I was not able to hear her side of the story.

How does any adoptee not take this personally? I tried to imagine how Helen felt at age 22 when faced with a missing fiancé (my father) and the bulge in her body that was me.

In 2010, I decided to get a copy of my adoption file so I could read the social worker's report and details Helen told them. I paid $75 for a court order to release a copy of my Wisconsin adoption file. Wisconsin mailed me a copy.

Let me explain what is in my adoption file:

1 - State of Wisconsin **Order for Hearing and Investigation**, where my adoptive parents petition in writing to adopt me: Laura Jean Thrall and the court ordered Catholic Welfare Agency of Superior, Wisconsin and the State of Wisconsin to investigate, as required by law. Odd this happened on June 5, 1958—I was born Sept. 9, 1956. I was living in "Legal Limbo."

2 – The **letter** to my parent's lawyer from the Wisconsin State Supervisor of Adoptions, Division for Child and Youth who wrote, "According to our incomplete record, it appears this child was committed permanently to the Catholic Child Welfare Bureau and that agency placed this child in this home (DeMeyer in March 1957). If that is true, no action is necessary on the State Dept. of Public Welfare. We are sure that if our assumption is incorrect, the

agency will so notify us and appropriate action of the state dept. can be taken upon receipt of the investigator's report." Dated June 9, 1958. ALSO in my file, the state of Wisconsin sent a **letter** to the Judge in Superior, Wisc., acknowledging the date of my adoption hearing: June 24, 1958. The investigator was the Catholic Welfare Agency who had complete control of me. Seven months of my early life, I was living in one of their Catholic foster homes.

3- Report: **Movements of Child while Under Care**: Catholic Infant Home, Foster Care in Superior (with their name and address) and Foster-Adoptive Home (DeMeyer). First Baptism: 9-18-56 (requested by my mother Helen) and a New Baptismal Certificate was issued on 2-21-1964. Wow—Catholics get this done quick and recorded. Up on the top of the form is Legal Status: Illegitimate and Mother's Name: Helen Thrall. My Birthplace: St. Paul, MN. In my adoption file is the signed **"Certificate of Baptism, Cathedral of St. Paul,"** listing my adoptive parents and my new name! It is signed by Rev. Barr and dated March 10, 1959 when in fact I had been baptized in Sept. 1956. This falsified baptismal certificate and my amended birth certificate are two fake documents made to hide my adoptee status—in case my parents decide not to tell me I am adopted.

4- **Hospital Discharge Report: The Physical Record of Mother.** She was admitted to the Catholic Infant Home on May 23, 1956. Her home address is in Chicago, IL. She delivered on 9-9-56. She stayed in the hospital 5 days until 9-14-56. Children living: One. (This is the proof Helen had already had a child who was also given up for adoption before me!) Delivery: Normal, spontaneous (Helen had an lml episiotomy with no complications). On 5-25-56, Helen's blood work: Her RH factor was positive. Helen was allergic to penicillin. No Sauk Vaccine given. (I am also allergic to penicillin.) ALSO: **The Child (me) Physical Report**: full-term, 10 lbs., 3 oz., 21 ½ in., Head Circumference 14" and Chest Circumference 14 ½ in. I was discharged from the hospital on 9-26-1956 as a normal female infant. Social Worker: Miss Underhill.

5- **Catholic Infant Home Report** – Their Address, Nurse: Sister Enid, Physical Exam at Birth and Physical Exam on Discharge from Hospital to Infant Home, 2 doctors signed. Feeding: Similac every 4 hours. (Obviously no breast milk for me!)

6- **Medical Exam** (Infant to Two Years, Wisconsin Child Center) —Laura Jean Thrall in Foster Care, General physical: Ok with Mild eczema on face. March 12, 1957.

7- **Medical Exam**—July 15, 1957—now named Tracy DeMeyer, General Development: Normal and lists all the various immunizations and vaccines I had. (My adoptive mother told me I was covered in rashes and bald on the back of my head when they got me.)

8- State of Juvenile Court, Vilas Country, Wisconsin, **Parental Consent to Termination of Parental Rights**, dated December 5, 1956. Miss Alverna Underhill (social worker) is the witness. "Father's consent is not necessary In case of illegitimate child." Signed by my mother Helen Thrall.

9- Leo Block, Director of Catholic Welfare Agency appears before Judge Robert Curran on May 28, 1958, in the matter of **Adoption of Laura Jean Thrall** and Mr. Block consents to my adoption on this legal form. Block's reason for consent: for the best interest of the child.

10 – Form letter: **Request** to the State of Minnesota Dept. of Public Welfare on April 9, 1958, states that Catholic Welfare Agency needs a copy of my birth record to be used as proof of birth to protect the interest of this child at the time of placement of adoption. Required fee enclosed $1.00. Signed Jean Johnson, Supervisor Protection Unit. Certified Photostat April 16, 1958 sent to Social Worker Miss Underhill.

11- **Copy of Investigation**, submitted by Catholic Welfare Agency, done March 17, 1957 through May 28, 1958 to the County Court in Wisconsin. Describes The Child (me) and Mother of Child (Helen). INFORMATION NECESSARY FOR CHANGING BIRTH CERTIFICATE in bold type. This is the story I wanted – all the details and dates. Helen had moved to Chicago in 1952 and dated my dad, Earl. (Helen doesn't say they were living together but they were.) In April 1956, she goes home to Minocqua, Wisconsin because she realized she is four months pregnant. Five months pregnant, she and her mother go back to Chicago to place charges against the alleged father. They were unable to locate him. Then Helen desires to go to a maternity home near her home and they decide her mother will drop Helen off in Milwaukee at St. Mary's on her drive home. Instead they choose the St. Paul (Minnesota) Catholic Infant Home because it is a work home. May 25, 1956: "Helen is using her own name at the Maternity Home as she saw no necessity for further protection…. This was her first physical exam and the doctors felt that she was further along and at least six months pregnant….Helen stated that she is very anxious to get out into a work home as soon as possible and was concerned she would now have one less month to work towards her expenses. She had no money saved and said her family would help as much as possible but she did not want to ask this of them. She wondered how soon she would have to pay her expenses at the Maternity Home. (It doesn't say how much money they charged her.) She was told that if we (Catholic Charities) could be certain that she would repay us as soon as she returned to work, we (Catholic Charities) would pay her bill at the maternity home and she could repay us in small amounts. This seemed to be a great relief to Helen. …She was uncertain about plans for her expected child and it was apparent she was very desirous of keeping the child is possible. She thought she would return home briefly after her confinement but would have to leave home very soon in order to find work. Helen was told that we could assist her with temporary plans for her baby for six weeks, during which time she could return home and make her final decision… Helen was with the alleged father for several months and has been under the impression he intended to marry her. She seemed to feel that if she could talk to him, they could work things out. He suddenly left his job in Chicago. She heard through others that he'd returned home." (The next page of the microfilm was missing.) My first months, Helen's life, and my adoptive parents life and their desire to adopt me, was revealed on four typed pages.

This is what to expect in an adoption file: documents, reports, letters, stories, arrangements, explanations, descriptions, maybe even a Baptismal Certificate, places and dates. Every adoptee **needs** this. Now I can see her struggle. I can live well knowing the truth.

What adoption cost me

Someone asked me what had adoption cost me personally. What a loaded question, I shot back in my email in 2012. I said I needed to think about it.

Obviously I didn't ask to be adopted!

This situation was thrust on me … If my soul wanted a big test this lifetime, this was clearly the route to take.

Finding out neither would ever look for me? That painful discovery cost me.

What kind of man would desert a woman carrying his child and who would tell a woman she cannot keep her own baby? Who made them this way? Belief systems, religions, social workers, neighbors, parents, judges, priests? Even your own family can be so damaged, it's risky to find them. There are times now I wish I had never looked but I had to know why I was adopted. Taking risks to find out the truth cost me years.

Being told by my natural mother to never contact her again? That rejection cost me.

I made all the moves, made all the calls, did all the travel and took all the risks to find both parents. I put myself out there to join a family who didn't even know I existed or cared that I did. That hurt cost me.

The adoption trade in babies was booming in the 1950s. In my opinion my adoptive parents were not carefully screened. Despite his raging alcoholism and their marital discord after two miscarriages, Catholic social workers still qualified them to be my parents? Very young I was molested by my adoptive dad. That betrayal cost me.

I had to pretend for years I was alright when really I wasn't. I tried to live up to their expectations and be the baby they lost. That impossible situation cost me.

My adoptive parents didn't know adopting kids won't fix a marriage and might even make it worse! I had to suppress my shock and disappointment in them for too long. It took me years to get therapy and counseling that worked. This delay cost me.

My lack of trust and being able to love someone cost me a marriage.

Many years later I was shocked to learn my ancestry. My father, who had the Native blood, didn't intervene to keep me. How did that make me feel? Betrayed.

I had no idea what to think about being Tsalgi since there was no one alive to reconnect me to my tribal culture. That cost me.

How can you measure cultural loss when there is no dollar amount or apology that can undo what happened? There is no way to get that back.

What did adoption cost me? Everything.

What did adoption give me? The strength to persevere.

Epilogue

Steps

It's very crucial I understand adoption issues. Adoptees are finally opening up about how they were affected. It seems there are stages to this, obvious steps. New research supports, not contradicts, what I already include in this memoir and albeit "brief" history of the Indian Adoption Project(s).

It's obvious Indian people are still recovering from a few centuries of good intentions. There will definitely be more stories from other Lost Birds/Split Feathers/adoptees. My next book "Split Feathers: Two Worlds" is an anthology , written with my friend, Patricia Busbee, a Native adoptee. We aim to have it published in 2012.

Not every experience is alike. I am not alone in my pursuit of truth and identity. I've known adoptees all my life but none had actually taken steps in challenging the system, as proactive or activist, writing about it. There were no "support groups" as there are now. Not one friend had successfully opened his or her adoption—not because they didn't want to, believe me. Eventually "time" did the trick and more adoptees were able to search successfully. (Google: Adoptee Search or visit Amazon for a growing list of books to help an adoptee-in-search.)

It's absolutely true that everyone else on the planet has the right to their identity, their name and their history —just not adoptees!

Why? Persistent myths by adoption professionals and by those same people who advocate secrecy. Secrecy should send up red flags. What are they hiding?

The majority of States and Canadian provinces still do not allow adoptees the right to read or possess original birth records, according to 2011 statistics.

Some stories have happy endings. My friend Rhonda said she was born too early (in the 60s) for the new open records law in Michigan to help her. She had only her non-identifying information, a common occurrence for adoptees in too many states. It appears adoption advocates believe secrecy protects our birthparents identity. Both of Rhonda's birthparents are deceased. Who would secrecy protect in her case?

Receiving her tribal ID card and meeting relatives makes her story so uplifting and inspirational. Rhonda met her relatives and told them she wanted to know about her father. They gave her that. She makes regular trips to her Michigan reservation.

Grateful

There is more good news. Finally—birthparents decided enough was enough and declared, "Damn the secrecy, damn the laws. Where are my children?" They are forming groups like Concerned United Birthparents (CUB) and working to draft new open records legislation. No doubt this will always be a sensitive issue for all sides of the adoption triad—that is certain.

Understanding the myriad of adoption issues, restoring my health and mental wellness, it's still enormously important to me. A new wave of knowledge is spreading, expanding and growing. With every news article, a growing internet and new books by adoptees—every adoptee is affected, so yes, I am profoundly grateful.

Struggle is too common a word in adoptee language. I am sure 10+ million adoptees are better off knowing the steps—how to open sealed records, and how to be reunited with birth family. Our unique experience has its own history now.

As adoptees heal and meet other adoptees, we all grow stronger. That is good. That knowledge is powerful.

A friend sent me a link to *The Adoption Show*, a web broadcast and radio program in Toronto, Canada, with Michelle Edmunds as Host Producer.

Michelle is an amazingly articulate adoptee. I listened to numerous programs as each guest expanded on their experience being adopted, and what they are doing now to increase awareness and hopefully change the system. I was overjoyed. All agreed it takes time to process adoption. It is huge. The obstacle is a billion dollar industry in America who doesn't want this kind of exposure.

A few more things I wanted to include in this book – for the record. When adoptees do begin to search, adoptive parents need to relax. You're not going to lose us. Let us heal this. Don't punish us for searching. Listen to us. Offer your unselfish support and love us unconditionally. Don't expect us to live a lie or be happy about it.

Many adoptees will wait until their adoptive parents die before they search. It's true. I didn't want Edie or Sev to know. If an adoptee waits, out of a sense of gratitude mixed with guilt, vital connections could be lost because birthparents die or adoptees cannot find them right away. Searching for years only adds to our trauma, believe me. Also, if we are illegitimate, birthfathers are nameless on our documents and it becomes more difficult to find him if our birthmother has died. Our siblings, if we have them, if we find them, may not know anything.

If paternity is uncertain, DNA testing is expensive now but a worthwhile solution. DNA testing with my father Earl was timely, since he died shortly after I found him. I am so glad I never gave up looking for him.

I've met more than a few adoptees who hope to find siblings as much as their birthparents; some have found that reunions with siblings are easier. Many times our brothers and sisters are thrilled when we find them.

Adoptees may not expect what they find out about their birthparents. Some adoptees will hurt with new pain, but in the end, we're better off knowing the truth. Adoptees might have to accept that our birthmothers may not like us or want to accept us, even years later. Her relationship with our birthfather may be too painful to revisit. So there is another possible rejection, depending on her circumstances.

I do not know if I would recommend an 18-year-old start this process. I was 22 and had prepared myself mentally and emotionally for a reunion over many years. I had some fear, of course, not sure what I would find. Expect healthy anger to erupt slowly and eventually.

For adopters, our trauma wasn't your fault, unless we were abused or molested under your watch. Please join a support group (there are many now) if you want to understand how an adoptee feels.

Guilt

I am not a medical professional, or a doctor, or lawyer. So I am not offering a pill or legal advice or Indian medicine. I just know what I did.

I know adoptees can heal, even without all the answers they desperately want. It is possible. Tell your guilt you are not looking for new parents—just answers.

I've heard this from other adoptees: "Help as many adoptees as you can with their guilt."

Adoptees can release damaging emotions in a safe way, in a ceremony, in a church, or in a prayer. It may take years, not just a few sessions of talk-therapy.

So I tell adoptee friends, "You may never find all the answers but you can wake up. You need to tell your side of the story. You will need support. Laws need to be changed. History will never change the facts you were let go by your birthparent or taken. Maybe she was coerced. Maybe she's afraid. She might be looking for you."

In my situation, years later, I am still having reunions, and I still make phone calls.

My advice to those in reunion is: "A reunion doesn't guarantee you'll hear what you expect. Many adoptive parents can't handle it. They have no idea the pain they caused you and they may not want to take responsibility for it. Once you meet your birth-mother or father, or siblings, you decide what to keep and what to leave behind. You have the opportunity to make your own decisions for the first time in your life. You create a safe zone and safe home for yourself. You become your own parent. You decide who to let in and who to let go. In other words, you decide to heal. No one else can do it but you."

Important days

Apparently 4,800+ adoptees, birthparents and their supporters signed an online petition in 2007 to open sealed adoption records in New York; it's believed 60,000 adoptees in New York are currently trying to find their birth families. Some surely will have Native American ancestry.

The goal is simple: open the adoption file, find a name, and then go meet them.

The most important days in my entire life were when I went to the judge to open and read my adoption file and later, when I phoned and met my father in 1994.

After 17 years of searching, in mere minutes, my father's voice restored much of my self-confidence. Yes, I was extremely fortunate to meet Earl before he died, to know my name and what tribe's blood and history runs through my veins. His kids are a part of me now, a part of my world. My entire life had been about my search for them. They never even knew I existed.

In 2006, when I met my uncle Bob, I didn't tell him that I needed relatives like him to help me understand my mother's rejection. Until I met Helen's family, I could not see my journey as completed.

Pedigree

I'm often asked: "Where should these orphaned children go?" Well, many will still go to orphanages or into foster care. Kinship adoption, placing children within their tribe, is still the best solution for American Indian children.

I don't object to adoption since every child deserves a home. A closed adoption, living a mystery, that's the bigger issue. Adoptees need to know who they are and the truth.

My mother's rejection was life-changing. Her second rejection, not wanting to meet me, was also life-changing.

Babies are not pedigree puppies. We don't live with our mother's rejection as easily as the world has been made to believe. Trauma can split a child's mind in many directions. If not handled properly, even with the best intentions of adoptive parents, their child's emotional health and future is in grave danger, even under the best circumstances.

I believe more birthmothers are becoming aware of damage their baby suffered. Some birthmothers learn this when they attempt a reunion, and find bitterness, anger and resentment in their birth child/adult. This is why many birthmothers will insist on privacy and secrecy out of fear. They fear this kind of attitude and don't want to face the child they abandoned.

Reunions can be tricky, some difficult, some impossible.

For many birthmothers, they live their lie their whole life. They hide it from others. They don't want to be judged or have to explain their decision, or recall their failed relationship, or the experience that led to their pregnancy. I understand this. Many women from that era were powerless and did not discuss what happened with anyone. There was tremendous shame in having an illegitimate child. There was fear. Some were coerced. Then it's difficult to face the child you erased from your life.

It's important to know this before you attempt to find a birthmother.

Old World Order

If you watch the *Discovery Channel*, you've learned there is no such thing as "race," per se, though this concept is not widely acknowledged. Most people don't grasp that skin color and pigment is a product of ultraviolet exposure, not about one human's superiority or supremacy over another, or who is more eligible for heaven.

I remind myself that sacred Indigenous knowledge is ancient and America is just a few hundred years old.

So why is the truth about "race" so scandalous?

"New World Order, Old World Lie," John Trudell said about exploiting human beings, with one group dominating another.

Even today, men rule and manage their institutions, except in Indian Country where women are honored as sacred. The Earth itself is a woman and called Mother in Indian Country.

One New World Order example is Americans adopting little girls from China. This was a political strategy to control their population and have more men, so Chinese families are allowed only one girl, but even this order has failed. There can be no marriage, or future generations without Chinese girls. The Chinese leaders are finally realizing their colossal mistake.

Some ideas are believable—but where did that idea come from? Women do not rule China. Women do not rule much at all. It's easy to see men have had more to say about this, and men exert much more control over women's bodies than women do. Even now, men rule countries, congress, the media and the church. Many more men denounce abortion and women's rights.

The Old World Order portrayed Mary Magdalene as a prostitute, and waited until 1969, centuries later, to apologize and revise their version of her story. What a strategy—making a sacred woman a whore. Something is definitely wrong. Women have faced this colonization of their bodies and reputation for centuries. The rules were not made by women or sacred Indigenous beliefs.

Birthmothers are traumatized, too, in this way. Secrecy may protect her but not erase her memory, knowing her baby is out there somewhere. Adoptees need to realize this and place blame where it belongs, on her society, on those organized religions.

As we prepare to find our birthparents, we're reminded her love was unconditional so she let us go because she loves us. Don't believe this entirely. Force, pressure, poverty, religion and laws helped her decide.

Reunion Pullback

I'd never heard of Reunion Pull-Back, which sometimes happens when adoptees meet their birthparent(s) and/or siblings. Pull-back explains what happened to me when I met strangers who were relatives and my siblings. I pulled back. I am still pulling back. New relationships take time. There is no set timeline for this.

There may be difficult moments waiting in these new relationships, with possible resentment, sibling jealousy, anger or disappointment. I found it impossible to fill in all those missing years in just a few short sentences with Earl and his family. I wasn't shocked to hear about abuse in Earl's family, too, who I didn't really know yet. It's not something I expected to hear, nor did I know how to deal with it. It appears that abuse is recycled in families, and happens over and over again. Indian Country is no different. It has its own problems to deal with and heal.

My first marriage was ending, and Earl was dying. I hardly knew how to deal with that so of course I pulled back. I knew I needed to process everything.

There was so much I didn't get to say to Earl. I didn't get to tell him I was rejected twice by Helen, first when she abandoned me and later when I found her. I wanted to him to know this hurt me deeply but there was never the right time.

It hurt that Helen was never ready to meet me. She didn't owe me anything. She could hide behind the law and deny the truth about me if she wanted to, but she didn't have the right to deny me my father, brothers and sisters.

I've learned some adoptees meet their biological parent and then distance from them, pulling back, wanting them to experience what they did when they were abandoned. All parents in an adoption need to understand these difficult issues.

For adoptees that recognize their pain and trauma, be emotionally prepared before you search for your lost parents. Accept that birthmothers often had no choice in the decision in that time period. Yes, knowing why you were abandoned or given up is still crucial to hear. Knowing why does have a healing power.

For those who will adopt, don't adopt us with the plan to erase who we are. Adopt us for who we are. Show us some respect. Honor our identity because we deserve it.

If people really understood, there would be no more closed adoptions. Those who conduct adoptions now need to take a much closer look at birth trauma, birth psychology, adult stress and mental illness.

The system of closed adoption, in the words of one lawyer, is barbaric. One day we will all look back at this and say, "How did we ever let this happen to innocent children?"

Four Names

The name I chose for myself is Three Feathers, tattooed on my right wrist, along with a symbol of happiness. I love this name. In 2002, I did a story about tattoo artist Dee Whitcomb (Lower Brule Lakota) and in return, he gave me my tattoo. This name suits me, three (split) feathers.

Today I am Trace *and* Laura (the name on my original birth certificate). I pray with my Lakota name *Winyan Ohmanisa Waste La ke*, given to me by my Lakota sister Ellowyn.

As Tracy Ann, I had no ancestry and no way of knowing. Barely alive, I had to create my identity. It seems that I have been dead more years than alive. Being abandoned tore my emotional fabric. There are times I wish I had just one mother—just one woman who could love me unconditionally, one woman who would keep me safe and not sacrifice me.

As Laura, I have parents, sisters and brothers. I look like somebody. My identity is Cherokee-Shawnee-Delaware and Irish. Some adoptees self-identify with one ancestry more than another. It depends on which ancestors keep you company.

Now when I visit my father's family, I learn about their lives, and their life before me. They tell me about my grandparents and relatives I never met. They fill in the blanks so I'll never feel invisible again.

Lost Birds/Split Feathers understand the importance of culture. Our blood tells us. Because of our adoptions, we don't take anything for granted. This is good. This is important. We recognize the beauty and importance of family. Languages must be learned and spoken, preserving it, keeping it alive for future generations.

I pray and hope those reading this will also make it their mission to understand Indian history and reach out to make peace with Indian people. Protect tribes and their sovereignty; protect future generations.

We can't undo what's been done but learn from it. We can't erase the past but we must never repeat it.

2012

This is how I see it. Adoption may appear complex yet it's simple: end closed adoption and open all adoption records. Sadly, in 2011, most lawmakers insist adoption records remain sealed.

Here are some complexities: the outcome for each adoptee will be different since expectations about reunion will vary. Each adoptee must come to terms with reunion, either failed or good. Adoptees might find relatives are ready to meet them, while others may not. Some parents may not have recovered losing us. Adoption lasts years and obviously adoption changes the adoptee. There is no doubt about that. As changed people, we may not meet our tribal parent's expectations or their idea of who we should be.

What happened with the Indian Adoption Projects was wrong. It was intentional and deliberate. It was damaging to Indian Country and to children who were forced to assimilate via adoption. That was Manifest Destiny. The end result: adoptees were erased from tribal rolls and lost their status and rights as tribal members.

We must regain our sovereignty and rejoin our nations.

For Lost Children, we cannot allow this history to be secret. We cannot be passive or grateful to those who committed this crime against us. We must act now in order to heal.

Acknowledgements

Thank you, Grandmothers, for staying with me all these years. You can let go now. I am safe. I am OK. I am all done chasing ghosts. Go, dance.

I thank my mother Helen for carrying me inside. I did not need to see you to know you. Of course I hoped to hear your voice. "Don't cry," you whisper. "Don't cry…. I'm here now." Don't worry, mother. I say these words for you. Thank you for my two sisters.

I wish to thank my mom and dad, Edie and Sev, for important lessons that brought me to healing myself. I love you. To their families, thank you for sharing your lives with me.

I wish to thank Earl Bland for a memorable reunion and answers. I wish I could have known you longer. Thanks Dad for my sister Teresa and my brothers.

Thanks to Uncle Bob, Sandy and Mary for your good words, for the kindness you showed me, and for the answers I needed in Minocqua.

I wish to thank every adoptee I have ever met. I especially thank my adoptee Think Tank: Adrian, Rhonda, Susan, Anecia, Suzie, Andy, Faith, Garnet, Paul, Mary Ann, Veronica, Tina, Bill, Ben (Ani), Eleanor, Wendy, Aaron and Dan. You are my relatives.

Thanks to God Bob (in Greenfield). Huge thanks to Gil Tennant, Stephanie Elliott and Linda Dombeck for their editing expertise.

Thanks to my friends and scholars: Dr. Raeschelle Potter-Deimel, Suzan Shown Harjo, Drew Hayden Taylor, Dr. Helen Rountree, Dr. Patty Loew, Michael and Marie Dutton, Joseph A. Parzych, Kitty Waitkus, Cynthia Bluh, Karolyn Kemp, Paul DeMain, Susan Deer Cloud, Jackie Willie, Von Hughes, Genealogist cousin Charles Bland and the Bland Heritage Foundation, Author Madeleine Blais for her inspired lecture on the art of memoir (which inspired me to rewrite huge chunks of this memoir!), The Adoption Show and Michelle Edmunds in Toronto, Dr. Karen Redfield for her help in Madison, Ann Tweedy and other friends on the journey who I will never forget.

Thanks to Karen Redfield and the Wisconsin Book Festival in 2008 who invited me to read from my manuscript. Thanks to the Superior Public Library and former mayor Herb Bergson for my reading in 2010. Thanks to Gary and Jitters in Duluth for the fun reading. Thanks to the Pequot Museum's Kim Hatcher-White and the Mt. Kearsarge Indian Museum in New Hampshire for inviting me to read in 2011.

I especially thank Black Bear (Stephan LaBoueff) for the patience, love medicine and phone calls, even if it made me cry for hours and days. I love you Uncle.

Mitakuye Oyasin to my family Ellowyn, Debbie and Merle in Porcupine and Boozhoo and Megwetch to my Anishinabe family in Lac Courte Oreilles. You healed me. You adopted me.

To my Connecticut friends (you know who you are) thank you for the love and laughter. I'll buy the mochas!

To my cousins Buddy and Peter, thank you for connecting me to my relations in Illinois and Ottawa and Quebec, Canada.

To Paul Burke, thank you for the genealogy and the miracles you gave me.

To Barb Burke, thank you for this beautiful cover design, the edits, thank you for letting me watch Jake and write, and your friendship.

And finally, I thank my husband Herb for his love and support. I never thought it would be possible to love you this much... I am sure there will be many more surprises ahead, Wild Cat. Camp Woodstock will always be an adventure.

Rest in Peace Mom... Edie passed peacefully on Dec. 9, 2011.

Rest In peace Teresa, my beautiful sister who passed Feb. 29, 2012.

Rest in peace Uncle Bob who passed in March, 2012.

FULL CIRCLE

Thirty years later, back in 1999, I'm living in Hayward, the same town where I went to my first powwow as a girl. I attend the Honor the Earth powwow in Lac Courte Oreilles. I feel the drum pound in my heart again. My Ojibwe friends take me by the hand and lead me into the circle, my first intertribal.

Thank you, Great Spirit. I made my journey home and have come full-circle.

Pray for mothers across the planet so they can keep their children with them until they grow big and strong.

Ea Nigada Qusdi Idadadvhn. All our Relations.

About the Author

Trace lives in western Massachusetts with her husband Herb. Her second book, "Split Feathers: Two Worlds," an adoptee anthology with Patricia Busbee, is pending publication.

Split Feathers/Lost Birds/Adoptees,
Email: **tracedemeyer@yahoo.com**
Write:
Blue Hand Books
Attn: Trace A. DeMeyer
PO Box 1061
Greenfield, Massachusetts 01302
www.bluehandbooks.com
BLOG: www.bluehandbooks.blogspot.com

TRACE'S BLOG: www.splitfeathers.blogspot.com
Twitter: @Trace15
Facebook: www.facebook.com/Splitfeathers
Visit Author Central on Amazon.com for more news about Trace.

CPSIA information can be obtained at www.ICGtesting.com
Printed in the USA
LVOW102242181212

312270LV00029B/2030/P